RICHARD TO MINNA WAGNER

Richard to Minna Wagner

LETTERS TO HIS FIRST WIFE

TRANSLATED, PREFACED, ETC.

By William Ashton Ellis

VOL. II

VIENNA HOUSE

New York

Originally published by H. Grevel & Company
London, 1909

First VIENNA HOUSE edition published 1972

International Standard Book Number:
Volume I . . . 0-8443-0012-8
Volume II . . . 0-8443-0013-6

Library of Congress Catalogue Card Number: 75-163797

Manufactured in the United States of America

Richard to Minna Wagner

152.

VENICE, 27. *November* 1858.

YOU ALTOGETHER GOOD WIFE,

Only to-day have I received your portrait from the Custom-house, as it had to be laid before the Censor first. You may easily imagine how it touched me! It was quite an excellent inspiration of yours, for which I thank you from my heart. Moreover—with all respect for Herr Klepperbein—I must confess that this photograph has turned out far more successfully than that product of his art you once sent me to London; though I have preserved the latter also, particularly since at least that good fat rascal, our lamented Peps, came out so well on it. The only thing I do not like about your portrait is the addition of those red lips; otherwise it is quite capital and has made a most moving impression on me. It lies on my writing-table now beside the portrait of my father Geyer; so I'm quite well supplied with portraits. Once more, accept my hearty thanks for the wholly excellent and kind idea!—A decent photograph of myself will never come off, and I'm waiting till some first-rate painter shall try his hand on me!

I have been confined to my room again the last 4 days ; what a deal of trouble I keep on having ! I had come by a sore on my leg, didn't think much of it, applied cold compresses, and bound them rather tightly to prevent their slipping, as I didn't want to miss the chance of good promenades in such fine weather. But the pain became fiercer and fiercer, the inflammation and swelling increased, till at last I grew alarmed and called in the doctor. At once I was ordered not to do any more walking, but to apply certain resolvent poultices ; which I continued for three days on end, with such an aggravation of the pain that I couldn't rise from my chair at last without screaming aloud. Now it has begun to suppurate, and I'm horrified at all the bad matter that is coming to light. I still have to take great care of myself, as the indurations still are there. In all my life I've never had anything so horrible on my body, yet it seems connected with my good nose, which is white as snow just now : a divertent, then.— The only pity is the constant hindrance to my work ; may God improve it !—

It's very shabby of me to be narrating you my little illnesses, when you have such great ailments to surmount yourself,—but I think it may divert your thoughts a little also. Thank Heaven for your last letters ! Remain like that, dear Minna ! Ward off your dismal fancies ; they are the deadliest foes to your health. Tröger and Pusinelli (with every physician who knows your complaint) agree on that in their reports to me. Your malady is painful and will give you trouble for long, and to the end of your life you will have to exercise the greatest care never to overtax yourself in any way, but always to spare yourself ; when true tranquillity of mind sets in, however, you soon will feel quite different and many of the distressing symptoms will disappear, so that at last you'll accustom yourself to certain, perhaps chronic, inconveniences in your condition, always be able to control them, and so lead quite a tolerable existence for long to come—for as long as your lease of life itself. But am I much better off? My nervous and circulatory troubles (*Blut-Leiden*) don't ever altogether cease disturbing me : how is it, then, that I still retain sufficient freshness and vigour of mind for creation, and have made my general condition so much more supportable than of yore ? Do you believe that if I had still been kapellmeistering, with that inner repugnance, that eternal annoyance, and the constant repetition of intense excitement at rehearsals and performances, things would go so endurably with me ? Eh, I should like you to see it : I should no longer be alive, take my word ! But each has a rift he retains for his life ; it is no good shutting one's eyes to it : we ought to learn wisdom with our riper years, instead, and cease sapping our vitals. On the contrary, if one orders one's life accordingly, and wins that fine repose I spoke of, despite that rift one can then enjoy one's life quite sensibly at last. That's what *I* have resolved to, and that's what you should do as well ! Man mustn't dwell too much upon the past ; whoever would keep himself on end, has enough to do with the present. In that respect remembrance is our greatest foe. As regards yourself, my dear Minna, I now have made it my most sacred duty to do everything that can possibly give you ease of mind about me, and therefore also to avoid whatever might excite you needlessly. I have written thus to Pusinelli also, and assured him that in his cure [of you] he will have a support in me on which he may rely.—So—rest ! repose ! trust ! reconcilement !—no more brooding !—

After my wedding-day presents I am expecting another letter from you in a day or two, in reply to which I'll tell you sundry things that I omit to-day (since writing now is somewhat difficult to me as well). I hope you then will also tell me you've at once put up your mantle bought in Dresden for re-sale ? Mathilde will soon attend to that for you, even if you lose a little by it.—Yes, I half expected I should have bad luck with my present ; you who always feel it too hot, couldn't you have waited just a wee bit longer? O you naughty Madame !

You will also have the new pianoforte score of the *Iphigenia* sent you ; I shall keep on getting sent to you whatever things of mine come out. But I forgot Tichatscheck this time, and am writing Härtels to send you yet another copy ; so give him either this or that in my name. And now God bless you for to-day !—Ow ! Ow ! —soon more, and always good, from

Thy

dear Man.

153.

VENICE, 30. November 1858.
Evening.

MY GOOD MINNA,

Only fancy ! it will be a whole week tomorrow that I have been caged up again. Since I wrote you last about my trouble, I have had to accept a new doctor, as the body-physician has fallen ill himself and can't go out. I passed three days without having my sore inspected, till at last I became really alarmed, as the hardness absolutely refused to yield, and the inflammation grew more and more painful. Now I'm in good hands, praise God, and the sore has been discharging for the last 3 days. It is by no means what we took it for at first, but a regular carbuncle of the largest kind ; the opening is at least as big as a two-franc piece, and I still daren't think of standing up, it hurts so. As in the last long period of my life I have committed no errors of diet whatever, but always chosen my food most carefully—as you know—this sore must certainly be regarded as the long desired and awaited crisis that is to free me from the secret mischief forever brewing in my blood ; in any case I have to thank the London diet for it, the first consequence of which was my Face-rose. So I mean to hope the best for my health, and together with this matter that my body will get rid of much upsetting it. Really I could do very well with that, to be able to keep to my work without a break at last ! Scarcely having resumed it after my last illness, of course I have had to give it up again for the present, and for the last 6 days I have been in a reclining-chair with pillows thrust under my leg to maintain it in a horizontal position ; thus am I lifted into bed by Pietro, and out of bed again next morning. A trial of patience ! And it's to last at least half another week ! Luckily I am well nursed ; my pock-marked but very intelligent and obliging *Donna servente*, Luisa by name, has the unpleasant office of putting fresh poultices on the discharging abscess 4 times a day, and always fulfils it with great cleanliness. Naturally she also reckons on a tidy tip.—

See, that's how it fares with poor me, true Lazarus with the sore !—Yet whatever I can write you in a very inconvenient attitude shall come to pass, so long as it will. I received your last letter the evening before last. In the first place I saw to my great regret that Karl had not arrived in Dresden punctually, to deliver you the [wedding-day] presents as early as the 24th. But it was an agreeable reassurance to me that at least the mantle pleased you, and you are going to sell the other one. Now wear all that for my sake, and think of me calmly and kindly when you do! Karl will soon be bringing me the presents I begged of you, I hope ? *

I also hope you have seen his mother ! If not, rest assured it is really through nothing but ill-health that she hasn't received you. You will be able to inform yourself more exactly on that, and her present condition, upon the spot. I had commended you heartily to her, and not breathed a word—you may be sure !—about the unhappy complications of recent date. Do give me credit for a little sense !—

Apropos, why ever do you enquire of *me* whether you ought to notify the Brockhaus's of your residence in Dresden ? Please act in that entirely according to your inclination. If you believe that silly rumours may have reached their ears, however, I should advise you the rather to do so, on purpose to refute them. Adduce as the quite natural ground of our passing separation my own wish to spend a winter in Italy, and your need to recreate and distract yourself in your native country, since you had a dislike of knocking about in foreign parts ; whilst both of us hoped to settle down in Germany again next year for good.—

But that *Julius* has inspired me with great dismay ; I cannot understand, particularly in your present state of suffering, how you should allow yourself to be pestered

---

* Clearly a Wedding-day letter is missing between Nos. 151 and 152.—Tr.

daily by that horrid blackguard ! Certainly I had my
fears of it before, and saw in it a point against your
choice of Dresden ; it is to be hoped, however, some
remedy may be devised. Don't vex yourself, but simply
beg Pusinelli to have a talk with the wretch and insist
on his not calling on you any more, if possible. He
might allege that you are in need of the completest
rest and freedom from excitement, whereas, upon enquiring the cause of a considerable agitation he had
observed in you, he had elicited that it was in consequence of his [J.'s] disturbing visits ; but he, Pusinelli,
had been authorised by me to keep a sharp look-out
for anything that might be harmful to your health, and
therefore felt pledged me to forbid his further calls on
you, otherwise he must report the matter to myself and
leave *me* to proceed against Julius. Promise the man
half a thaler a week if he doesn't call on you again ; I
fancy that will do it. But no other tenderness towards
him ! I have reason most profoundly to despise that sort
of men, who live moreover on nothing but gossip and
scandal, and to deem them absolutely worth no pity.
I beg you *most earnestly* to turn this unsavoury visitor
for ever from your house without exciting yourself in any
way ; and forgive me also for my kinship having ever
placed you in the predicament of having to deal with
such a vagabond. I know your strength in instantaneous
mastery of your aversion, but you should save it for
something more imperative, not waste it on such scamps ;
for it really is a great strain on you, and the results are
not far to seek.—Reassure me by an intimation that you
have leant ear to my wish.—

Why on earth do you ask me, also, whether I mind
if you go on visiting the *Devrient ?* By all means do so,

and above all give her my kindest regards : she still stands for nothing in my memory except the great and grand, just as she has remained the beau-ideal of dramatic singing that looms before me ineffaceable with all my works. Already I had promised myself to present her through you shortly with the poem " Tristan " (of which you will receive 10 copies, the distribution whereof you're to attend to for me), and to write her in addition a letter reviving to her mind my recollection of her splendid feats. This shall be done, and purely from a certain gratitude for what she was as stimulating artist to me even in my earliest days. For that matter, I anticipate no abundant sympathy with my *present* works : it would be another thing if she still could perform them herself ; but she moreover isn't very quick at grasping.—

Your being satisfied with N. lifts a great weight from my mind. God grant duration ! Salute her from me, and tell her she must go on proving herself, when on my side I will also faithfully observe my promise to her.—

I might have expected you to bestir yourself for my acquittal, and my thanks would almost be an insult to you. Only thus much : don't build too much on it ! I enclose the answer to your questions, however ; make what use you think fit of it. For my part, I believe Prussia alone can assist me, and almost hope so too. They could allow me to go there in King Johann's despite ; and if he remains obdurate, I know already what to do to compass that.

Now farewell for to-day, and rest assured you now have given me, as well, my first true calm. Continue thus, and trust

Thy

R.

I occupy the room on the first étage with the projecting *oriel* and the two windows to the left of it.

154.

DEAREST MUTZ,

I have just received your letter—in bed, in fact, where I think of staying all day tomorrow also. As it's so dark in my bedroom that I can neither write nor read in it by daylight, I am falling to at once this evening to answer you a little, since I have the lamp at my bedside and can see to my heart's content. Luise has had to construct me an impromptu desk and bring my writing materials ; she speaks Italian and I French, which often leads to confusions, as a moment back.—

Yes—here I am, for the third week of it indoors ; carried 14 days from chair to bed, and from bed to chair. The abscess luckily has done discharging, and the wound, which was exactly deep enough for one to place six four-groschen pieces in it, is on the high road now to healing, so that I feel no more pain from it worth mentioning. The doctor therefore allowed me to walk a little in the room a few days since, and as that answered and it was such lovely weather, the day before yesterday he even sent me in a gondola to the Piazetta, with permission to walk from there to my restaurant. The air and splendour of the day were a thorough treat to me, which made me somewhat overweening, and tempted me to do more walking than was good for me. The consequence was that my leg took to swelling very much, and has given me such increasing pain even with the smallest use of it, that I decided patiently to keep my bed until the leg is altogether sound again ; which in *this* way is certain not to take much longer.—That's how it is with me, you see ; not dangerous, but very bothersome and demanding patience.—

It has fared strangely with me in this lonely interval, when for almost 3 whole weeks I haven't seen a living soul except the maid and doctor. Prince Dolgoruki called on me just once, and once young Winterberger ; but I confess, they each remained too long for me, and I was glad when they took themselves off. In truth I can dispense with all society, and above all I never need amusement ; I need nothing but health and an untroubled frame of mind for work, because nothing but my work really uplifts and sustains me.—Yet I'm by no means becoming surly through my solitude ; on the contrary, the doctor and maid have mostly been astonished at my cheerful humour if they tried to comfort me. Yes, yes, that's how it is, when one has his life behind him !

I foresaw Karl's remaining away longer than he told me ; nevertheless, I believe he will come back to Venice : moreover, he has retained his lodging and left his things there ; but to think of the queer fellow never writing me a word ! I am greatly looking forward to your presents, only I'm sorry that the piano-mat should not be hoarded for the new establishment when we are together again ; I only say that for its saving, though, and am looking forward to it much. My last supply of Paris snuff gave out entirely a month ago, which is a true disaster, as one can only get disgraceful Austrian here ; but it's an incredible undertaking to get any through the post : one hardly catches sight of it at all. The nicest present I've already had, your photograph. The more I look at this portrait, the better I find it, so that I really don't remember having ever seen such a successful one. The eyes and their expression, in particular, are quite excep-

tionally speaking; you have something in them that
becomes you very well, something tender, melancholy,
not unrestful. No doubt that comes in part from your
late sufferings, poor woman ; but otherwise, unless the
photographer has altered very much, you look considerably better than when I left you. Once more, many
thanks for the portrait ; I only wish I could shew you a
similar one of myself, instead of the sickly physiognomies
they have reflected from me hitherto. But what pleases
me most, is the tone of your letter to-day ; I see you are
living again, have the present and future before you ! O
stay like that, turn your life to advantage, take inconveniences and hardships lightly ! Then a great alleviation of your physical sufferings also will not be long
delayed, and—the evening of your life may amply recompense you for its sultry noon. That is what I hope for
myself too !—

Greet our acquaintances ; your having so many callers
is really quite unheard of. If only it distracts, and
doesn't fatigue you ! So soon as you remark the latter,
be merciless and shut your eyes to all other regards.
Your answer as to Julius made me laugh ; if you are able
to help yourself so pat, by all means I have no advice to
give you. To be sure, it's the simplest plan to give such
tramps short shrift : " Close the door ! " that's best.

I can't say much more on the Lohengrin-Dresden
project, only the Ney must have incredibly changed to
her outward advantage if I'm to believe your description ;
in London she looked to me exactly like your poor
brother's wife, only a great deal commoner in face. She
is an excellent singer ; but dramatic expression, true soul,
she has not. I cannot possibly conceive her as Elsa ;
rather as Ortrud. But don't press this opera so in

Dresden : in the first place, it will bring me absolutely nothing in there ; in the second, it revolts me still to think that, where *I* intended to present it first, so exquisitely mindless a conductor as Krebs should have its getting up. Let us wait and see how things stand next year. Already you are putting my Dresden affairs in the best order, you know, and I begin to believe the thing can be adjusted soonest that way. It would be your masterpiece, and I gladly will follow your lead.

For the rest, I beg you to inform me precisely how long you expect your supply of money to last you, and when I ought to be holding some in readiness for you again. I told you I would make you a New Year's present of the *one* expected Berlin tantième ; but a second performance has since been added to it, and the hoped-for little sum thus wins enough importance for me to wish to have the whole of this receipt at my disposal. With so many outstanding Zurich obligations now, I'm really growing a little anxious ; for no less than everything is hanging fire : if Hanover still pays up, it would be a stroke of luck—as I could send that money straight to Zurich. Therefore the tantième comes in very handy for me to have something to live on myself, and unfortunately my living isn't cheap here, as you may well imagine. For instance, I'm looking with horror toward my doctor's bill now. That prince's body-physician fell ill himself, and I had to send for another ; when they despatched me the chief visitors'-doctor in the place, who certainly has treated me very carefully and well, but as a wealthy foreigner.—I tell you all this, so as to keep no secrets from you ; but don't let it disturb you : you know how things come and go ; very possibly I shall have good tidings in a few days, and everything will stand differently again. So it's agreed that you shall deny yourself nothing—do you understand? As much as you frugal wife require, will always be at my command. Consider that about the Berlin tantième as nothing but a precaution on my side, to prevent my being suddenly left dry; but any day may make it needless. So write me exactly by when you'll want money again; in any case I had reckoned on sending you a fresh supply between New Year and Easter.—

And now about my diet. Each day that God creates, I eat my veal-cutlet with spinach; either before it some fish—or after it a little chicken or game. I haven't any high opinion of those horrible sea-lampreys; probably it needs Herweghian epicurism for that.—Every evening before going to sleep, a glass of lemon ice, which Pietro fetches me.—

Here comes Luise with the tea, to accompany which I have some cold chicken to-day. God only bless me with sound sleep, which hasn't been the case since I have lacked all movement. I must conclude, for my writing seat is so inconvenient that one arm and leg have gone to sleep already; let's hope I soon may follow their example, and fall asleep entirely.—

Good night! Soon renew me the pleasure of your writing a thoroughly good, informal letter like to-day's.

Adieu, good Mutz!

Il tuo caro sposo
Ricciardo.

155.

VENICE, 15. *December* 1858.

My very best thanks, dear Minna, for your tidings; your efforts, of course, do not require my thanks. What

I have to say in reply, is not so easy to make clear as it might seem. So much is certain, the time has arrived for taking a definitive step with regard to the future ; from various sides I see myself driven to active and decisive intervention myself. From Devrient and Carlsruhe I have received no answer at all ; the Frommann keeps dinning into me that I mustn't expect the smallest thing from princes, nor even build hopes upon Carlsruhe. True, Liszt made out that they firmly hoped to get me into Germany, for a moderate time at least, for the first performance of a new work ; but beyond that I must entertain no hope of amnesty as yet. On the other hand, if Härtels are to engrave the Nibelungen (which is in negotiation again), I must give them the firm assurance of a first performance ; even in the case of Tristan a definite engagement is now becoming indispensable. Lastly, the pair of us must soon be coming to a stand, know *where* we may set up our domicile from next year forward.—Consequently you doubtless will perceive the weight I attach to the negotiations initiated by yourself, and—so far as I'm concerned—I wish nothing more heartily than to see my repatriation finally arranged on this path, which to me seems the only one open. It is a calamity, however, that I haven't a single truly influential acquaintance in Dresden ; a proof how isolated they left me there in days gone by. If you knew, for instance, the past career of this Herr M. (a fine name indeed !), you would be able to judge what I am bound to think of him. I made his acquaintance in Röckel's company at Hempel's ; at that time he was a Red, came from Frankfort, where he had belonged to Blum's clique, and profited of the Democrat era in Dresden to get himself made a democratic public-advocate (*Staats-*

Anwalt) by Oberländer. Thenceforth he became a reactionary, and when the Oberländer ministry fell, to retain his berth he offered the succeeding Reactionary ministry not only to change sides himself, but to set a sure trap for the Democrats, whom no one knew better. Such a man was welcome, and exactly so did Napoleon turn one of the most notorious thieves and swindlers, Vidocq, into his Minister of Police, because he knew that a man like that was the very best sleuth-hound for hunting down rogues.—You may readily imagine that Democrat and Reactionary are all one now in my eyes, but such a person is an arrant knave, with whom one should have no more dealings than extreme necessity requires. So I beg you not to get too intimate with him.—

On *his* fine talk I couldn't bring myself to run into the noose at Dresden, albeit I admit he isn't to be sneezed at, and what he says mayn't be without foundation. So hear what I intend to do. The new Minister of Justice, *Behr*, stands in fairly good repute ; I don't think I shall prejudice my cause if I express myself to him at length about my situation. Consequently I shall write to him, saying I am now compelled to come to a decision affecting the whole of my life, and begging him to get the archives laid before him to judge from them the charges made against me ; would he then inform me what I might have to expect, whereon I should determine whether to apply for a safe-conduct to place myself under examination ? I shall represent to him that my health renders it impossible for me to undergo a long, or even a short arrest ; because, if I couldn't take proper daily exercise in the open, my nervous agitation and sleeplessness might quickly ruin me and make me incapable of ever pursuing my art again. Wherefore, if he could not give me the assurance that in any event, providing I made submission to the King by the very act of presenting myself to the tribunal, His clemency would absolve me from detention whether for examination or as a punishment (were it only in view of my long exile), considering my age, and in particular your ailing health, I should have to make my mind up now for good and all to settle outside Germany, and never set foot in my fatherland again.—I shall see what he answers me, and all will depend on *that* answer. He is sure to propound the matter to the King; consequently, if his letter does not contain definite, or at least satisfactory assurances in the event of my voluntary surrender (just to fulfil the letter of the law), and if it is merely couched on the contrary in the well-known dry juristic tone, then I owe it to myself to say Valet to all hope of Germany.—

Reflect, since Johann has been king, not a *single* case has occurred in Saxony which could afford me the smallest hope of an exceptionally lenient treatment unless I obtained definite guarantees beforehand ; on the other hand, what odious things have I to fear ! In the first place, that two-month trial itself : after 10 years now, imagine how it must strike me to be confronted with this and that witness, set at certain variance with Röckel and the like ; and then the cross-examinations and plaguy pedantry.—Aren't you afraid yourself lest my irritability might play me a trick in the end, and I might lose my patience in a manner to make me regret it the rest of my life ? And then the penal detention : a room to myself and my piano ; oh yes, it sounds very fine, but we'd better wait and see.

All this, I admit, is nothing to a man who hopes by means of sacrifices and transient hardships of the kind to re-enter, let us say, his old position, enjoyment of his property, his family, and so on ; but what have I strictly to gain by it ? Oh, do let us look at that closer ! In the first place there still remains Lüttichau with his claim for that advance of 5,000 thlr. Good : I settle that by binding myself to supply my operas gratis for the future, and to rehearse them etc. myself. But what have I to seek in Germany at all ? The hearing and conducting of performances of my works ? Very pretty, if experience didn't so irrefutably teach me that I shall have *more* annoyance, worry and exertion every time, than profit and enjoyment ! I know myself, alas, and how often I let myself be carried off against my own conviction ; I shall embark on productions to which I'm invited, and they'll make me horribly *repent* my share in them. Please remember my folly with that Tannhäuser at Zurich ! Enough,— with my continually augmented loathing of this whole ruck of theatres and singers, it positively makes me *shudder* to think of mingling in that stew again ; *I*, more than any one else, feel *what* I sacrifice there. Even *you*, I know it, do not understand or comprehend that fully.—*What* do I *gain*, then, by exposing myself to all the chicanery of a legal prosecution ? Nothing, for sure, save fresh occasion for self-sacrifice and over-exertion ; whereas it is the world alone that strictly gains thereby. Comical notion, that I should first have to pay for it by letting myself be maltreated in Dresden !— There'd be a chance of my very soon and bitterly repenting it. Consider that yourself as well.

Then, *where* to settle really down ? In Dresden under no conditions ; for a hundred reasons not.—In a small

city, *à la* Weimar ?   I've had my fill of these small cities.
So nothing but a big city, where one at the same time
can keep quietly to oneself, and yet find pleasant entertainment through the theatre and society as need arises.
This chiefly for your own sake, too, as you cannot altogether share my penchant for retirement, in which I really
am best off.   Consequently—Berlin or Vienna.   Good ;
but as first condition, no appointment there either, no
obligation, but complete independence, merely lending a
hand when I chose.   What tells against Vienna, is its
entire foreignness to us at bottom ; which is a consideration, you see, with a definitive last place of sojourn.
Berlin—well, we shall see ; but neither does *it* truly offer
me such attractions that I should care to be locked up for
them first, and perhaps I could live much more agreeably
in any other large town.— So—well considered, *what*
should I strictly be winning ?—By all means the chance
of looking round the theatres, to make my choice for first
productions of my works.   Capital ! but that also would
be *all*.   And even that might be made good if I did *not*
return to Germany ; it wouldn't be impossible.—For, if
the Minister's answer proved of such a nature that I must
renounce all future prospect, I should definitely choose
Paris for my abiding domicile.   There we would go to
Passy, close to the Champs-Elysées, definitively install ourselves modestly but quite comfortably—and remain there
even if I were allowed thereafter to return, which would
only then be necessary for stray performances, accordingly
on visit.   Then I should make *Strassburg* the place where
I should always give my operas first, beginning with
Tristan at once this summer, when we two could meet
again there.   I know how to set about it with Strassburg
now ; on that another day !—

There, I've thrown together quite enough to let you form a notion of my frame of mind. It is needful you should know that precisely, and enter thus into my views. —

I beg you, as a beginning, to give me the exact address and titles of the present Minister of Justice. Then I will write to him forthwith ; and rest assured I shall write very calmly, becomingly and temperately, but also very clearly and decidedly, so that he may learn in particular that my interest [in the return] to Germany is less great than must necessarily be that of those for whom I should then exert myself.—Perhaps I shall forward you the letter, for you to hand to him yourself ; then he perhaps will also give yourself the answer for me. —

And now I must conclude for to-day ; I am still below par. True, I'm out of bed again, but walking is still quite a misery. They've put my leg into a fearfully tight surgical stocking, meant to keep the rush of blood away from the inflamed and swollen veins. What things they are !

You don't mention whether you have received from Karl the score of Rheingold.—Anyhow you already have *two* pianoforte scores of Iphigenia, haven't you ? You don't mention that either. One of them is for Tichatscheck ; if you don't know what to do with the other, why, make it a present to the Devrient.—You will also receive 10 copies of the *Tristan* [poem] ; you should distribute them as follows :

      1 For the entirely good Minna.

      1 ,,   the Devrient

      1 ,,   Heine

      1 ,,   Fischer

      1 ,,   Tichatscheck

                        1 For Pusinelli
                        1 ,,   Ritter
                        1 ,,   Kläre Wolfram
and put the others by to be disposed of later.

   And now a thousand times the finest farewell! I
can't write any more. I still have no news from Hanover
or anywhere else. It's ebb again ; but just have patience,
we shall not want for money in future. And so farewell,
you party-goer! Go on giving me joy through good news
of yourself.

                                              Thy R. W.

156.*

                                   VENICE, 3. *January* 1859.

WELL, YOU ENTIRELY GOOD MUTZINIUS,

        You gave me a great delight with your letter on
New Year's Eve. I was in great anxiety again, as you
hadn't written for so long, and your last letter had made
me fear you were feeling worse. I was on the point of
writing to N. [about it] when, together with yours, came
a letter from Karl announcing his approaching return and
at the same time assuring me you were decidedly better
than [when he saw you] last at Zurich, also that N. had
confirmed your feeling better. My God! where would be
the use of all the good and the better we hope for this
year, if you didn't take such thorough care of yourself
that your restoration to health should make you capable
of tranquilly enjoying what we hope for? The knowledge that I had been too anxious, and you were in better
spirits again, gave me a very pleasant, kindly New Year's

---

   * Between this and no. 155 another letter is clearly missing, since
Minna wrote a friend Dec. 29, '58, that she had heard from her husband
"yesterday"; see my Introduction to the *Mathilde* volume, pp. xxvii and
xxxi.—Tr.

Eve. I was glad to hear that you also meant going to
bed early that evening, for I had purposed doing just the
same myself. I turned in at 11, and my only anxiety
was to avoid hearing it strike 12 ; at last I dozed off :
suddenly the tower clock struck ; I counted in vexation,
but—it struck 5 in the morning. So, slept luckily over
into the new year ; may you have been equally successful ! !—

On New Year's morn I telegraphed to you in the
best, serenest humour ["with all my valuables in pawn"—
letter to Liszt], and only hope the despatch reached you in
good time for breakfast ; you must let me know that.
In the evening Karl arrived, against my hope ; he was in
lively vein, and had a lot to tell me, but I didn't get
your nice kind presents till next morning. The cigar-
cases are famous, and do you great credit, as myself a
great pleasure ; I return you my best thanks for them.
With the so long and ardently desired snuff I really had
hard luck : how I was looking forward to the first pinch !
Then I am seized by a violent cold in the night, and by
morning have lost all sense of smell, so that—when Karl
at last brings me the snuff—I have no sensation from the
pinch at all ! Isn't that shameful ?

Your intending to forward me the beautiful piano-rug
later really pains me ; it looks as if I still had to make
myself thoroughly at home here. Nevertheless it will
give me great delight to compose the third act of Tristan
on your mat, and so I say : Why, send it on as soon as
finished ! Simply put it in the post ; there's always
some to-do this end, but that won't matter. When we
come together again, though, I shall have to get a small
van-load sent after me, I've had to add so many things to
my domestic comforts here.—

I have commenced this year with a tranquil mind and honestly good hope. A voice tells me it will be a luck-bringing one, resolving much, and furnishing a good desired solution. To myself it now is also certain that in a few months I shall have obtained my amnesty. Hurry nothing, I beg you; don't ask for that safe-conduct of your own accord. Whatever is the good of first consenting to submit myself for trial, when so much now lets me hope I may assume that I have done enough already with my own two letters, to the King and to Prince Albert, and the result will soon appear entirely of itself? Even Liszt, who always has been dubious, writes me this time (New Year's Eve) that he firmly hopes to see me back in Germany this spring. Anyhow, then, prospects have been opened, so let us wait for the answer from Carlsruhe first; at any rate for that—as we thence shall learn quite plainly how the Saxon Government is minded, and we can direct our further steps accordingly with greater safety, should any such be needed still. I wrote you on this question quite calmly the last time again *; let me hope you agree with me that, *if* it is possible, this agony of a trial etc. must be spared me. No doubt it will not suit the Herr Staatsanwalt, who would like to swell his own importance; nevertheless, however excellent a man he be, I've no desire to gratify him that way.—So—a tiny wait!—

Your communications always give me great delight, especially when they're framed in that humour peculiar to you. I had a good laugh at Fipsel's "mask" and Jacquot's terror of it. The dear good beasts!

The new Tannhäuser performances have been an

---

* The "zuletzt noch einmal" is a further indication of that letter which my last footnote assumed to be missing.—Tr.

agreeable surprise to me. Why, you should be quite reviving now, dear Minna, under such fine and refreshing impressions! Wasn't I right when I kept feeling that the Zurich winters, in particular, were bound to have something very depressing for you? My fancy is constantly occupied with my projects for work, which can make me finally forget and do without all else; but you, poor woman, what had you? It really must be quite heartening and livening you up now!—For that matter, I perfectly believe you as regards the Ney; only I mustn't be blamed for not having been able so of a sudden to efface the impression I had gained in London of her personality. So, that has changed now, she has become slim; which of itself does much. I also know quite well what one can do with such a glorious voice; if she gradually makes friends with my music, I've no doubt I shall find in her a very weighty pillar for my further representations in Germany. In that sense this experience has procured me a new, quite unexpected artistic aid, upon which I shall reckon in future. Please call on her, and give her my kindest regards; thank her in my name, and convey her my hopes for the future, for my Isolde, my Brünnhild or Sieglinde, and so forth.—You see, I am no hardened sinner!

I should have written you yesterday or the day before, if I hadn't wanted to wait for a message setting me in certainty whether they had forwarded you twenty louis d'or from Hanover—as I gave orders there. Even yet I've no full confirmation that this has also been done, but merely a general intimation that they will send me the fee for Rienzi (as to which I wrote at last); I'm bound to have the point cleared up, though, within the next few days. If you have received the money, I shall know you're a little flush again for a while, and will make it my first care that you never run dry. Rely upon me.—In general also this sort of affair will soon get into satisfactory trim now, so that I shall soon have discharged my few remaining obligations (the Zurich bills were paid forthwith by Heim out of the 1000 *fr.* I sent him) and both of us may look forward to a bountiful year free of care. I have particularly great hopes of Vienna ; in a few days they'll be giving their 17th performance of Lohengrin, for the benefit of the Pension Fund (better than ever !). In every way Vienna gives me great delight ; every remark from there about my opera is always so respectful and unconditionally admiring, that I am bound to infer a great impression. Who knows :· Vienna [for our home] after all, as you have wished so often ?—Thus much is certain : if all fruit fails, through Minister v. Bach I can get the Kaiser to allow me access to all his realms in spite of Saxony and German Bund. I have received quite definite hints to that effect.—So— another door would be open ! In short, this year I *must* pass in ! May Fipsel only not get too fat by then, but rather lend yourself a little.—

Karl has this moment arrived for his evening call ; he is greatly attached to me now, and I have grown equally fond of him. I am trying to help him onward in his works just now ; Liszt wants him to write an opera : I am plying him too, and think it will come off ; anyhow he has the stuff in him.

For the rest, I'm as well known here already as a spotted dog, particularly through my grey fur-cap ; every-one nudges his neighbour and points me out. At the glover's to-day I heard I was the greatest composer of the present day ; that comes from the number of visitors, and through Vienna. I have accepted no invitations as yet, and shall abide by it ; at the restaurant, however, a little group has already organised which always waits for me there, and with whom I'm glad to chat sans gêne from time to time. There is Prince Dolgoruki, an Austrian Count, a Venetian music-master (a terrible enthusiast of mine), and Winterberger. Others form audience at a distance.—

The good little leg is so-so again ; we have splendid weather, and I enjoy my long-discarded promenades once more. May you also be having fine weather at last ; enjoy it right calmly and comfortably ! But no more punch, please, else I'll peach to Pusinelli ! A thing like that won't suit you now.—

Give the excellent N. my very best thanks for her ingenious attending to your Christmas present. How glad I shall be if she proves herself, and becomes what she can and should be to you ! Now farewell ; a thousand hearty greetings, and God with you !—Soon more and better— once again, Good luck !

Thy

R.

Have you distributed the copies of Tristan, like a good girl ? Particularly to the Devrient—which interests me highly. And to Ritters ?—

157.

MY GOOD MINNA,

My kindest greetings and thanks for your letters ! The one received to-day, however, was too long overdue ; every evening when I came home from dinner my first look was at the table where my letters are always placed,

as they generally arrive in that interval : as I found none,
and had intended waiting for your answer to my last, I
likewise postponed writing to you, since I kept thinking
—Her letter is sure to come tomorrow, and then you can
answer that as well.   You mustn't ever take it ill of me,
that I like to have frequent reports on your condition ; even
when it includes complaints, a letter always reassures me
very much—the mere sight of it makes me feel that.   I
shall write to Pusinelli one of these days.—Dear Minna,
nothing concerns me so much, as to have good and gratifying prospects of your health.   Everything else lies
in human power, and what I cannot attain I must strike
from my mind, to turn what remains to me to the utmost
advantage.   By which I mean, as regards the final settlement of our patriation question : let it fall out in this year
as it will, in *our* hands it lies to decide for ourselves—
according to circumstances—and establish our domestic
hearth as well as possible.   But—health : that's what *you*
have to bring to it, good Mutz !   Take thorough good
care of yourself, and think of nothing now beyond procuring yourself everything, and observing everything, that
is of service to you ; that is your duty, not only to yourself—but also to me.—

The symptoms which alarm you now and then at
present are truly no matter for wonder ; all your organs
have been taxed in the highest degree by your incessant
heart-trouble and sleeplessness.   In a lower degree that
was also the case before, particularly in the form of
prolonged debility after agitating conditions.   But if the
heart-beat only improves a little (as indeed you have
assured me, to my joy !), the principal cause disappears,
and—after rest, recreation, a good cure and cheerful visit to
the country—the organs will regain their strength at last,

and—ultimately your good constitution will enduringly conquer, especially if all moral sufferings stay more and more aloof. And that lies in our own—in my hands ; I'll see to that, I promise you !—

I am fairly melancholy on the whole now ; I have to keep on calling to myself with all my might : Hold out ! Patience ! Sit firm !—Neither should I care to pursue this sort of life for long ; though I mostly choke my longing for varied activity and an ampler, more stimulating life in general by recalling my past experience, and reflecting that this world can only yield me more annoyance and dissatisfaction, at bottom, than contentment and uplifting. When I think of the celebrity I now have reached, the number and variety of those by whom my works are admired and loved, and yet that I cannot even attain to so much as to be able to exist and move about in unmolested safety, the question can't but haunt me, What can be the matter with the whole of this world ? All have words, words, regrets, condolences—but definite, thorough-going help occurs to none.—My sole remaining trust is pinned to the Grand Duke of Baden.

In a very short time, the next few days perhaps, I must know the last answer from Saxony. Devrient wrote me last time that the G.D. had instantly expressed his readiness to grant my wish and make definitive enquiries forthwith at Dresden concerning my projected visit to Carlsruhe ; at the same time he [the G.D.] sent me word that, after the declarations already received, he was sure of obtaining no refusal to his request, and consequently I might count on it as positively as one could count on anything in matters human. Devrient is so sure of his affair that I have already had to forward him the first act of Tristan for copying out [of the parts], since his

copyists are very slow and he would like to have something rehearsed before the summer vacation.   So let us
wait for that definitive answer from Dresden.   If it turns
out according to the G. D.'s expectation, I think I shall let
that suffice for the present, and do nothing further in the
matter.   Once I'm at Carlsruhe and can get into personal
contact with the young Highnesses, I hope for sure to bring
the whole affair to a definitive conclusion there.   Should
there be nothing else for it, however, I am determined
then to go from Carlsruhe to Dresden with a safe-conduct,
to bring the matter to a legal head and final clearance ;
you have my word on that !   So—everything shall certainly be set in order *this* year.

Should King Johann on the other hand revoke his
promise to the G.D., against all expectation, it then
remains agreed that I address myself exhaustively to the
Minister of Justice, as we settled before, and—if there's
nothing else whatever for it—surrender myself at Dresden
before Carlsruhe.   It surely would be disgraceful, though,
if these grudging hard-hearted folk should think needful
thus to torture me first ; but—I can't conceal it from
myself—one may credit them with anything !   Even here
I have recently heard that the Saxon ambassador to
Vienna had actually demanded my instant expulsion from
Venice : that was the time when my pass was redemanded
of me.   The Vienna ministry replied by asking the
ambassador whether he would present a formal request for
my expulsion in the name of his Government : Austria
would be very loth to comply with it, more particularly
as I had a good Swiss pass and stood under the protection
of Switzerland, whilst Austria was on very friendly terms
with Switzerland at present.   The ambassador thereon
said nothing more about it, and—I was allowed to stay.—

This was reported hither through an official of the Vienna ministry; therefore your communication to a similar effect finds me already acquainted with the matter. All the more reason, now we see what pleasant little gentlemen these are at Dresden, for my not wishing you to give yourself away. Indeed it will avail you nothing: in the best event a few fair words, but without any serious results.—

Now I have shewn you the way I mean to go, I hope you will agree to it. I shall know something quite definite very soon, you see, and hope for a good issue; for— as I told you last time—even Liszt, the mysterious, writes very confidently at last. He simply points to the fact of the Duke of Coburg (who—*entirely between ourselves*— wants to dedicate his new opera to me !!??) having lately taken very serious counsel about my situation, and—as it seems—set measures on foot (perhaps in the Bundestag) which have inspired Liszt with such great confidence. So I really think it's bound to come to pass in a fashion honourable to myself at last.—

Liszt is quite disheartened about his position at Weimar, and has given the Opera up entirely.— It has been a singular tale with Rienzi. You know how long that opera has been going to come out there. It seems that Liszt had been put off at Court, particularly through Dingelstedt. I had commissioned Liszt to extract me a specially handsome fee for it; even then he thought I had better not set it too high, as he had difficulties in bringing out the opera at all. In itself that riled me. Finally Dingelstedt sends me an official letter of enquiry, a short time back, about Rienzi and what fee I should ask. I answered him just as tersely, that I had never asked a fee from Weimar, but received what they deemed becoming !

Reply : he offers me 25 louis d'or, to be paid after the first representation.   I forwarded that letter to Liszt, made somewhat merry over it, and simply remarked that I was accustomed to receive my fee from every theatre immediately on its receipt of the score.   After a while he begged me not to leave Dingelstedt without an answer, as the latter made a point of it.   Then the thing disgusted me at last ; I wrote Liszt a letter for him to shew, telling him I didn't care a rap about the Weimar production of Rienzi etc., yet giving him to understand they still might salt me if they sent me a respectable fee *at once*.   Honestly, that was my only real object ; but Liszt, who has long been in strained relations with Dingelstedt, and was merely watching for a good excuse for rupture, seized this occasion to withdraw Rienzi and proudly declare he would conduct *no* more operas.—Really that was too much for me, and I answered Liszt, with humour, that he had taken the thing too seriously, I had simply meant to give him a weapon for threatening with and quickly extracting a good fee.   Well, *he* has taken that amiss again.   Nonsense without end !—

Now I'll answer a few things in your letter.—I can only understand X's silly behaviour to you on the assumption of his being (between ourselves) a good person.   You are the friend (probably he also believes, the confidante) of his wife, and that is enough to make him suspect you.   Just leave him alone for the present.— But tell me for Heaven's sake, what is all this about a " *Hôtel de Saxe* " story which I am supposed to know already, and regarding which you make use of strange expressions to me ?   *I haven't a notion :* let that suffice you.   Moreover, accept my assurance that I have not made X my confidant with a single word ; never have I

mentioned the *least thing* to him. Another piece of
rubbish ! !—

Would you like to know how I brought about the
acceptance of Rienzi at Hanover after all ? You having
written me that *Niemann* had taken fright as to getting
through the part after hearing T[ichatschek] in it, I
wrote and asked him if he hadn't detected that T. was
really covering up his true weakness with that immense,
often quite needless parade and display of staying power ;
or if he believed there was nothing else in Rienzi than
just one everlasting cheerful outlet for the voice ? By
all means [I told him] T. imposed thereby, and his strict
object was simply to prove that nobody could imitate him
in that ; with thorough love of mischief, he had done this
for the benefit of Niemann also, who is young still and certainly nothing like so distinguished a singer. So I shewed
him how the rôle should be conceived, to solve my task,
instead of merely cloaking it with staying-power. Then
I told him that if he gave the rôle so originally, [i.e.]
according to my own conception, he for the first time
might shew T. himself what there lay in Rienzi. That
is my honest opinion, and I may tell yourself that T. is
by no means my ideal Rienzi. In this part, where nothing
ever serves him save his strength of voice and staying-
power, he does me positive harm ; and I want a more
intelligent performer to solve the task, and at the same
time prove it isn't *only* T. who can sustain it.—Well,
that gave Niemann quite another notion ; and the opera
at once was set down for performance in H.—Perhaps you
will reproach me with a little treachery to T. ; but reflect,
dear child, how oppressed and contraried I always have
felt by intimacy with this sort of people, who strictly
stand the breadth of heaven apart from me. I can't

deny it, I do not make much account of friendships of this kind. His attachment touches me, however, and so I take a good deal else into the bargain.—

In general I have grown rather fastidious toward the Dresden art-world, for example, through my long exile ; a certain class of trashy talk has become very painful to me. Had even the *Devrient* nothing better to say of my Tristan, than her remark about the long death-scene in the third act ? So this act is nothing save a death-bed ? Well, *I* can see in it a deal besides, and even the practical side of its execution has been well thought out by me. Really, the lady is only cut out for the stage ; to which, I'm astonished to hear from you, she would like to return. Can she never conceive of art as art, then, but merely as stage-routine ?

Ask Papa Fischer if he knows of any poet who wrote a drama in a state of amorousness (*Verliebtheit*) ? As if Schiller must have written his " Robbers " among a pack of bandits, or Shakespeare his " Othello " as a jealous husband ! One can depict nothing truly (*nichts wahrhaft dichten*), particularly in Drama, which does not stand outside one, so that one sees it as if in front of him ; if one is involved in it, he is incapable of clear poesy. But that is not given to everyone to comprehend, and least of all that the poet, just because he is a poet, can even portray a world he has never seen, as Jean Paul an Italy he never had travelled.—I still can remember Count Redern's surprise when he made my personal acquaintance in Berlin after the Flying Dutchman : " Good God —he said—but you're quite a pleasant sort of man ; from your opera I should have expected to find a gloomy, forbidding character." Ah—no doubt I shall have plenty more of that kind of stuff to hear, once I get about

in the world again ; but I also shall grow indifferent to
it ! For the present I'm mostly a trifle too melancholy ;
I grant it, my seclusion has its shady sides. Moreover,
I'm never quite well ; my susceptibleness is always
increasing. The long want of movement has put my
liver (*Unterleib*) out of order. What I chiefly suffer from
are chills ; never have I frozen so much, as in Italy.
Certainly my apartments are only reckoned for summer,
as they have no sun, the bedroom never ; what that costs
for firing in these wretched stoves, with these badly fitting
doors and windows, is enough to make your hair stand.
My only hope remains an early advent of Spring, when I
mean to enjoy my lodgings thoroughly at last ; but it
will then be getting time to think of turning out ! !—

Doubtless Karl has told you of my soirée ? An
Italian music-master, a great enthusiast of mine, had
played the Minstrels' Contest on the piano to Prince
Dolgoruki ; then I told them they could form no notion of
it that way, they must come to me one evening and I
would sing it. And so it befell. To wind up, I gave
them ices. For that matter, it won't be repeated.—

Here come my evening callers, Karl and Winterberger ; so I suppose I must conclude here, as the brats
won't take No for an answer. I will write you about
Karl another time : he has shewn me his piece ; it has
great beauties, but also great defects, which he's altering
at my suggestion.—I am instrumenting at present, and
think of sending Härtels some manuscript again at last ;
God grant I may be able to go on undisturbed now. I
may tell you so much : I have never written such a
piece of music as this second act ; all my other works are
indifferent to me now in comparison. Only trust me ;
when I *do* compose, it turns out nothing ordinary.

But farewell for to-day, dear good Minna ! Put your best foot forward and defy the scurvy climate, which seems indeed to be exquisitely bad in Dresden. Here it's nearly always bright, even if somewhat cold on account of the North wind. If I could only give you ever-smiling skies and fine soft air ! Even for that, tho', means may yet be found. Meanwhile—just a little more patience and calm ! Good times will come !—

Give Nette my best regards, and thank her in my name for her care of you. Should anything good turn up, you shall hear of it promptly ; otherwise—always an answer by return. Adieu, hearty greeting and kiss from

Thy

RICHARD.

158.

VENICE, 25. *January* 1859.

Well, dear Mutz, I mean to write you properly at last to-day. It's always the same with me, when I'm at work ; then I really have to crowd my time up, and how other people often have so much to spare for parties or card-playing, is beyond my comprehension. I work till 3, and can take up nothing else all morning if I am not to be made useless for work. Then I take my consti-tutional, generally get to dinner by $\frac{1}{2}$ past 4, and am back home about 6. If I rest a moment then, I have only just time to write a letter before 8, when Karl usually comes ; but I often have to countermand even Karl, if I've a number of letters to write. Working another short hour in the evening occurs very seldom, as I always have letters to write ; a little reading still seldomer, in fact only when Karl doesn't come. I have been to the theatre some three times in all ; I'll tell you of that by mouth

one day.   Lord knows we always have such a number of
more serious things to discuss, and in particular you
keep giving me so much renewed anxiety yourself, that I
really never have the heart to entertain you with such
a thing.

The amount of letters I have to write is appalling !
Everybody is so dull of apprehension, and the simplest
things have to be put on paper three times to and fro
before I even can get the plain answer I ask for. They're
all like that, especially Härtels and of late good Ed.
Devrient.   From the latter, however, I at last have
elicited exactly how things stand with my projected
descent upon Carlsruhe.   I can't say I'm dissatisfied with
this last information, because I see that the production of
Tristan in my presence is at any rate ensured, and no
longer depends on the grace of King Johann, which
might have made it doubtful to me still.   But what I'm
going to tell you is in the very *privatest confidence :* as
women never gossip, only men (of which you've lately
given me such an infallible proof again !), I may count
upon your strictest silence, mayn't I ? Of course I didn't
even need to say so to you ; for, as you will perceive that
its success depends entirely on the greatest secrecy, it
goes without saying, that the secret will not reach the
public ear through you.   It is this : the Grand Duke [of
Baden] has decided to let me come to Carlsruhe entirely
on his own responsibility, and not enquire at all again in
Dresden first.   Once I am there, the Saxon Government
may demand what it pleases, he'll let them talk and hold
them off till I've done and the production is over.   He
has considered it in all its bearings, and is sure of his
affair.   Only if anything leaked out *beforehand,* if the
Saxon Gov. got wind of it, and opposed it with distinct

demands, that might make its execution impossible to
the G.D. ; whereas he knows how to excuse himself for
the accomplished fact.   That's how it stands ; and so
it's fixed and settled now for all eventualities.   So—the
6th of September ; we'll keep your birthday together the
day before.   The Devrients shall hire me a lodging close
by them for us two and our animals, where you must
arrive if possible before me, to receive me in it.   Thenceforward, good Minna, we unconditionally remain together ;
whither we next direct our footsteps, will be likewise
all settled by then.

This would also fit in with your prescribed summer
cure in the country, which you would have finished by
the end of August in any case.   God grant I may receive
you back strengthened then, and full of good trust in your
health !   I hope so !   Your sadly bitter promises in the
event of your not feeling pronouncedly better, I don't take
as so seriously meant ; I should think you must know
that every creature, every animal, stands all the closer to
me when I know it to be suffering, and how much more
my poor dear sore-tried wife !   You won't therefore
suspect you'd be more indifferent to me if you were not
suffering, will you ?   Enough on that sore point !—

I haven't arrived at writing Pusinelli yet ; my God,
I'm owing so many other letters !   But it shall be done
within the next few days.   Like the true and valiant friend
he is, he has undertaken all responsibility to me for your
cure.   It is nothing new to me, that you cannot be
radically healed of your heart-trouble; even Dr. Ehrismann
told me as much from the first : but I have repeatedly
sought to console you with the knowledge that it looks
worse than it is.   At all events your ailment can be
mitigated to such an extent that it becomes quite

endurable, and you accustom yourself to it as thoroughly as almost every person in his second half of life has to get used to some chronic complaint.   It will not prevent your attaining the full old age appointed you by Nature ; but the principal thing needed for that, and no mistake, is peace of mind.   With *that* you are rescued, and for that your physician is—*I;* I know my obligation, and faithfully shall fulfil it to the end of my life.   First of all, whatever may decide itself about our future habitation in the next half-year, I am chiefly attending now to that which may and will contribute much to giving us such ease of mind that we can jog along anywhere : and that is plenty of *money !*—I am springing every mine now, to get all the profit I can from my works.   I shall even renounce the printing of the full scores of my Nibelungen, since that entails sacrifices which would be simply deducted from *me* in the end ; whereas I expect to be doing fair business in time with the piano-forte scores.   I may count on 12,000 *fr.* income this year for certain ; but more on that another day, when I shall have further definite results to state.—

Yesterday evening I received a telegram from Bülow on the success of Lohengrin at Berlin on the 23rd.   All it says is : " Great success.   Applause more decided than with Tannhäuser.   Representation tolerable, especially Formes."   Perhaps you already will know more details than I,—it is only through yourself that I heard of his scene with the public [at B.'s own concert] ; silly snappish fellow !—The notice you also sent me about Liszt, to be sure, is very spiteful ; indeed he didn't deserve *that*, neither was the scene at Cornelius's opera so bad as all that.   These newspaper writers are thorough hounds. You know that that sort of thing doesn't affect me any longer. The paragraph about the G.D. of Weimar and a production of the Nibelungen amused me, especially the chorus of 200. Still, I have reason to suppose that something decisive has occurred at Weimar now, and it is precisely the pitiful conduct of a certain Court clique (with Dingelstedt) *against* Rienzi, that has contributed to this. Liszt is still silent, which makes me believe it this time. For that matter, the G.D.'s *wanting* it [the *Ring*] is nothing new.—

The news about *Heubner* profoundly distressed me, as you well may imagine ! At first I believed I must make up my mind not to take another step with the Saxon Government ; on regaining my calm, however, I saw that everything else I propose to do *then* can only have its due effect after I have done my uttermost with Dresden. Under no condition shall I submit to an examination ; but I'll presently write to the new Minister of Justice, and put forth my last endeavour to win this man as friend and gain my amnesty through him. Should that fall flat, with a good conscience I can tell those to whom I next address myself that I have done *everything* to attain the selfsame end I should have attained long since with far less trouble if luck had only made of me a Badian, Austrian, or even a Russian subject. The Bundestag, dear Minna, cannot compel the King of Saxony to pardon me ; but if the King will not accede to its representations in my favour, it can permit me to take up my residence in any other German state excepting Saxony. And that—I shall attain. As soon as I have the final refusal of the Saxon Minister of Justice, I shall draw up my petition to the Bundestag, and get it supported there by the Grand Dukes of Baden, Weimar, and Coburg, also the Emperor

of Austria (through Minister v. Bach) I hope, and
perhaps the Prince of Prussia. Eh, it has recently been
suggested to me that, if I addressed myself to the Emperor
of Russia (who has recalled all political offenders exiled
to Siberia, and has now made one of them the Governor
of a province), I should find in him an energetic mediator.
No, good Minna, luckily I have still a card to play !

And now to get my work done first ! I have sent
Härtels some manuscript to-day ; by the end of February
I hope to have the third act itself in front of me. Ah,
if all-bountiful God would but grant me the boon of
remaining in fairly good health, not getting waylaid
by too great cares, and above all, of always having
right good tidings from yourself ! Then—once I'm
thoroughly in vein again, after that hideous interruption
—I know I shall bring the last act fluently and finely
to its end within 3 months. Meanwhile you'll be
commencing your country cure ; where ?—that is just
what I mean to discuss with Pusinelli. Then if we
really have money, no doubt you'd better take a little
recreation trip until I can be beautifully received at last
in Carlsruhe by my flourishing old woman ; when we
shall meet again as if re-born, to learn the reason why
we ever nagged and plagued each other so. I fancy that
is pretty much how everything will hap ; do you
agree ?—

I can thoroughly understand the Tichatscheck furniture being disagreeable to you now. Please do yourself
no violence, but get whatever you want sent from Zurich.
You may easily believe you'll be receiving some more
money shortly ; so don't gêne yourself, I shall not let
you lack.—

Once again, then, let this be enough for to-day ; I'm

quite done up.—But tell the Devrient she is perfectly right that there's no artist like her nowadays, for she's a genius ; but one oughtn't to make oneself angry about it, and above all, not turn bitter.   To *know* a thing like that, is the true exaltation, not to quarrel over it.—

Now farewell. Greet the whole tribe also, which would please me thoroughly if it consisted entirely of women ; because no scandal would reach your ears then, since it's only males that gossip !   O you stupid Minna ! Never mind, be a thousand times saluted by

Thy

RICHARD.

O Nette !   O Fips !   O Jacquot !

159.

VENICE, 7. February 1859.

DEAR MINNA,

I see very well, I was a fool to let myself be betrayed into any share whatever in the odious gossip that continues to surround you, to my deep distress.   I thank you, also, for having returned me the letter in which I expressed myself to you about it ;* I should really have been obliged to attach more reason to your declaration that I had offended you afresh thereby, if I had not had this opportunity of reading it through again.   *How* you understood those lines, is your affair ; it is my own satis-faction, that I seriously and honestly meant to enlighten you concerning a slur on my character, and whatever may have offended you in them reposes on your own misunder-standing.   However, it has given me an experience the more, how circumspectly I must deal with you, and that

---

* Obviously a letter originally falling between this and no. 158 but subsequently destroyed by the writer.—Tr,

I had better put up with any and everything, than endeavour to explain things to you in my favour.—

I beseech you by all that there is in this world, Shut close your ear ! Don't let reports be brought to you by X or by anyone else, but think how we old folk may yet conduct a supportable life to its end. Really things are hard enough for us without that ! I am beleaguered with care upon care,* and never have a merry day, God knows, to win me but a semi-peaceful evening from this wretched mundane existence. It is becoming hard, very hard to me, to keep my courage up, and my weariness of life is greatly on the increase. I often feel of late as if it would be best for me to put an end for ever to this constant battle ! Whence should I gain but a vestige of joy ? Impeded in each and everything, restricted to news from without, I've got the length of picking every letter up with fear and trembling, which unfortunately prove only too justified. How can I help being so profoundly dejected that even tidings such as the Frommann's last make all but no impression on me any longer ? To pre-pare a time of kindly rest for both of us at the close of this wearying life, to tend yourself and sweeten your toil to the best of my power, is my sole remaining aspiration on this earth, to which I else hardly belong any more. Daily do I ponder how I best may set about attainment of this final goal, take this and that step toward it :—then another letter comes from you—the whole old misery is opened up afresh : I had once said this or that—so-and-

---

* Only three or four days previously he had received marching orders, not rescinded until after the present letter. His sparing his wife the upsetting intelligence (*cf.* no. 162) is so characteristic of his treatment of her, that I feel bound to break my rule concerning footnotes to these volumes, and direct the reader's attention *in loco.*—Tr.

so can tell this or that,—and all has been in vain once
more ! !—I try to rectify ; I only make bad worse !—How
long is this to last with myself, too ?—I'm always poorly ;
not a day [passes] on which I am not plagued with this
or that disorder.   For a long time I've been suffering
increasingly in my lower regions again ; added to it,
a fresh severe cold : I couldn't go out again to-day, as
I had fever (also, my legs are swollen).   I had been long
impatient to receive an answer from you ; it comes,
another shock for me, and self-reproach that I had let
myself for once be tempted into intervening in your
everlasting gossip—you women and (to please me) men !
A sensible man should at least know what he intends and
with whom he has to deal ; and as soon as he has cleared
his mind on that, he should let the world talk as it
pleases.   I might have been entirely at ease thereon, for
I know what I intend, and can also tell myself that it is
good : I intend nothing more on this earth, than to cherish
you, to deal honourably, faithfully and well by you—God
is my witness—and so my reckoning might have finished ;
but alas—I still am a little mistaken as to whom I have
to deal with : unfortunately I have to keep experiencing
afresh that such insane misunderstandings can arise,
as now again.   Will this source of trouble ne'er dry
up ?—

A few days since I wrote to Pusinelli, and assured him
that he and his faithful interest in you were the only
thing that stopped me from repenting having ever let you
go to *Dresden ;* otherwise you had dropped into the most
atrocious scandal-hole, where you were always being
stung up afresh.   As your summer cure will take you
away from Dresden tittle-tattle, I mean to build good hope
on it, else I should have proposed to you to join me at

once; for it is to be hoped I should then at least be so far master in my house as to keep this eternal hearing "something," now from this person, now from that, at arm's length from you. Believe me, once you're with myself again, I mean to tend you better than your good lady-friends, who have nothing better to confide to you than Mad. T.—And I am even to hold my tongue when such an ass as that X behaves so rudely and insultingly towards my wife, who had received him in her house with open arms! I had only meant to let it depend on your answer, to write *to him* myself, and give him a piece of my mind about his insulting behaviour after I had particularly commended you to him as well; but God preserve me from it now! Heaven only knows what fresh proof of my want of affection for you I should be furnishing thereby again!—On the contrary, if it eases you, also believe that I've told the B.s about the Hôtel de Saxe story! Believe anything, and interpret everything as you think fit, I'll stand it all; for I see, my words and protestations avail me naught!—

But enough of that, I am horribly sick of it! God grant I very soon may hear you're out of Dresden. I heartily repent not having influenced you to go to Weimar; you would have been admirably looked after at the Altenburg, and in any case very intelligently and considerately treated. But I expected something different [from this], and didn't want to oppose you.—

My good Mutz, I can't tell you much more to-day. My not having written you earlier was because your intermediate letters seemed to contain nothing of equal importance to the letter I expected with an answer to my last. Everything else, the whole Berlin Lohengrin, doesn't chain my interest enough. If you want to go and

hear it, though, please do ; you will shortly be receiving
10 louis d'or again which I've assigned to you—from
Mannheim (through Härtels). For the rest, I've much
trouble and weariness ; to-day I feel aching and ill all
over, and wish I—

Child, child ! fulfil your promise, and—not another
word about the past !—

If I feel a bit better and freer tomorrow or the day
after, I'll write you again, but hope to be never prevailed
on again to wade in that pitiful mud with you !—

Salute our house-mates.   If you are suffering, console
yourself with me ; I'm suffering—also !—

Farewell ! Very soon more from

Thy
very bad Husband.

160.

VENICE, 10. *February* 1859.

MY GOOD MINNA,

I haven't felt well the last few days, and have had
to break off work ; [whilst] I've had to spend my utmost
capability of writing anything on all kinds of letters, none
of which has given me pleasure.   Added to which, I
should like to write you in as good humour as possible : I
think your rug will assist me to that at last.   The certificate has come, and I'm to get it from the Custom-house
tomorrow ; so I shall reserve the close of these lines until
after I've seen it.—

Yesterday I also sent off an important letter to Dresden :
my last attempt to ascertain what I have to expect from
there.   After mature reflection, though, I haven't addressed this enquiry to the Minister of Justice, from whom
I no doubt should have got nothing but a dry evasive
answer.   No, I hunted for a high-placed, influential

person, of easy access to the King, and with whom a word could really be exchanged ; and I hit on my old Lüttichau, who after all stands nearest to me of them all, and to whom at the same time I could make a proposal for the regulation, in a happy event, of that advance from the Pension Fund I had left in the lurch. The letter naturally turned out a long one ; if I can any way manage it, however, I'll take a copy for you from the draft and enclose it by and by. It was of importance to give definite reasons once and for all why I cannot entertain the suggestion to present myself for trial after these 10 years : I have declared that this regard for my state of mind and health, thereon depending, is absolutely due from me to the claims of the art-world on myself and my works to be still created ; but I deem it of moment that the King should definitely know that I *cannot* consent to it. So I shall make everything hinge upon Lüttichau's answer ; I've written him in such a tone that I may assume he will do all that is possible to procure me perfect certainty. Should that fall out adversely, I then should try the other path of which I told you lately, through the German princes.—

Well, I shall have to wait that while before I can give you my final views about next winter and the fixed habitat to be chosen for the pair of us thenceforward. Is it to be in Germany, or is it to be abroad? That is the question, and as the answer doesn't stand within our power, we will not break our heads on it at present, since that would lead to nothing. Nevertheless I've been enquiring as to the climatic conditions of certain places, and among other things I have learnt to my sorrow that Vienna has a very bad climate. Strassburg is said to be quite unhealthy, and a miserable hole all round ; neither could one count upon the place itself at all, and I could far more easily bring off a German Opera in Paris, where there actually reside 100,000 Germans. However, no brain-racking on that point now, as said ; once the other is settled, that can soon be arranged. No doubt your own state of health will also have to be taken into consideration then ; perhaps suitable winter quarters in a nice mild climate may be of decided benefit to you, at least until your radical improvement. Venice, for instance, hasn't been precisely hot this winter, but I must say I've never enjoyed such clear, pure air, with blue and cloudless skies, almost throughout a whole winter before. November was stormy and raw, as everywhere ; but since then, on an average, we have had bright clear weather nearly all the time, mild, yet often fairly fresh ; and now we're also getting the beginning of Spring warmth. I almost think this climate would be bound to do you good : only I doubt if Venice itself and its canals would please you otherwise ; also, I'm not exactly mad on passing another winter here so soon. Karl's not having needed a fire comes from his living on the Riva, where the sun beats from its rising to its setting; also from his room being only about half as large as our little dining-room at Zurich, and as low again. It is a regular Venetian attic, and must be absolutely unbearable in summer. Moreover, Karl wasn't in Venice from November 20 to January 1, *i.e.* the coldest period, whereas it has been bright ever since, that is to say, sun in his room ; which counts for a very great deal in Italy. It would never have occurred to myself to take rooms on the Riva, as in all this else so tranquil Venice it is the only spot where from morn till eve cries, bagpipes, barrel-organs, Punch-and-Judy shows, and now at Carnival time even the music of rope-dancers

etc., never cease. I take my daily promenade the length
of it, and am as if in pieces when I've got through all the
hubbub ; so that I keep asking Karl, who always has his
windows open for the sun, how he can stand it. He
declares he has got used to it now, and indeed had done
no work at first whatever. That's true : at the outset he
rummaged Venice like a madman for pictures and art-
treasures, and was never to be found at home ; even now
one mostly cannot catch him. But I, on the other hand,
have my big room on the solemn, still Canal, and—for
the winter alas !—no sun. Added to it, a bleak corner
where the Messieurs Winds often come to quite terrible
blows when they're changing. Then, miserable stoves,
very badly fitting windows, and—with the exception of 2
to 3 hours—I'm all the time indoors. That makes a
fearful difference. Indeed, I should have moved out in
the end if I hadn't the Spring in front of me ; which
begins very early here, and precisely in this apartment,
lying as it does, should compensate me richly for the
winter. Already I'm stoking much less, and fancy I
soon shall leave off altogether.—

I can't tell you of any further special incidents, except
that they want to give my operas in *Moscow*. Härtels
forwarded me an enquiry they had received about
Lohengrin ; as the people there are not obliged to pay at
all if they can only manage to obtain the scores another
way, I believed it prudent to take counsel with my
Russian prince. So the latter has commissioned a friend
in Moscow to procure me advantageous terms there just
for honour's sake ; such a thing has always to be done
through personal influence, if anything decent is to come
of it. Then, still waiting for word from there, I learn
to-day through the Leipzig theatrical agent, who had

addressed himself to Fischer for the purpose, that he
had applied to Härtels specifically about Lohengrin,
but at the same time had orders from Moscow for the
whole of my operas.   So I cannot do better than await
the first Moscow answer, as I am sure to hear from there
then that it really is a matter of all my operas.   It would
be highly desirable if something quite decent should
result from it soon ; but I won't build too great hopes.

Give Papa Fischer my very kindest regards, and
thank him for his letter.   His news that there are no
more scores of Tannhäuser at all is certainly most fatal.
Just to lay in a small stock, I had recourse at once to
Boom and A. Müller, to whom I had once given copies,
and begged them to exchange the Tannhäuser, which
they must know quite well enough by now, for the
Tristan which they should receive from me instead next
autumn.   That would make two copies, which Fischer
has probably received already ; a *third* might be extracted
from Frau *Uhlich*, as Karl says he made a present of his
copy to poor Uhlich.   The widow might be offered the
former shop-price of 10 thlr. for it, which doubtless would
be welcome to her ; Fischer, or even yourself, will
perhaps be so good as to transact this.   He might
simply give the lady an intimation to hold it in readiness
in case it's needed.   Fischer might also take advantage
of the opportunity to have another thorough search
among Uhlich's papers for those lost portions of the
Rienzi scores, of which he tells me to my horror.   How
could such a thing have got lost ?   Can any part thereof,
by chance, be lying still at Fürstenau's ?   Please ask
Papa to set my mind at rest soon.—

God knows, nothing ever goes off smoothly, without
bother !—I'm thoroughly sick of it.—

Bülow writes me from Berlin of Hülsen's comical wrath at Lohengrin's "impertinent success," as he is said to have expressed himself because he can't give it as often as it's asked for : he would never have expected that ; and now Johanna's going to marry soon, what ever is he to do ? Every seat booked for six performances which haven't [all] been given yet, and constant fresh orders—it's really quite amusing. Presumably the Tuczek will have to take on Ortrud then.

For that matter, dear child, these young folk worry you too much ; let them be as they are, I don't believe they're half so bad, tho' everybody has his weakness. With such very *young* people, you see, one mustn't be too particular ; that's how I get on with them now quite well myself. Don't let what you hear from here and there disturb you too much ; Hans is bursting with zeal for his masters, and just as he is passionately devoted to myself and my successes, he also is incredibly susceptible to all attacks on his papa-in-law, attacks so often very spiteful. His behaviour at that concert was perhaps injudicious, but at any rate does honour to his character and ardour ; moreover, the consequences seem to be turning out quite well : the young Jews were furious, but he impressed everybody, and the cause isn't standing half so badly in Berlin now, even for himself ; in a few days he'll be giving his second concert. The immediately next piece after that scene was the prelude to Lohengrin, which was so frantically applauded that the audience was only annoyed, in turn, at its not being repeated.—

Liszt certainly seems to be in a state of profound ill-humour now, and I can discern that it isn't the scurrilities of the newspaper Jews (to which you might really pay a little less attention now and then !) nor the insignificant occurrences at the theatre, etc., that are to blame for it, but his experiences of the gross ingratitude, disloyalty and treachery, of those to whom he had shewn nothing but kindness. The man is palpably too grand and imposing a figure for our mass of German Gothams. In France a man like this, with such goodness of heart, such zeal for the advancement of others, and such eminent abilities, would be otherwise esteemed and honoured. It grieves me very much, and I shall make it my business to hearten him, for I almost fear he has become distrustful even of myself.—

I thank Herr Bürde very much for the attentions he is shewing you ; it is uncommonly gratifying to me to hear of such a thing. Don't you forget to remember me cordially both to him and his wife [the Ney].—

So I'll wind up for to-day, and save the blank space for admiring the rug, which I'm to receive from the Customs tomorrow, as said. The amount of red-tape in these Customs is wellnigh past belief ; so I'll conclude by telling you the tale of my cigars. As I didn't want to pay double duty [by bringing them] through Sardinia, I got Frau [Karl] Ritter to send these cigars after me from Lausanne, the beginning of September. Since then I've had to correspond as far as to Vienna, even to get permission to import them ; every week there has been something to attend to for them, and money to fork out. At last, with the beginning of February one has got the great length of permission and all, but—the cigars have been sent back to Lausanne ; merely two pounds of snuff had arrived, which I had got sent from Geneva, and for those I was asked to pay—40 francs duty. Prompt as my thanks for the snuff, I naturally would not accept it, and wrote off to Lausanne merely to keep the cigars there till I fetched them myself.—What eyes you'd make, if you could see me with my long *Turkish pipe!* For one gets excellent Turkish tobacco here, but wretched cigars. So, at breakfast just think of my long pipe and the ashes you'll have to knock out for me some day!—

11. *February.* (*Forenoon, during work.*)

This moment, dear Mutz, the rug has arrived, been unpacked, laid under the piano, and already made music on. It touched and moved me very much! How gladly would I have got yourself to spread the carpet for me, and let you witness my delight at this beautiful kindly work. There is something very doleful in my having to receive such intimate domestic presents from you at a distance now, and I cannot fight off a great sadness.

Dear good Wife, we have a hard life of it; let us conquer it at last! But only from the inner fortress of the heart can it be overcome; so rest, calm, peace to the heart! Everything is still to hope, and I hope it from the bottom of my soul; but for God's sake, oblivion! Keep Present and Future firm in eye, and vanquish by their aid the demon Past, and with it every feeling of revenge! I'm preaching you no sermon, and should not be elect to; but I am expressing my sincerest, heartiest wish. For—I do so want to recompense you yet for all the sorrows of your life; myself I now have hardly any other than those of knowing you not yet released from yours. What else in life can truly pain us, than the belief that we had been betrayed? And what alone can remove that pain from us, save recognition that we really had deceived ourselves, and even our enemies were only suffering and

erring mortals, no wicked culprits? I know no better
and more thorough balm. And yet, so feeble is the
making of the human heart, that we scorn this best of
balms the fiercest, because we won't admit to our own
selves that *we* mistook. Thank God, I've overcome that
fatal vanity ; Heaven grant you soon this balm yourself !—

And now farewell ! Rest assured, your lovely rug
has given me great, affecting joy, and will do every day.
Accept my thanks, my greeting, and my hearty kiss
for it !

Thy
RICHARD.

161.

VENICE, 16. February 1859.

MY GOOD MINNA,

No, believe me, it isn't Venice that is harming
me. How should this ever-pure air, this cloudless sky,
be guilty of that ? But I might even be in Paradise,
and whence could I derive a sense of wellbeing ? Is
there aught that does not give me worry, care, unrest, or
everlasting labour ? What on the contrary affords me
merriment, nay, so much as distraction—to say nothing
of joy ? What gloomy thoughts have I not to digest
every day ! It is medically established that the majority
of human beings go to ground through an excess of cares
and troubles given no sufficient counterpoise by exhilaration, and that this is the cause of most illnesses. I have
found this plainly verified since yesterday and the day
before. Your last letter came the day before yesterday,
and just as I took it into my hand with the usual mis-
giving, thinking, " God, what will the matter be this
time ? " so the reverse effect of its calmer and brighter

contents was highly beneficial to me ; so that I suddenly felt as if a cramp, that had been wringing my vitals, were loosing its hold. And yesterday's letter from Pusinelli confirmed this good effect still more. His faithful, circumstantial and very minute report on your case and cure is the first thing that has really had a profoundly soothing and comforting effect on me for an inconceivable length of time. Tell him so, I beg you, and thank him a thousand thousand times for this benefaction,—for he thereby has given myself as well the best physic to help me now. So courage, confidence and hope ! Keep faith with Pusinelli ; give rout to that frenzy of fancies ; look free and clear into the world ; take people as they are ; make things as pleasant for yourself as possible, and attend to your health : when it will soon improve perceptibly and greatly. And if you won't let Pusinelli talk you out of Consumption, why, stick to it : after all it's better to imagine such a thing, than to have it in reality, when one generally refuses to believe it ! No, I have been relieved by our good friend in all respects. Keep watch on your heart, and all will be well ; and one ought to end by getting that a little under one's control !—

Only leave me here for the present, at least till I've finished the composition of the 3rd act : then I can instrument it somewhere else. Where?—What do I know ! I'm longing for mountain air this summer : Lucerne pleased me much the last time ; perhaps I shall ferret out a quiet cottage there, and thence make regular excursions up the Rigi and upon the mountains. But all this is merely scheme and dream ; I've settled absolutely nothing yet.

I am delighted with Schandau for yourself. It is

really very pretty, and you will remember what youthful pranks we played there, which may make the place not altogether disagreeable in your eyes : just think of that brown Rüpel with the tortoise. The air will do you good there, and as for money, I'm already seeing to as much as you can anyhow require.—

Dear Mutz, only the other day I wrote you at considerable length ; next time I'll write you more again : to-day I merely wanted to tell you that I feel somewhat better after these last letters. My fingers are perfectly stiff with writing ; I wrote to Tichatscheck yesterday.—I will tell you about business the next time. As to the dress for Frau Pauline, I must wait until I've money for it ; which also is bound to arrive.—You already know of my letter to Lüttichau, also that I will *never* submit myself to a judicial examination in Dresden : give the four gentlemen my politest and profoundest thanks for their beautiful self-sacrificing sympathy ; but never and under no conditions would I tread the road on which they thought of helping me, and I therefore thank them also most profusely for their noble aim.

Farewell and let this be enough for to-day. More again shortly. I thank you for your last letter, and breathe a little freer ! Be greeted heartily, and go on being of benefit to me and to—yourself !

Thy
RICHARD.

162.

VENICE, 27. *February* 1859.

BEST MINNA,

Either I must give up my work, or engage a secretary ; no longer will the two things go together. It is incredible how my connections and necessities for correspondence have been augmenting in the course of years, and particularly for some time past ; and yet there's very seldom anything delightful in it ! Your letter before last—besides itself requiring an immediate answer—at once occasioned me *three* business letters (to lawyer Schmidt, about Kriete's—to Boom again, about the scores —and to Härtels, about the preparation of new scores of Tannhäuser) : the fourth letter—to the King—I luckily had written and sent off already ; not to himself, indeed, but to the Minister of Justice, which is more expedient in my opinion, than to the King himself. I had already hit on the idea, myself, of laying all the emphasis on my (somewhat exaggerated) ill-health.—The expulsion affair here, I admit, you weren't to have learnt from me till later. The malignance of the Saxon Government—for it had occurred on *none* but their initiative—had so revolted and upset me, that I believed the news of it must make the same impression on yourself. As you were quite upset enough already by the last back-biting, I held it my duty to tell you nothing of this new act of meanness for the present. I'm very sorry for you, if you want to foist upon me any other motive ; naturally other people don't shew you so much consideration, and let you know. I had told it to Pusinelli at once, but begged him to spare it you ; a course he accordingly deemed wise to follow.

I was advised by the local police, as it was merely a question of furnishing a good excuse for my remaining here, to address myself to the Archduke [Ferd. Maximilian, Governor of Venice] with the request to let me stay here till a warmer season of the year for considerations of health. That had the best results, and at once came the order to leave me in peace. The success of this expedient then gave me the notion of trying it with the Saxon Minister

of Justice also. In my letter, which will be laid before
the King in any case, I have submitted myself entirely to
the wisdom of H.M., acknowledged the justice of the
condition imposed for my pardoning, and declared that
I should feel prepared to present myself for trial if my
physician had not most urgently dissuaded me in view of
my extremely imperilled nervous constitution, etc. The
letter is simply of such a nature that, if they don't
exempt me from that condition *on the strength of it*, never
and under no conditions do they mean to. So that is
done with :—now let us wait for the issue !

What you tell me of X [Lüttichau] made me positively
laugh. I had written the man in a way to make the
heart leap in his body ; thereon I receive from him a snub
—which I enclose for your amusement. That snub he
wrote all warm from an immediate perusal of my letter ;
consequently he has betrayed his true feeling. All his
behaviour toward yourself I treat as comedy ; the ancient
must have learnt that much in his many years of
managing a theatre. Away with all these courtiers and
comedians !—Well and good : I'm doing all I can to
have left nothing undone ; [but] I nurse no hope, and
am quite resigned already. I—don't require their Pardon
any more, and really shouldn't at all know what to do
with it !

In what big town of Germany should I settle down ?
Not one of them attracts me. To put an end to this
eternal hovering, I've accustomed myself more and more
to the thought of our going to Paris. At bottom I can be
of no more profit to myself in Germany ; they are giving
my operas there without me, and they go ; I spare myself
annoyance, and couldn't expect any larger receipts if
I were present myself. But in Paris I am personally of

need, and that not only for a season, but in permanence ;
then it will also catch on, and we may arrive at decent
funds at last. I am resuming my negotiations with Paris
already.

For the present, however, I have only one care— : to
get done with my Tristan. I need this new opera ; thereafter I can devote myself awhile to outward activity,
which will do me a heap of good. I haven't reached the
third act yet ; I must take care not to be disturbed again
by anything so soon as I've begun it. But I neither
could, nor should I care to, stay in Venice so long as that ;
so I'm already meditating leaving here by the end of this
[next] month. I quail at the thought of setting up
[alone] again elsewhere, however ; so Wille's invitation
of a few days since, to spend the Spring with them, came
most agreeably to me. Certainly I haven't quite made
up my mind yet, but nothing could better meet my wish,
than to occupy the Bissing's [Frau Wille's sister] first étage ;
I should enjoy the lovely hill walks there, have Wille's
cheery company, and even the youngsters I like. Above
all, too, the saving would be most important to me ; for
I should have very little to pay out, which would be
a godsend to me after the fearful expenses of my stay
here ; and there would be all the more for you to fling
about at Schandau. I hope you would agree with me,
and not grudge me this agreeable interval for work at my
third act ; the piano and beautiful rug I shall take with
me. I expect to have done in 3 months ; then a rapid
hunt [for rooms] in Paris, and to pick you up at Carlsruhe.—More plans, you see !—

And now for the very latest : New York ! They
make me an offer to-day for *five months* at 30,000 *fr.* and
travelling expenses. It seems as if they want to tempt

me ; so I have roughed out my plan as follows :—I shall ask for 50,000 francs, also *Klindworth* as assistant, so that I may have only *my own* operas to conduct and Klindw. to help me even with those.—While they are thinking it over, I shall aim my pistol at the breast of the Paris director, and demand Tannhäuser or Rienzi of him for next autumn, with a contract guaranteeing me a similar result.   To attain this, I shall tell him that my opera will still be available to him only this year, and if he didn't accept, I should wait till I came to terms with the *Grand* Opera, and then he would *never* get anything of mine.—Well, we shall see which way the dice fall ; in any case it's good to have [two] chances.—

Boom has written me that he and Müller won't give back the scores presented to them ; so there I sit !   But to think of even Papa Fischer having let things come to such a pass !   Now I beg him—Papa Fischer himself—to put an advertisement in the Theaterchronik etc. (also in the musical journals) that the composer would be assisted if anyone who formerly had bought a copy of the score would re-sell it to Fischer on repayment of the purchase price.   Perhaps something may come of it.   I shall assign him money shortly.—

Your looking better, old Muzius, rejoices me uncommonly.   Ah God, how willingly and gladly do I hope !—But I cannot conceal from you that your last letter but one contained another passage which again deprived me of all hope, so that I passed a totally sleepless night and felt *wretched* the whole next day.   Let that suffice you !—You see, I am better again now.   I shall attend to more money for the beginning of April, unless you want some even earlier.   Take care of yourself, deny yourself nothing, and count on my loyalty, which means to do you nothing but good !—I shall write you again soon, notwithstanding that I must lay aside my work again for the next few days to write letter on letter, as you may well imagine after what I've told you. It really is terrible ! In that respect I was better off in my younger years ; how little people troubled their heads about me ! Now it's increasing ad infinitum.—

So farewell. Don't be cross if I've forgotten anything ; my head always gets dizzy with letter-writing.

Greet the three live-stock ! They're to give you great joy, and then they'll give it me as well !

Best greetings to all, and best of all to yourself.

Thy

RW.

163.

VENICE, 1. *March* 1859.

DEAREST MINNA,

Your last letter has just arrived. The draft for a letter from myself to the King gave me such great delight, that I really cannot help letting you know my amusement. That there should be any person in the world, and a high-placed one to boot, who believes *me* capable of writing a letter like that, made me laugh out loud. By—God ! I might also ejaculate, *How* is it possible, and *where* is it possible, that anyone should think me *so* contemptible ! Eh, that could only happen in my precious fatherland, of course, to which my heart is so breaking to get back, that I presently must pine away if I can't breathe the divine air again in which such wonder-plants thrive as the author of this high-placed letter !—But tell me, did you forward me the letter as a joke ? You surely read it ! Or are you so endresdened again, as to have become insensible to the ridiculous absurdity of such a style? Believe me, on the strength of this letter the King would have unconditionally *rejected* me ; for he really would be too acute to take such a letter in earnest !—

Well, time will shew. Rest assured, my letter to the Minister of Justice was the best thing I could do. I believe I shall be pardoned off it, in fact, just because it's almost more than immaterial to me now. And if anything could have contributed to that feeling, it is the glimpse I've had again to-day into the miserableness of my beloved fellow-citizens.—

My yesterday's letter [*i.e.* 162] will have already told you more on that.

Ah, how it delights me, too, to have received an invitation to an Album with Reissiger's signature. Reconciliation ! Sweet reconciliation ! O how that does one good ! With the best will in the world, however, I shouldn't know what I could honour the gentlemen with just now. I've nothing in the world for such a purpose, and have never written such a thing to order. The Weber monument is all very fine ; when I'm allowed to come back, I'll conduct them a concert for it. If they need money before, X has such excellent pay and appointments, that it will be a flea-bite to him to make up the deficiency. God forgive me, I am a trifle bitter against the whole silly crew, and—would rather have nothing to do with them. Not one of them asked after me when there was need ; but now that I've become a famous man, why, I'm Ew. Hochwohlgeboren again.— Leave me quite out of the trash ; I've other and more serious cares than such tomfooleries, God knows !—

If they would only find me scores of Tannhäuser instead, or form a Wagner Committee to sell my 3 Meserian operas better, that I not only mightn't be reaping no reward for all my trouble, but mightn't still have debts for it as well ! The idiots !—

But when are you going to Berlin to hear Lohengrin ? I am always expecting to get a report from you.

Give Frau Karl Ritter back, please, the *Rheingold* score for me ; everything has fallen through again for the present [with Härtels]. Don't forget it.—A couple of packets of Paris snuff would also do no harm ; you fancied you had sent me 3 pounds, but they were only 3 halves. Even if I go to Wille's the beginning of April, it will be difficult for me to procure any, as I shan't stir a foot toward Zurich, and shall also try to keep my presence at Mariafeld as secret there as possible. The invitation is very agreeable to me, not *because*, but *although* it is near to Zurich ; for that, at any rate, would be the *last* place I should care to go to. The other amenities, however, incline me very much thereto.—

Last evening I played to Karl and Winterberger (my " two little boys, fair, fine, young and wise ") the second act of Tristan, which sent both of them downright crazy. Winterberger swears by bell, book and candle that even *I* have never made a thing like that before ; to-day, I hear, he's already playing bits of it from memory.— Yes, *beautiful* the act is. But there, you'll think I'm giving way to " vanity " again ; which, as you believe you've been assured by me, I had given up entirely. I don't quite know on what it's founded, but thank you for your good opinion, and really shall strive not to be vain any more. Of course one is only *vain* of *fancied* merits ; of one's real ones one is *proud*. But if it were not for my *pride*, how should I ever hold out in this heavenly world ? Nevertheless, if you wish it, and if it serves to pacify you, I'll put off *that* as well. What more do you want?   Anything, so only that you're fully pleased with me!—There : And yet he's a good husband !—

And now congratulate me on tomorrow, when I have to write to *Frankfort*, *New-York*, *London*, *Faris*, *Prague* and *Hanover;* to Härtels, too, would be as well.— Next time I shall write you about a secretary. You *must* procure me such an individual in Dresden. But on that next time.

For to-day a thousand charming and delightful things from

Thy

OLD VAGABOND

on the brink of the grave through longing for the Waldschlösschen.

164.

VENICE, 9. *March* 1859.

No, good Mutz, I'm not *provoked* against you, but only very much *concerned* about you, about our future.   I know that peace can only come from within, and there- fore feel unhappy when such thoughts as " God's punish- ment for insults put upon you," * and the like dark and passionate fancies, are still so alive in you. After all, however, it is scarcely to be expected that you should already be quite clear and composed. Were I a colder,

---

* Something similar will be found in that letter of hers to a feminine friend of the end of 1858 (*cf.* p. 418*n.* *sup.*) in allusion to little Guido Wesendonck's death : " May God hold every blow of Fate away from that cold woman spoilt by happiness, but I believe there is a Providence. I was always thinking, if only our Lord God would suddenly check such sauciness through the illness of a child—and now see! O it gives me a shudder."—Tr.

more phlegmatic being myself, no doubt I should be able to judge all this at every moment in the same way as I know how to take it when I allow a little time to pass ; but unfortunately I myself—who have so few agreeable or encouraging experiences, and always am over-exerting myself—am often so irritable and touchy that I cannot maintain the needful cold-bloodedness, and then I tell you frankly. But now that my mind has grown clear again on this, I beg you to regard my last complaint as unuttered, and let everything rest on itself ; which is better than its weighing on us !—What gives me most hope for our future, and even most delight for the present, is the progress in your own condition. You can't think how that revives me, and how I thank Heaven when I hear anything so comforting as Pusinelli's last report, and now your yesterday's. Only keep on that way ! *Everything, everything* will then go well and happily ; I *know* it !—

I should have quite a lot to talk about with you, and should so like a pleasant hour's chat ; I always lose my patience with this curs.— writing. Therefore I must be a trifle briefer than I otherwise could wish. So, in the first place :—I really would rather *not* go to *Wille's*. Lord knows, I had only cast my eye on the convenience of board and lodging for my unfortunate work, also a little no doubt on the saving, but overlooked at first the difficulty of quite avoiding Zurich, which could scarcely have been escaped in the end ; even the callers from town would have gêned me, and in the long run it would have been very conspicuous, and afforded fresh food for remarks, if I had so carefully avoided Zurich. That would never have done, and as I also haven't a spark of affection for Zurich now—for which no one can

blame me—I have definitely declined with thanks.
Consequently you were quite right to leave me that
to settle with myself ; believe me, you did thoroughly
right, and I thank you much for this reserve of yours.
I only needed to think it well over, to recognise that
such a visit would have yielded me more annoyance,
than tranquillity for work. Moreover, when I once
have shut a place behind me, as you know, I've done
with it.

But Switzerland [itself] will be most refreshing to
me now, and I'm longing much for mountain trips.
Well, the Lake of Geneva is quite unsympathetic to me ;
it's no true Switzerland, the whole length of the shore
nothing but wearisome vineyards, and only the one fine
distant view. I shouldn't know where to go there ; all
is stiff. On the other hand, *Lucerne* pleased me greatly
last summer, and you know my penchant for the
Vierwaldstädter See in general. There I have observed
quite lovely summer-houses, with pension, on the verge
of the forest. In the months of April, May, and June,
there are no strangers as yet, and I fancy I quickly could
find what I want there with little pains ; perhaps even
at Brunnen itself. So—my work here is nearing its end,
and in any case I think of being on the move before
the end of this month. Probably I shall send the piano
off a little earlier, so that I may feel at home in my new
quarters at once, and ready for work. If the sky doesn't
fall in, I thus hope for good undisturbed work at the
third act, and once that is finished—I am free as a king ;
for I then shall have unloaded for a longish time, and
can devote myself exclusively to outward activity again.
For my recreation I am vastly looking forward to the
Rigi and Pilatus, which I think of duly riding up on

horse-back. Then excursions to Brunnen, Seelisberg, and—na! who knows if our little summer-house at Brunnen mayn't come true after all!—

But now for the big fish!—Fie, Mutz, don't speak so disrespectfully of America!—Don't be alarmed, but—it's something to think of. Five months might easily be flung away, if I could thereby make us free and independent *for the rest of our life*. And that might be done as follows. If they guarantee me so much that, after deducting the cost of maintenance and journey (which latter is free), I could bring back 50 to 60,000 *fr*. net, we should have a sure and handsome income for *five* years, could put aside *all* other takings during those five years, and thus reserve ourselves our 10 to 12,000 *fr*. annually for a number of years beyond. The advantage of which would be, that one would always know exactly how *much* one had a year, and *when* one could touch it; whereas the present haphazard style of income remains so disconcerting even if one ends by getting in enough. Besides that main condition, however, I have set up the following: *Klindworth* as second conductor at 10,000 *fr*.—*I only for my own operas;* 5000 *fr*. to be prepaid at once in Europe, the remainder to be deposited with a business firm in New York; liberty to conduct concerts in Philadelphia and Boston (where they already are enthusiastically interested in me). By the way, do not exaggerate the cost of living; if I got through in London with 500 *fr*. a month, I'm sure to do it in New York with 1000 *fr*.: one has the very best pension there for 10 to 12 *fr*. a day.

Well, you may readily imagine that nothing save the prospect of so momentous a result as I have just described could have induced me to take the thing into somewhat

more serious consideration ; for it is an infamous suggestion to me otherwise, to make such an abominable journey.
You can imagine that, no doubt. Therefore I have
also knocked at another door, in order, if it opens to
me, to be able to leave New York on one side with *good
conscience* even if all my conditions are fulfilled. Now
admire your husband's cunning ! I have written to *Paris*
and given the director of the Théâtre lyrique to understand that, if he doesn't at once decide on mounting
Tannhäuser (or Rienzi) *for next season*, fulfil all my
conditions, and pay down 5000 *fr.* premium (in addition
to the tantièmes), he would *never* have an opera of mine
for his theatre (for I should then go to America for the
winter, and come calmly back to Paris, with my
American money in my pocket, to push the production
of my operas at the " Grand Opera " *con amore*) ; and
I shall keep my word. So I mean to see what the man
will decide upon. If he satisfies me—good ! Then valet
America ! Then I shall have things more convenient
and closer, pretty much the same pecuniary result, and
both of us will be comfortably seated in Paris this next
winter. Naturally I should like that best. If on the
other hand it didn't come off, whilst the New York
director fulfilled all my conditions, then it would be a
case of biting at another sour apple to be master of my
own position from that time forth. We two should meet at
Carlsruhe, you would accompany me to Paris, where you
might really do best to continue straight off, and could
get everything nicely into place after your own mind
during my last journey, so that on my return in the
Spring I might find the new home all in apple-pie order
and comfort—for which I'm longing so. Ha, how will
you feel when I slip a matter of 10,000 *fr.* into your

hand, and say: "Here, Mutz, now go and rig us nicely up!"

I am only afraid I shall develop into a terrible miser in time, I've such a passion to become a rentier!—For the present, however, we won't go into all that stuff, nor do anything precipitate, but make ourselves thoroughly acquainted with everything. The final hard-bought and slowly to-be-won last comfort of our old age depends upon it!—Nothing is decided yet; everything just merely plans: but—you surely must admit there's something in it.—My mind is thoroughly made up for Paris. There alone *can* I be of any considerable use to myself now; things in Germany will go at a pinch (especially as regards receipts) *without* my person. If I have the amnesty—, so much the better; for I could run over whenever it's a question of anything out of the ordinary. But it revolts me now, to think of settling permanently in any such a German Gotham. In Paris one can live so immensely sans gêne. An agreeable dwelling would be the chief point, one where you also would have something to look at—on to the Champs Elysées, for instance, where Fipsel can also amuse himself. In short, I intend having a good time in my old age yet (for I have a terrible amount of grey hairs!), and you, old girl, shall have it too.—

Now a little hasty business!—

Meser—Kriete—lawyer Schmidt and the rest—if I only could — them all!! However, here's for another go at that hash!

Enclosed find a billet to Kriete—read it, and then seal it.—A second to Herr *Müller*, Meser's worthy successor:—read that also, then close it and ask Papa Fischer to hand it himself to the gentleman so as to receive a prompt answer, i.e. the declaration, which I beg you then to despatch forthwith to Breitkopf and Härtel in Leipzig. This tag-rag makes me altogether frantic. Lucky that Härtels have declared their readiness to engrave the Tannhäuser full score anew ; otherwise I shouldn't know where to procure any from. A. Müller has written me now, tho', that he will send his and Boom's copy to Fischer.—

I certainly could not suppose you *hadn't* read that splendid letter I was asked to write the King of Saxony ; consequently I return it to you, as I may firmly hope it will give you great amusement, and you will then under-stand the humour it put me in. Believe me, I have done the best thing in this matter now, and accordingly also —the last. I shall do nothing further, and never mind if they don't amnesty me, I know (as you see) how to shift for myself !—The Serre broth another time ; one shouldn't undertake too much at once !

Karl told me the other day that he isn't expecting his wife now ; I don't know what is up about his pass, and in general can't quite make him out. So wait for my further instructions about the Rheingold [score].—*Winter-berger* left for Rome two hours ago ; he made a fine hullaballoo taking leave of me ! This whole tribe really seems to get fond of me ! Apparently I shall leave Karl behind here ; he would like to finish his new piece before he decides on his next step, which I think very sensible. For *myself*, work this time is driving me forth ; nor should I care to wait here for the *war*. We'll come to an understanding about the future revolutions in Paris another day ; till then continue doing honour to your dear doctor, and joy to your good man ! Ah, if I find you quite well and good in half a year, I'll carve Pusinelli in marble !—Fare terribly well, embrace Fips and Jacquot,

and give Nette my respects. Shoot the bolt nicely on
Julius ! Don't trust Lüttichau too far, for after all he's
—a courtier ! Don't learn to jewdel (*jüdeln*) at Auerbach's ; rather get the Devrient to teach you to yodel
(*jodeln*). And above all, love, honour and esteem

Thy

beautiful grey Husband

R.

165.

VENICE, 23. *March* 1859.

MY GOOD MUTZ,

I really am robbing myself of a couple of minutes,
to send another couple of lines after my telegraphic
despatch of to-day. As you will know by now, I am in
the act of departure, and have a terrible deal to attend to
first, particularly in the way of correspondence. Besides
which, I'm very flustered and sleepless ; I drafted this
morning's despatch in the night. My blood gives me a
lot of trouble, for which the Spring is probably to blame ;
nor is the thumping of my heart to be despised. Neither
can one say that this climate is particularly beneficial to
the nerves, though I haven't found myself either better or
worse on the whole than in other winters. In any case
I'm going away most willingly ; the dearth of walks
becomes unbearable in the end. I'm looking inhumanly
forward, on the contrary, to the mountains and their air ;
I shall make an expedition every week.

For the rest, good Mutz, everything is turning out
passably. It rejoiced me much, that I was able to allot
100 louis d'or from Härtels to you alone, I being indemni-
fied by the Vienna sale of Tannhäuser. I'm also paying
Heim completely off to-day.

I have now declined the *Ritter* subsidy for good and all. Taking your hint, I learnt through Karl that the Ritters had had great losses on their Russian investments through the last war [Crimean], and that Frau Ritter had only not apprised me of her difficulties because it was the very time when that quarrel arose with Karl, and she on no account would let it look as if her aid were stopped in consequence of that. That sufficed to make me address myself to Frau Ritter, as early as last November, and assure her that my prospects for this year, and my future in general, were so rosy that it would be wrong of me to lay her under contribution any longer. This I accompanied with a heartfelt and sincere acknowledgment of her uncommon, never sufficiently to be thanked-for service to myself, and so on. She was so affected by it, and thanked me so fervently for my " kindness " and " delicacy," that I may term the close of this relation almost still more beautiful than its commencement. She is an extraordinary woman, and the whole family, for all its oddities, remains to me a great and most precious exception. Salute them all from me again to-day most kindly.

So, dearest Mutz, we stand entirely on our own legs now, and as you see, they'll carry us quite well. Enjoy the 100 louis d'or right merrily and free from care ; one may hope they'll last you till we meet again ; if not, I'll soon attend to more : I attend to you gladly, you see, for it gives me great joy. Please deny yourself nothing. Take a still finer lodging at Schandau ; you *can* indeed : reflect, I herewith am giving you over 100 thaler a month. I want you to move in perfect freedom and plenty ; so— hire a nice lodging. I like to lodge nicely myself, and can't permit my wife to be worse off. Take a carriage twice a week too, or as often as you want, and do all the

beautiful drives to the Kuhstall and other parts. I
implore you, enjoy this summer to your heart's content,
and let no consideration deter you from anything that
might enliven you or do you good. Your health will
thereby take a decided turn for the better, and I shall
then have the agreeable duty of maintaining and ad-
vancing you on that good road. But that's the very
way you'll make it possible to me ; so don't let it trouble
your conscience. If your money doesn't last until the
end of August, when we're to meet at Carlsruhe, I'll send
you more; I am looking ahead, and shall not leave you
stranded, you see.—

I too am looking forward to this Spring, and think of
nestling at Lucerne quite comfortably for my last act.
The *perfect* solitude, without *any* acquaintance, will do
me much good in those splendid surroundings. Now and
then I shall go to Brunnen and up the Seelisberg, and
shall be quite contented with a little chat with folk there.
So—we'll each install ourselves right pleasantly, that we
may meet again refreshed and merry.—

I can't possibly write any more to-day. At 6 tomorrow morning I start for Milan, where I shall spend a
day looking at the Gallery and churches ; then viâ Como—
Lugano, Bellinzona, Gotthardt, direct to Lucerne. Piano,
bedding etc., are already en route. I hope to find the
proper lodging quickly *now*, and in any case shall write
you immediately after my arrival ; for this once please
write me *poste restante*.

So a thousand hearty, hopeful greetings ; be good to
me, and stay firmly convinced that I'm sincerely and
heartily good to you.

Thy

R.W.

166.

LUCERNE, 30. *March* 1859.

Address : *Schweizerhof,* Lucerne.

To my delight, my entirely good Mutz, I found your letter on my arrival at Lucerne ; but your having brought back such an agreeable, exhilarating impression from Berlin would have still more delighted me if the Frommann hadn't at the same time written me that she really found you quite agitated still, and with feverish hands. No doubt good Pusinelli knows what he is doing, if he wouldn't consent, for instance, to this journey to Berlin. But you always were a bad, refractory patient, and often have given me trouble in this respect before ; learn better now, deny yourself even an expected pleasure so soon as it involves a possible interference with your improvement ; and once you've decided to make your lot depend upon your confidence (in this case, in Pusinelli), repose that confidence implicitly and endeavour to circumvent nothing. Live for your health now, your health—and nothing but your health. Whatever you can wish besides, is now assured you ; a bright and pleasant evening is prepared your life, if you only will support me through your health. But I therefore ask you to be good and docile. I forgive your Berlin this time ; but since it has made you more agitated again, you must now keep very quiet.

Obey me also as regards your Schandau lodgings ; a pleasant, well-equipped and thoroughly convenient home does much for outward rest. Rainy days come, when one feels it painful to be cooped in narrow shabby walls. I admit my own foible for roomy, nice surroundings, and that I deny myself nothing to indulge it ; but I consequently wish *you* also to deny yourself nothing. The means are in your hand, practise no false economy ; you can make up for it by cutting presents down a little (with which you're partial to the open hand). Above all, never do *aught* except what promises some sort of ease to you, some service to your comfort. Remember that, there's a good girl, and tell yourself :

> " The wise things which these children say
> be graven in my heart for aye."

—And so I'm back beside my favourite lake ; it seemed quite like old times, to be looking at Flüelen, Seelisberg and Brunnen again, in fine weather and glorious light. Only St. Gotthardt behaved rudely. After my great joy at sight of the splendid blossoming of the fruit-trees in Italy, Father Gotthardt put himself into a grizzly mist-coat stuffed with flakes of snow (which kept falling out), and pommelled me quite violently in the infamous sleigh on to which they jammed me with an Italian tailor. A pretty tale, this snow-passage through wind and weather, on an open sledge reaching only as high as one's ankles. A charming cold is breaking out with me to-day : hatishoo !—

I looked for lodgings yesterday, and found it much harder to fulfil my wish than I expected. The choice of pensions isn't large, and everywhere I learnt to my horror that orders had already been booked for the middle of May. Nobody would let me have the big chamber I fancied, since it was the dining and reception room in every case ; beyond that, nothing but bedrooms anywhere. So at last I found it most convenient to come to an arrangement with the landlord of the Schweizerhof. He has a fine dépendance with a glorious view, a building where no visitor is taken in before the end of June ; so I can be entirely alone there for the next quarter, occupy a splendid salon with balcony, get my meals and attendance from the hotel, and the whole thing together will after. all cost little more than at a pension, even if they would have given it me there, though of course it's not precisely cheap. I'm expecting the piano tomorrow or the day after, and hope by Sunday to be seated at my work, for which I'm very well disposed, as all else is shaping fairly well for once.

Here it occurs to me that I really must beg you to go to Herr Advokat Schmidt—get his address from Pusinelli —and ask him what sort of a * * * * * he is? These people will drive me crazy. You write me that all the music was packed up and sent to Härtels directly after my letter to Schmidt ; but *they* write me that, in spite of my latest assurances, they still have no notification from Dresden (! ! !). Moreover, Härtels offer the most advantageous conditions, and are certain to let one screw them up to 2000 Rthlr * ; but the thing must be clinched at once, for Härtels naturally consider that the business may simply exhaust itself in time. If you're not afraid of its exciting you, I beg you to try and procure me a definite explanation and definite answer. Otherwise nothing particular has happened with me. I ought to be receiving a declaration from the Paris director soon ; from America probably not till the middle of April. I am prepared for everything, and merely determined to do my utmost, without giving myself away or engaging in anything quite repugnant to me, to ensure us a future free

---

* About £300. It was a question of their taking over from Wagner's creditors his publication-rights in the three operas, *Rienzi, Holländer* and *Tannhäuser*, excluding the orchestral scores : a very long story, its first chapter dating from 1844.—Tr,

of care and altogether independent of the favour of any prince or other person whatsoever.—

I was a couple of days at Milan, went to see splendid pictures and other works of art, and clambered all over the colossal white-marble cathedral, gigantic and sumptuous to weariness. 100,000 Austrian soldiers, all quartered in Milan, formed my body-guard ; let them go nutting behind me as they will, not one of them shall come to Lucerne. The Swiss air is doing me good, and with all my heart I should like you to breathe it again. That, too, will come !—For the present make use of the summer, good use of it ; 'tis yours entirely, you have no other duty than to make it pleasant to you and take care of yourself. Let me soon hear good news again, and rejoice with your heart's calm

Thy good

St. Gotthardt-Husband.

How I miss Fipsel ! ! My resisting all temptations to obtain myself a dog, may shew you the sort of man I am !—Greet Nette, and let her also lack nothing. Does she go on tending you well and kindly ?—Ask Jacquot if his name is Kakkarakak ? ?

167.

Lucerne, 9. April 1859.

So, dearest Minna, I'm installed once again. I am uncommonly pleased, and find myself very comfortable. It would be impossible, too, to be better lodged ; this marvellous view on every side, an elegant large salon, every convenience, excellent attendance, and—the only person in all the house. What more could I wish ? The mountain air is doing me a deal of good again. The walks are heavenly, much more beautiful and varied than at Zurich. I'm feeling very well. My having absolutely *no* acquaintance here is also of some account. Boredom—God knows—I never suffer from ; on the contrary, rather too much occupation, so that I cannot even get much reading. The whole morning till 4 belongs to my work, which I resumed yesterday ; then after dinner I make my big promenade until 7, rest it off a little, drink my tea about 8, read the newspapers, write a letter, and usually am so sleepy by 10 that I cannot so much as open a regular book. I won't say this is to continue for the rest of my life, but it suits this last spell of work at Tristan admirably ; afterwards I think of making a longish pause and mixing more with people, for which I shall have opportunity enough in Paris.

The piano unfortunately arrived somewhat later than I had expected after my precautions. In the first place, conveyance in Italy was much hindered by the enormous army-transport, which absorbs every truck ; and then the poor chap had to wait a long time on the Gotthardt before the bad weather and quantity of freshly-fallen snow would let him pass. Nevertheless he was still quite in good tune, so that I was able to dismiss the tuner again. It really is an incredible instrument, for which I mean to revenge myself duly some day. Naturally your foot-mat is with it ; but I've had yet another great joy. I had written to Heim about my big divan, as I could beat up nothing like it here ; several other things were packed with it, as you will know, and among them —the beautiful Swan rug. Well, I haven't spread it out badly before the divan, so that I feel quite at home already. I really set very much store on one's abode and everything connected therewith,—of course I'm not dictating anything to *you* in this regard, but console myself with the thought that, if you're not better fended, after all it isn't *my* fault, as I heartily wish it you and am doing all I can towards it.

Nothing further has occurred yet ; but I have to keep answering useless letters, such as Präger's, and of late again honorary diplomas from Holland and suchlike absurdities. Since absolutely nothing can happen round about me, moreover, I hardly know whence to draw matter for tidings. You at all events are living in the big world, and can let the swan in Berlin nod you something which appears to have made a great impression on you. All due respect for your assurances, however, with the best will I can't yet form a favourable idea of the Berlin production ; everything is strictly insufficient there, and not a single singer fit. At no price should I care—unprepared—to witness such a representation. In Vienna, on the contrary, I would have gone straight to the theatre to see Lohengrin without a qualm ; by all accounts the production there has been extraordinarily happy. For instance, the first big (long ? ?) scene in the 2nd act, between Ortrud and Friedrich, is said to create a furore every time ; both seem to be equally excellent. No, when I think of that Berlin Krause, I can't help bursting out laughing, and try to blot the whole Berlin picture from my imagination at once.—At Dresden everything is sure to be better ; indeed the singers are so well suited, that my only fear is for the Kapellmeister [Krebs], who is certainly incapable of seizing aught in the affair. Let's see, then !—

That the L.s also intend going to Paris this autumn, was a—very disagreeable piece of news to me. In my life I unfortunately have often had to do with riff-raff, and my only true progress consists in having cut myself

more and more adrift from such worthless connections.
But I consider the L.s, in fact both of them, quite ragamuffins in Sulzer's downright sense, and *her* moreover
such a shameless, dishonourable beggar and swindler that
I'm really filled with apprehension by the thought of
living in the same place with these people again, and
being exposed at every moment to the wife's sponging
on the tolerable competence I hope for.   I am really so
outspoken, dear Minna, as to call your present intimacy
with this lady a great weakness, and to reckon it to you
as such ; and if it were only for reason of my rooted dislike
of this woman, perhaps I might hope that out of regard
for *me*, who never force my likes upon yourself, you
would somewhat restrain your relations with her.   Maybe
I've nothing further in my mind at present, than the
vexation it would cause me if this female swindler should
wheedle you out of some of the money I have assigned to
your comfort with such great delight ; but that's certain
to happen.   In Italy I heard things about this lady which
really make me frankly determined to hold her at arm's
length.   Enough—it is and always will be a pair of
ragamuffins living uselessly and aimlessly from hand to
mouth, and shamefully exploiting every friend ; and—
that sort of person shall come into as *little* contact with
me in future as I can help : at least as much freedom of
living as that, would I fain ensure my future.—

I hope, dearest Mutz, the L. has not yet twined
herself so tightly round your heart, that the above will
seriously excite you ; but remember we have mutual
duties, whose fulfilment itself has the object of giving
our future an endurable and pleasant shape.—

Get away to Schandau as soon as ever you can ; it
will do me good as well as you.   How much I regret

your having chosen Dresden of all places, I've said already, were it only on account of that dreadful person Julius ; I tremble with rage every time you write me about him.   Couldn't you manage to shew him the door for good and all?—However, Schandau will shoot the bolt on that too ; and then it is to be hoped you'll come direct with dog and bird to Carlsruhe !   What the next move will be, whether a definitive Paris at once, or my American journey first, must soon decide itself ; but even in the latter event you perhaps could remain behind in Paris, get everything prepared for the Spring, and await me there, where we'll thenceforth live together.

Well, that also will soon clear itself up.—Farewell, take care of yourself, and fare sumptuously !

Salute friends and household.   With the best of wishes,

Thy RICHARD.

168.
LUCERNE, 14. *April* 1859.

O Mutz, what an impatient woman you are ! To answer a letter on the third day, when one has simply nothing of importance to relate, is none so rare a thing, and you often let me wait much longer !   When will you grow a little calmer?—Besides—I delayed instinctively, since I had a horror of saying something to you about the L. that lay at my heart all the same.   Indeed, if I had put off my letter another couple of days, no doubt it would have been still wiser ; for I should then, perhaps, have wholly overcome it, and—not mentioned it at all.   Now it has happened, don't take it too seriously, and attach no further weight to it ; neither seek anything special behind it.   Enough—you know that I prefer living completely retired, to having all sorts of tainted company ; I am leading so plain and—I might even say—so nobly-still a life at present, that the thought of such a renewed *potage à la* L. really pains me.—However, that will all arrange itself ; lay no too great weight, as said, on my last remarks.

Your news about the Devrient was a great shock to me, as you may well imagine ! Great God, what dangers you women are exposed to ! ! That so-called " certain age " and " certain period " really is a terrible time for you. Surely your own sufferings, good Mutz, are to some extent connected with that period : in fact, it even is certain ; but as you were already more inclined to an affection of the heart through repeated violent moral agitations, it has taken that turning with you, and perhaps spared you the other, to which the Devrient has fallen victim. Much as you have to suffer through that turning, you have a great consolation herein : even should you never *quite* get rid of them, your heart and nerve troubles may yet be assuaged and abated by a quiet life, agreeable impressions, avoidance of all great exertions and excitements, and good dietetics in general, to such a degree that you will certainly attain the age appointed you by Nature in a very tolerable condition, even of comfort, under circumstances,—whereas with that terrible turning a brief respite leads irrevocably on to agonising death. Oh, but it is awful !—And if you still should have to bear a rift about with you, as said, praise Heaven that you are spared the poor Devrient's fate ! !—Sure enough, an injury she sustained in her last confinement, which also was the cause of her bearing no more children after (I know that from H. Müller, to whom she confided it), much predisposed her for that turning ; the more do I thank God, that

that is spared yourself !—Forgive my going so closely into
the matter, but indeed it lies so close and is so serious.—

If she could be saved after all ! I really have heard
that the water-cure has had decided effects in such cases ;
perhaps it isn't too late yet. I'll enquire after *Vaillant*,
then write at once ; I think he's coming to Geneva soon
again. I have unbounded confidence in him, and if the
poor Devrient can be helped at all, it is by him. Do
speak to her about it ; but—lose no time.—

As regards yourself, I know you're under quite good
treatment now, and moreover am convinced that morally
good influences, i.e. composure and removal of excitants,
are the principal point in your cure ; let us hope we shall
always succeed in procuring and preserving you those
remedies !—

For the rest, I too am having heartily bad weather
now. That at least was different in Italy, and to give
you an idea of the Italian climate, so decried to you,
I may tell you that if at Venice it ever was dull and
rainy, it lasted but *one* day, *never longer*, and clear sky
with bright sunshine so predominated that I retain almost
nothing of rain etc. in my memory. No, the climate
is another thing there, than this side of the Alps ! But
what I lacked, to my greatest detriment, were the long
walks, hill promenades, green sward and air of higher
regions. And doubtless that is what I've somewhat
suffered from of late ; with the present true Föhn weather
here I feel quite miserable, so that it was only with pains
and trouble I could piece a couple of bars together
yesterday. But I need to be light and bright of heart
now, if I want to work well ; and no doubt that has its
very natural, human grounds. By next November, when
I shall have quite finished my Tristan also, it will be *six*

years since I began composing again.   In those 6 years,
accordingly, I shall have written *four*, we'll call them
four big operas, a single one of which would suffice in its
fulness, depth and novelty, to be the labour of 6 years ;
compared with these works, in respect of wealth and
interestingness of detail, my earlier operas are mere rough
sketches, as a single glance at the score will shew any
musician at once.   All this I have drawn from my inmost
being, without the smallest outward stimulus or support
from my sphere of art, under the oppressive feeling of inability to see any of it represented, forever thrown back on
myself and my innermost fount.   Who hears these works
one day, will be astounded when one tells him that these
4 were written in 6 years,—I know it !—But—I also feel
—tired, very tired ; and I need a course of coaxing,
strengthening, to lure the tones I wish for from the
greatly run-down inner strings.   Solitude does me good
at present ; but merely because I know that the society at
my disposal can offer me no true refreshment.   Now God
grant that when I quit my solitude again, harmonious
company, invigoration and refreshment may also be my
lot.—If you will only grow calm, gentle and—well,
yourself you'll do the greatest share toward that ; so tend
yourself : 'twill strengthen both of us !   Farewell, good
Mutz, and ever be good to

Thy

also good

husband R.

169.

LUCERNE, 18. *April* 1859.

MY GOOD MUTZ,

Your latest letter has done me a power of good
once more.   I had become so anxious, that I really was

afraid my attack on the L. might have upset you again
and put something else in your head ; so it certainly
was a great relief to hear you make such excellent fun
of the lady. All I'm really sorry for in the end, is the
10 Rthlr this latest attestation of her friendship costs
you, and my only solace is that Sch. has also had to part.
God the all-merciful keep such friendships off your neck
and mine in future ! I always had an antipathy to *her*,
and no doubt the greater part of it came from her roguish
physiognomy and her rollicking ways ; she is demoralisa-
tion itself, lost to all manners and shame. On the other
hand it perhaps was a little excusable that her husband's
more elegant, refined and better-cultured personality
should have let me uphold a more favourable opinion of
him for a length of time than I certainly can maintain if
I finally admit to myself the truth. Particularly since
I discovered that his intellect also is of no great account
—which with so entirely unoriginal a person can be
concealed for a time—he can no longer pass muster before
my judgment and feeling. That eternal tavern life too,
with all its concomitants, has lowered him more and more
in the end. G. himself strictly ended by leaving me
with no very favourable impression ; this going to the
beer-house every evening fostered *his* failings also more
and more ; he has become a thorough washerwoman,
like all this tavern brotherhood. With his real talent,
activity and estimable attitude towards his family,
however, he naturally remains a very different chap in
my eyes from brother L. ; of that there can't be any
doubt.

Apropos of that, dearest Minna, I now have a
communication to make to you which I hope will be
welcome. Listen ! For a long time I've felt that a

bold front must be presented to the mischief which precisely these washerwomen and their like have wrought, a mischief so closely affecting the honour of so many concerned, your own as well, and at any rate originated by my so startling departure from Zurich. I'm glad to say, the possibility of doing so has gradually been paved. Last autumn Wesendonck informed me of the death of his Guido in a very touching letter ; I answered him in the same tone, and we have remained in correspondence ever since, from time to time. It wasn't this, however, that determined me to quarter at Lucerne ; for, notwithstanding my having given Heims the prospect of a visit this summer, I did not propose to touch Zurich. But Wesendonck invited me a few days back : I was to put up at his house, he would send his carriage to the station, and gave me to understand that he wished to put an end to all exaggerations and perversions through so open an act of friendly intercourse. So I accepted, went to Zurich last Saturday, got into Wesendonck's carriage there, slept the night in his house, and travelled back on Sunday afternoon [yesterday], after driving to the Zeltweg in the morning, in Wesendonck's carriage again, and paying a solitary call on the Heims. This was a very salutary demonstration, as both of us hope, and all the world will naturally infer my footing with the family, which of course has made a great impression even on the servants. He was very glad and happy, and from myself, no less, it has removed a great embarrassment. You too, I hope, will draw the same conclusions from this as have been so reassuring to Wesendonck. Before I quite leave Switzerland again, I think of accepting a second invitation of his, when a larger party is to be bidden.—

I scarcely need to tell you that this does not make the smallest difference in my and our mutual dispositions for the future. Everything remains as fixed ; only, behind me—and I hope, behind yourself—all is clear and bright now, and there are no more clouds or vapours to dispel.—-

Thus it also is very good news to me that you have decided to come on from Carlsruhe to Paris with me, even if I should have to pass the winter in America. I am convinced you will feel quite happy there, even without me ; and Kietz shall be wholly adopted, that is self-understood, as youngest child of the house. It would be a great advantage to you, then, if you would take regular lessons in French ; I cannot but think they are bound to afford you a very agreeable, and at last a fascinating distraction ; in fact I even believe it will have a peculiarly beneficial effect on you, as it is an occupation that doesn't tire one in the slightest and also has quite a definite object, which would · multiply your enjoyment of Paris by ten. We'll have another talk on that ; I must first know exactly how I stand with Newyork, which is bound to decide itself within a month from now. I may merely tell you that in this affair that good soul Wesendonck has already been co-operating. It came very natural to assure myself through him about the Newyork undertaking ; he has written about it, and if it comes to pass, I shall know it is something solid ; for the money is to be deposited with his American house.

God only grant my work may now go quickly forward ; so much depends on it. Last week the weather continued so abominable, that I could only go for two brief walks between the showers and under difficulties. I felt infamous, and had to lay aside my scarcely started work again. In the circumstances, Wesendonck's invitation was also quite a welcome diversion. When I returned last evening, together with your own I found a quantity of other letters I still must answer ; a lot of useless stuff, thanks for diplomas etc., also to our lawyer Schmidt— oh dear ! but probably that will be an end of it. An order for Tannhäuser has also come from *Pesth ;* Fischer must be so good as to rectify one of that pair of scores at once, but not despatch it until after receipt of the certificate I've given the director. That *Müller* (of Dresden) still has a score ; in my answer to Schmidt I am insisting that he shall give it up to Fischer. Russia and America may be coming along yet, and I'm in the greatest fix. By the way, give Papa F. a thousand greetings, and tell him I should be immensely delighted to get a sight of him this year. Now he's a free man, I think it would be best if he came with you to the Carlsruhe Tristan ; but if he wants it earlier, let him visit me in God's name at Lucerne. I shall be here till the end of *June* for certain ; after that it will be difficult, as strangers come in streams then, the pensions and hotels get packed, and my beautiful repose is done for ; besides which, I of course should have to pay much more. God only grant I may have done with my act by then !—If that's the case, I unconditionally shall go to Paris, and in the event of nothing coming of America, have a good hunt for an abode to suit the needs of both of us : *quiet* for myself, and amusing for you, giving you something to look at when you peep out with Fipps. Well, all in good time ; but now for my other letters : I've a stack of them before me still. Only don't get so impatient at once, if my answer happens to be a couple of days behindhand ; I could really do nothing but write letters the whole time.

And fine weather has come to-day at last ; so I'm looking forward to a rousing walk, and hope to have a willing head for work tomorrow. Keep writing me such nice things as the last time, and especially if you sing Pusinelli's praises, which I always am so glad to hear : God, then stones fall off my heart, and I say to myself—So, a bright and tranquil evening is to come at last !—

So, do your part of the business, and be very much ' away ' to Juliüschen. Salute the watchful N., Fipps and Jacquot, and hold dear

Thy
Thine.

Zurich, for that matter, was monstrous indifferent to me, and the only wish I felt, was—not to return there again—at least for many years. This parochialism—I can stand it no longer ; I must have the biggest now, and some measure of outward activity. I mean to procure those in Paris.

The Above.

The notice is borrowed from a Correspondence of the Allgemeine Zeitung, where there have often been bene- volent reports on me from Venice, though I've no idea from whom.—

170.
LUCERNE, 24. April 1859.

O Mutz ! how can you seriously believe I've been dancing ballet here ? You know that, spite of every invitation, I never have been able to consent to it even

in the largest towns of Europe ; and I'm supposed to
have done it before the little public of this place, where
it wouldn't even have been duly reported ! No, that's
just another of your fancies.—For that matter, the good
Lucerners are nuisance enough to me with their promenades in front of my abode, where I like taking a bit of
a stroll up and down of a morning, before work, on the
gallery that runs all round the house ; I have to submit
to being nicely gaped at, and don't quite know whether
it is due to my celebrity, or to my lovely dressing-gown.
As regards the latter, I've long been waiting for you to
ask me after it ; for you might have presumed that the
old one fell at last in tatters off my body. But, since
you have shewn yourself so unconcerned for my chief
passion, I mean to let you guess hard how the new has
turned out. It is very beautiful, and although I had it
made for me in Venice days, it's still as good as new, I
spare it so.—

I really felt no great enthusiasm for the dress you
destined for the X [see p. 452], and probably shall leave
it for the present on your shoulders. In things like that,
I stick to it, you are a shade too generous. What has
the lady done, then, except to get out of having to take
you into her house ? You might have accepted that as a
simple return for his reception into ours ; had he lodged
and boarded at the hotel instead, probably he would have
had to pay more than you now would owe them for the
hire of their furniture. If people of this sort behave
absurdly, I generally make up my mind *never* to ask
anything of them again, and so we're strictly quits ;
however, as you promised it her in the first fit of
sentimentalism, you must give her the following message
from me now :—I meant to buy the dress in Milan,

especially as there would have been no duty to pay from there, but unfortunately I chanced upon two feast-days when all the shops and magazines were closed ; I'll see to sending her a dress from Paris in its place. And there's an end to it for the present. Don't *you* go spending money on it, do you hear ?—I shall turn disgracefully stingy to friends in time—as I've told you once before.

Child, you're mistaken about the number of Lohengrin performances in Berlin ; I have it in black on white that down to the 1st of April only *seven* took place, which haven't quite covered the advance yet, leaving 50 thlr of it still to be worked off. If there have been another two representations in April, so much the better. I hear from Vienna that *Ander* is going to Berlin in May, and will sing Lohengrin there ; of which I'm uncommonly glad. He is certain to have a great success ; for if *Formes* is somewhat better this time than he was in Tannh., it's only because (after having grumbled at the " tedious " part) he heard Ander in Lohengrin at Vienna, and so at any rate acquired a different opinion. I know everything, you see !—

I read your letter of to-day with great delight at breakfast on the open balcony in beautiful bright weather (at last !) between puffs at my Turkish pipe—concerning which you've made me no reply as yet. I treated it as a little gossip hour, and so, to round the gossip off, I'm writing to you at once before I set to work. What puts me in good humour most of all, of course, is the news of your improvement ; one can see it from your letters at a glance, and when you specially assure me of it in addition, I can wish for nothing better. So continue ; so will all be well, and this summer cure will crown good

Pusinelli's work—(who in return is also to get a morsel of his capital paid back ! *)

Nothing certain from America as yet. Yesterday Wesendonck sent me a letter from his brother-in-law, according to which the director was away and not expected back before 2 days ; consequently, definite news soon. Meanwhile he merely intimates that the director has big ideas for next winter, but had just lost money in Philadelphia. At this very time—he writes—they have given Tannhäuser in Newyork at a second-rate theatre (with very insufficient means) ; of which I naturally knew absolutely nothing, and owe it to that absurd Herr Kriete, who— in spite of my counter-orders—kept urging the Dresden publisher to sell full scores as well; whereby I suffer double injury : in the first place, no more copies to be had ; and 2ndly, cheating out of my fees from Holland and Newyork. I really should like to sue Herr Kriete for compensation : he is getting the uttermost farthing of his capital, and I shall still have to pay him the interest as well ; but who will pay me anything for my damages ? And when the lawyer is proving to me clear as day that the lamented Meser did me out of at least 2000 thlr !— Please rub that under Kriete's nose a little, and somewhat lower the pitch of his pretensions.

And now for something about this precious war which stands in immediate prospect. Child, this infamous war *will* not do me damage yet, for it *is doing* so already. Lucky I got my piano out of Venice in time : my box of books, music, manuscripts (among others the Young Siegfried), linen etc., I haven't *yet*. Three weeks ago the carrier wrote me from Venice that the military trans-

---

* Opera-publication affair again, Meser's successor (H. Müller) taking over the business.—Tr.

ports had taken exclusive possession of the railways, and
he must wait until the lines were freed again. You may
imagine how vexatious that is to me ; but I may congratulate myself if the box doesn't get lost entirely !—
On the whole, however, I don't believe the war need
alter anything material in our plans, and for the following
reasons : *either* it will be confined to Italy—when it won't
make any difference ; *or* it will become a *universal* one—
when *every* place will be unsafe, but Paris the safest of
them all. Should the French Emperor *lose*, that will be
decided somewhere else, and apparently the Orleans
would return to power ; what preceded that, would be
more a military matter, and it wouldn't arrive at a revo-
lution in Paris at all. Should he *win*, however, Paris of
itself would be completely unaffected. But whatever
happens, in such an enormous city one can live so
tranquilly and unmolested, you see, almost without
learning what is going on. I also think we shan't take
rooms exactly in the Rue St Denis, but farther out,
towards the Champs Elysées, whither an émeute never
trends. Moreover, as I'm no longer a German (thanks to
the beautiful Saxon Government !) but come from *neutral*
Switzerland, under no circumstances will any obstacle be
placed in the way of my journey. Should it come to a
war with Germany as well, I should certainly have to
return to Basle first—on the détour for Carlsruhe—and
go on thence to Baden ; similarly, we should both have
to cross the Swiss frontier from Carlsruhe to Paris. For
the present I can foresee no greater difficulties, and only
wish I hadn't to go to America first, but to Paris straight
off for good. Consequently I should like the Tannhäuser
there to be brought about this coming winter ; a point on
which I also am awaiting definite tidings.—

My Amnesty affair isn't worth wasting another word
on.   I saw this issue in advance ; still, I had to take that
final step as well, just to be able to appeal to it in
the proper quarter.   At Carlsruhe I shall see how far the
Grand Duke means to meet me, then to make my last
attempt with the Bundestag : namely, to effect that
individual princes such as himself, the Prussian and
perhaps the Austrian, should be released from the extra-
dition proviso with Saxony in the exceptional case of my
wanting to reside in their territories awhile for the production of my operas.   I have the chance of such an egress
being found in course of time, and should then have strictly
all I need ; for I am determined now in any case to settle
down in Paris.   So—no more commotion on that !—

For the rest, I'm awaiting the " lucre " you so
thoughtfully dreamt of with my ballet-dancing.   I fancy
everything will turn out well, and indeed have no ground
to be dissatisfied upon the whole ; last year cost an awful
amount of money again, and yet in the end so much
came in that we both had enough, and I—no debts !
Everything at Zurich is paid off to the last farthing.
Even if America and Paris were to yield no tribute for the
present, we could manage abundantly with what I have
in prospect, and—*all* of it's earned by myself ; *not a
creature* is contributing me anything more.

So congratulate us, and—be of good cheer !   Charming greetings to all !   Get well, and hold

Thy

splendid Husband dear.

171.

LUCERNE, 12. *May* 1859.

Look here, dearest Mutz, you really don't behave
your best towards me !   I might have had an answer to

my last letter 5 days since. I don't think it's the fault
of the Post, for date and post-mark have always tallied
hitherto. With the telegram it was different : that
certainly went off at 8 in the morning, but only as far as
the Swiss frontier; the Swiss bureau won't answer for
delays arising at the German stations. The brief letter
you wrote me in consequence of that despatch I had
already answered in essence through my letter of the
same date,* and so I hoped to receive a reply to *my* letter
in turn, by the beginning of this week. Moreover, it
propounded various points on which you were to give me
your opinion ; so I shall hope to hear something from you
tomorrow !—

   To-day it's miserable enough again. We had a lovely
sunset yesterday, all was so vivid, and I expected a fine
day to-day for certain :—this morning everything in mist
and cloud again !   I've really had bad luck this time with
Switzerland : my plan of residence was altogether reckoned
for fine weather ; cut off from all society, nothing for one's
recreation or distraction except Nature in its beauty, an
abode which is only beautiful through offering a lovely
view,—and now : that Nature and this view continually
cut off and veiled !   In a big city that of course matters
nothing, or certainly much less ; there one often scarcely
remarks how the sky is looking. To be dependent on it
alone, however, is another pair of boots.

   Speaking strictly, what brought me to Switzerland in
general and this neighbourhood in particular, was the
hope of remedying the troubles in my lower regions—
which never cease plaguing me, now in this form, now in
that—by frequent and considerable excursions, climbs,

---

* Another missing letter.—Tr.

and a taste of the pure high-mountain air. But they
have become almost worse ; each morning I awake with
heavy head and aches in every limb, to gaze out on such
another cheerless day that stops me from everything.
And one is to preserve good humour with it all ! Work
—yes, that's mighty fine, it helps one to forget much in
the end ; but all the worse if work itself becomes impossible. No, this sort of thing cannot go on much
longer ! I still hope to effect a radical alteration, and
reconciliation with my surroundings, through the advent
of settled fine weather ; if that favour isn't granted soon,
I really don't know what to do, especially about my
health. I have a horror of all springs and spas, because
I'm not the man to abide by the cure so systematically
that it does some good ; and then, on the contrary, it only
makes bad worse. What might be of the most radical
help to me, and lead to a great change in my slack state
of health, I know well enough :—to be able to arrive at
decent outward activity again, delight in a fine performance, stimulation, etc., etc.—But how wretchedly and
pitifully does the whole world leave me in the lurch,
everybody, everybody. Bah ! and yet one has so many
" friends," such influential, high-placed friends !—
Abominable ! !

Liszt wrote me recently again : " Only complete your
Tristan, and then we will see ! "—to which I answered :
" Capital ! But how if I didn't complete it, couldn't
complete it, because I need refreshment *first*, not *after ?*
Have I perchance supplied too little yet, to earn the
Germans' energetic interest in my fate? Must I first
make this or that besides ? "—

Well, I shall help myself ere long, and presumably
then turn my back on some of them.—For the present, as

said, I'm still living in hope that the heavens will at last take pity on me and shew a friendly countenance to my Swiss cure ; things *can't* go on so wretchedly ! In any case I shall keep my birthday on the Rigi, let the weather behave as it chooses. I shall ascend the previous evening, and awake in the morning atop ; then down again to receive the lovely presents with which it is to be hoped you'll congratulate me.—Otherwise I'm sent to Coventry, the whole world holds its tongue ; 'tis as if they all had a bad conscience in my regard.

The *war* is most absurd, that's certain ; but the Theatre always comes out of it best in the long run, as people fight shy of larger outlay in the lump, such as for pictures and works of art, but gladly invest in a bit of a ticket for an evening's distraction. 'Twas ever thus ! Nevertheless I admit I regard the American offer now with more and more favourable eyes, and—as you will uphold in me—am quite determined to accept it. After all it's an absolutely safe way, independent of any European complications, of amply insuring ourselves against every contingency for a number of years ; and consequently it is quite invaluable. The voyage on the extremely comfortable big steamers is said to be really not so disagreeable, and at any rate nothing to compare with that we once went through.

Under these circumstances I still hold fast to *Paris* as the best, nay, only place for us. Even if I take nothing at all there at first, that will not matter, whilst it certainly is the most agreeable of all large cities, and the one that offers most from every point of view. If I get in a regular huff with Germany, I might even decide next Easter, on my return from Newyork, to embark on a good (superfine) German Opera enterprise (in the Italian

Opera-house), so as to bring out my operas, including *Tristan for the first time.* Lord bless me, there are 100,000 Germans living in Paris, and it would also make a prodigious sensation among the French public ; I shouldn't be at all afraid of the success, a downright *German.* And what joy for me, from the heart of the enemy's country first to shew these mouthing German-patriotic swindlers a German work in the fullest sense, and then to ask what all *their* German swinery was worth ! !—It really is unaccountable how they behave to me, and I can't help thinking they're all * * * * * * * fellows who cannot trust themselves to use the proper language in the proper quarter.   Devil take it—if the fire there were only duly poked, and the disgrace of their still keeping me out of Germany regardlessly shewn up to them, they would be bound to feel ashamed of themselves and do something respectable.   But it's just *this* cowardice which so disgusts me that I mostly turn away from them all with nothing but contempt.   However, I shall help myself ere long, as said— : but in my own way then !—

Lord, the weather cleared up so nicely yesterday, that I really got back a little zest for life.   On a three hours' ramble, such as one really can make nowhere else than in these glorious environs, I had much to observe which delighted me.   I sat down by a mill-race to cool myself till I could take a drink, when I got into a good frame for observing : inside clacked the works, outside cackled the hens ; pigeons sought their provender between them ; on a small wagon heaped with straw the sparrows hopped about and pecked stray grains ; I heard the ox in his stall, and asked myself what still was lacking? Aha ! the cat came out of the door, seated herself on the sill, attended to her toilet, and watched the birds.   At last a

girl sallied forth to draw water, and behind her bounced
a great big dog, who never harmed me.—Then I thought :
Eh, such a *genuine* country life might also suit me for a
change. I'm so fond of keeping company with animals ;
and that no superficial company. One always has something to give one little cares and blameless joys, with
them ; every day has its interest, for one learns to know
each beastie personally, they depend on us, and that
flatters us.—Then I passed over the hill, through the
forest, with the heavenly concert of woodbirds, in which I
keep believing I discover some new song. But it was
superb on the pasture-lands. Such beautiful chimes I
have heard nowhere else : almost every cow wears her
big fine-toned metal bell, on which these people seem to
spend a lot. Standing in the midst of them, it was a
true Power of Sounds to me ; and the cattle are so
friendly, all come close up to one and look at one
inquisitively. Long did I hear those lovely bells, from
farthest distance ; ay, even at night I heard them on my
balcony across the lake, for the cows remain upon the
pasture all night long.

If everything went thoroughly according to my wish
for once, I should like to pass the winters in Paris, but
every summer we should have to be able to lead just
such a homely country life in Switzerland ; perhaps at
Brunnen after all. I don't mean to give the latter
scheme quite up, and shall resume it with Aufdermauer.
America ! America, thou must help !—With money, you
know, one can do anything !—

Tell me, bad woman, do you honestly deserve my
painting you such pretty things as the above, and on
pink paper into the bargain ? (Which reminds me of my
barber, who wished to speak thorough *heigh* German with

me yesterday, and since the Swiss always pronounce *ei* as
i—Isen, for instance, instead of Eisen—jibbed at saying
Pap*ier*, and offered me instead "Pap*eier*." I had to
explode with laughter!) And there I go telling you
such a fine anecdote into the bargain! What have you
done for it? You prefer not to write me at all. I fancy
it's a sign that you're having as much entertainment as I
by all means wish you from my heart; but I don't particularly respect your large correspondence elsewhere. What
you women have to hatch among yourselves isn't worth
much as a rule, and your father was perfectly right not
to consent to you girls learning writing. Na, mend your
ways, and give me in exchange the greatest joy you can
afford me, by sending me fine reports on your state of
health. Ah, so much is based on that! Our remaining
apart till the end of August or September, looked at
sensibly, has the sole aim of your going quite smoothly
through your summer cure, from which we all indeed
have hoped so much. Meantime I shall jog aimlessly on,
hoping that good summer weather here will yet bring me
the proposed benefit to my own health, that my work
may thrive therewith and get completed, I may then
attend to everything in Paris nicely, and finally we both
may pitch our tent a little solidly again and fairly snugly:
when mutual cosseting and recreation will do both of
us good!—

Now adieu, you bad Mutz-wife! If I don't get a
letter tomorrow, I shall become still more personal!
Adieu! Best greetings to the menagerie!

Thy
RICHARD.

It will soon be a full quarter of a century now, that
we have known and made eyes at each other! A lovely

time—how will it be after the next quarter of a century??—I fancy I then shall be amnestied.—

172.

Lucerne, 18. *May* 1859.

You often give me cause, dear Minna, to ponder
whether of the two is better, to stay silent as to certain of
your utterances, or reply to them.   As a rule I think it
of more benefit to both of us, to pass over this and that
in your letters in silence, above all when it only deals
with *me ;* and I have also found this verified by thereafter
learning from yourself that I had attached too much
importance to your observations here and there.   The
case is different, however, when I have to see that it
concerns ideas which so often recur for *your* self-torture ;
then I am bound to feel I ought to do my utmost to
explain things for your reassurance.   Above all I
see, to my regret, that a readily excusable feminine
vanity prevents your ever realising what one strictly
means by *love*.   With me this feeling comes into play
when another's sympathetic interest in me moves me
to thank him no longer in words, but by deeds ; so
long as I feel compelled to make return to anyone by
an assurance of my gratitude and friendship, I feel that
things are not quite straight between the two of us as
yet ; only when I feel I need no longer do so, but may
accept the boon conferred upon me as a gift which, I may
rest convinced, delights the giver almost more than
myself, the receiver ; thus, when I have no further need
of words and protestations, but must even account them
superfluous and out of place,—only then do I also feel
transferred to the position of rediscovering my own welfare
in another's, of recognising the good turn I do him as a

charity shewn myself ; when he suffers, of setting his interest on a thorough equality with mine ; and when he suffers *very much*, even of subordinating my welfare to his, since it becomes clear to me that my personal welfare can repose on nothing save the restoration of that other's.

In your very exhausted condition you must be allowed to overlook the fact of my finding myself in the said mood and position towards yourself ; yet, in spite of a seemingly contradictory experience, you ought to judge that if at the end of 25 years I am now behaving the most pronouncedly thus towards yourself, it must also constitute the leading feature of my whole relation to you.—What one has accordingly to understand by Love in its noblest sense, however, never comes out between husband and wife till their relation has matured. What begets that relation is something quite different ; it is a charm of shorter or longer duration, but fleeting of its very nature : in common parlance one calls the condition when one is under the spell of this charm, being in love *(Verliebtheit)*. This phase—for it is only a phase, and therefore changeable—makes us eager and selfish ; for it is nothing but the longing to possess the other exclusively and for one's will. Hence that prodigious jealousy which is almost a preponderant factor in this passion : to ensure ourselves a right to jealousy, i.e. to keep everyone else away from the coveted object, we enter engagements without reflection, without pondering whether other circumstances permit, yes, even without regard as to whether we are ensuring the happiness of the coveted object of our selfish longing, or may not rather be endangering it in the extreme,—engagements and alliances that have no other aim whatever than the making us legitimate owners. This is the

foundation of all marriages for so-called—love. No heed
is paid to outward circumstances ; perhaps a simple glance
around, a moment of calm reflection, tells us that under
present circumstances, the insecurity of our outward
position and everything connected with it, the consequences
of a precipitate marriage must inevitably be embarrassing,
disheartening, full of want and care ; but the blind lust
for undivided possession of the other blots out all reason :
self-will conquers, and the consequences, cares, sorrows,
hardships and distress—which unavoidably follow in the
train of an immature and outwardly precarious situation
with no civic bottom to it—not only do not fail to appear,
but become the more serious and painful, the more high-
spirited and passionate the individuals who attract each
other.

Now see, dear child, when I wished to give people a
notion of the genesis of my works, and consequently of
my psychological development, I could not pass over such
a momentous crisis in my life, as that which attaches to
our union, without remaining unintelligible. It would
have been foolish and entirely opposed to my real object,
if I had sought to narrate our love-tale at full length ; all
I required were just a few brief strokes to indicate an
episode of some importance which, for that matter, occurs
in the life of so many, nay, of most men, and need
be only briefly touched because one presupposes that
everyone knows well enough what here is meant : to wit,
the necessary consequences of a youthful marriage contracted at the behest of passion, without calm consideration of outer circumstances, against all obstacles and
objections raised by that practical common-sense which
foresees trouble.

That you will not get it out of your head that I meant

to expose and even accuse yourself, to me seems so nonsensical and perverse, that I hitherto have scarcely known how to reply to you ; because I couldn't see in what way to enlighten your mind on a thing so simply understandable that I really hope to find no misconstruction of it has occurred to others, saving perhaps to persons of the Sch.'s intelligence and so on, for whom at all events I never wrote my book.

I am very sorry now, at any rate, I had that Preface printed then ; for it was far too poetically (*genial*) written for the majority of readers even half to understand. Thus I also have to regret that in the whole of this Preface you still pay no heed to anything except that passage,* and maybe could wish that I had seized the opportunity of writing a fuller account of my life, when I should also

---

* By this "Preface" is meant the *Communication to my Friends*, originally published at the end of 1851 "*als Vorwort*" to the poems of *Der fliegende Holländer, Tannhäuser* and *Lohengrin*. Here is the "passage" in question, with the simple omission of half-a-dozen lines not bearing on the conjugal dispute in any way:—"The modern requital of modern levity soon broke in upon me. I was in love, married in obstinate ardour, tortured myself and partner with the sordid experience of an indigent home, and so fell into that misery whose nature it is to bring thousands upon thousands to the ground.—Thus an impulse developed in me to a consuming desire: to find a way out from the pettiness and paltriness of circumstances governing me. This impulse, however, had only secondarily to do with real life ; its front was directed toward a brilliant career as artist : to get away from all the pokiness of German theatres and try my luck in Paris. . . , My household difficulties (*häusliches Trübsal*) increased; the impulse to extricate myself from an unworthy situation mounted to a violent craving to begin something grand and inspiring, even if I had to leave my immediate practical object unregarded awhile. This mood was fed and fostered in me by the reading of Bulwer's 'Rienzi.' Out of the squalidness of modern private life, whence I could nowhere glean the least material for artistic treatment, I was snatched by the presentment of a great historico-political event, in the enjoyment whereof I was bound to find an uplifting distraction from cares and conditions which to me seemed nothing less than absolutely hostile to art" (*cf. R. Wagner's Prose Works* I. 297-8).—Tr.

have been able to give yourself a handsome testimonial in
the eyes of all the world for your self-sacrifice and loyalty.
If you understood the whole, however, you would also see
that it never struck me to write a biography—a thing I
really should have thought absurd and droll enough,
to say nothing of puffing my wife—but on the contrary,
that I touched in brief hints merely on such points in my
life as seemed needful for displaying the course of my
artistic development. So, if anyone should speak to you
in future of that passage with a dubious look, just laugh
them in the face and say : " Bless my soul, after leading
me a pretty dance with his ridiculous jealousy, just to
prevent anyone else coming near me he insisted on
marriage ; and in such unfavourable and beggarly circumstances, that my calm reflection told me in advance
what misery we should have to undergo. But what was
I to do ? I loved him also. And so we pair of callow
youngsters rushed into a misère which soon enough
became so grievous and acute that I myself believed I
couldn't bear it any longer ; and since besides my head-
strong young husband's heavy load of debts, with a
summer out of work in front of us, he further plagued me
with the fiercest outbursts of an intolerable jealousy, one
day I ran away."—

Thus, dear child, might you answer in full keeping
with the truth, and you would have explained that passage
correctly. But I presume that no one but a stupid person
could put you in a position dictating such an answer ;
since a person of sound intelligence would understand the
passage by itself, and never think of driving you into an
explanation that would end by rather raising doubts about
your love for me, than mine for you. For a really
intelligent person then would ask you in reply : " So you

could run away like that from your young inexperienced husband in the sore plight he was in, as well as you? According to that, you did not really love him, did you? For a wife who truly loves her husband, and *cannot help* loving him, no doubt may feel very wretchedly injured by his outbursts, but so soon as her simple love-instinct reminds her that even those outbursts sprang from nothing but the passion of love (you know, of course, that passionate love and jealousy have made men murder their beloved !), moreover, that the unhappy, hard and grievous plight in which you left him was after all itself a consequence of the imprudence with which he had insisted on marriage when it would have been better to await a more propitious season, and therefore had strictly proceeded from his ardent affection for you,—so soon as she remembered that, she couldn't possibly run away from him ; since that very misery, at bottom, must have borne witness to her of the uncommon strength of his affection."

As a fact, dear child, there are many would answer you thus ; and as you're so particularly fond of indulging these old reminiscences, I will simply tell you that a very calm and intelligent man of great feeling actually gave me this to reflect on at the time itself—when, accusing myself in excuse of you, to reconcile him to your conduct I had given him the elucidation I have put into your mouth above for future use. You know him quite well, and doubtless will not have much to say against him ; it was Hermann Brockhaus,* whose letter of that epoch also lately fell into my hands again. —As said, though, should this serious reply be ever made you, then without detracting from your honour

---

* Married to R. Wagner's sister Ottilie.—Tr.

you might answer somewhat thus : " Undoubtedly my
love for Richard had vanished in those troublous days,
but I do not believe it would have gone that length
if a man of good position and ample means had not
approached me at the same time with so strong a show
of heartfelt sympathy for my sufferings, and protested
that sympathy in such alluring fashion, that under all
these conflicting impressions I wavered for a while ;
and since Richard's love for me only manifested itself
in such wounding explosions that I could scarcely
recognise it any more, I was unable to perceive in it
sufficient recompense for all the misery this unfortunate'
headlong marriage had brought on both of us. Yes,
I must reproach myself with having allowed it to
unsettle my mind awhile, and anyone who takes account
of everything will be able to forgive the young wife for
so far yielding to temptation that she kept away from
her husband at first, treated him hostilely and misled
him as to her steps, and faltered in her choice between
him and another to such a point that that other, alas,
could give himself the look of my having shewn more
favour to him than really was the case. But that
relation itself was my ordeal, and in *it* I first gained
full conviction of my love for Richard, which finally
emerged as the fruit of that regrettable aberration. For,
precisely when it had to come to a decision, I plainly
recognised how fond I was of Richard, so that I prevailed on myself to confess my fault to him—who had
meantime abandoned all hope of me, and taken up an
engagement in far-off Riga—and to ask his forgiveness,
averring that nothing save the gotten consciousness of
my great love for him could have moved me to do so.
Richard himself, too, had meanwhile had much to get

over, and in particular his love for me had been put
to a hard test: appearances had imbued him with the
suspicion, indeed the belief, that I had completely
betrayed him and surrendered myself to another; newspapers had been sent him from Hamburg, in which he
read that I had been staying at *the same* hotel with that
other; what else could the poor fellow believe, than just
the worst? Indeed, he had received letters in which
he was positively taunted on account of my behaviour;
whilst covert and overt insinuations were made him
even by members of the theatre at which he was,
ridiculing him as a cheated husband. He stood that
test, however, and it proved that his earlier fierce and
froward passion had made place for a true and earnest
love. He answered me at once with devotion, forgave
me all, called me to his side, and never afterwards
discussed my lapse with anybody, even under the
sorest temptations arising later. So love, belief and
loyalty had taken their abode with us, and the trials
of our youth were past, even though the hard trials of
maturer life itself remained in store for us. With
Richard's individuality, which on the one hand
qualified him for the creation of such important works,
and in the end for such unusual successes, it could not
but be, on the other, that strong shadows also thereby
fell upon our life. I am not referring to the constant
outward cares and trouble, although they sorely taxed
my strength: but it could not be avoided that his
original artistic temperament, the peculiarly emotional
and enthralling fervour of his works, should keep him in
the same state of excitation as was conveyed by them to
others, and thereby troublings of my own repose must
necessarily arise. So considerable an artist as my

Richard, and constantly at work with such passionate tools, retains throughout his life a certain juvenility which often, no doubt, must become alarming to the wife at his side ; whereas in the accustomed narrow circle of the household that wife remains near him as an ancient possession, which one often doesn't notice any longer just because one is so familiar with and certain of it, from without new figures may present themselves toward whose effect the anxious wife may have to be forbearing. Luckily he was cut off from the world during the time of his actual triumph, and perhaps many an anxiety thus passed over my head ; yet I was not left without painful experiences, which affected me all the more violently as the constant distress and unrest of our life unfortunately had made me and my health intensely sensitive. In exchange, however, I have also reaped the comforting experience that when it came to an extremity, and sorrow overwhelmed me, I could rely on Richard once again ; for it was precisely then he proved the faithfulest and most unselfish to me, thereby justifying me in the conclusion that he most heartily reciprocates my love and loyalty, and finally would bow to anything and give up everything, to raise me up and be a good husband to me to the best of his ability.—That's how things stand with us, and now— ask me no further questions."

I believe this answer would be thoroughly truthful and wise, and thereafter you might hold up your head with tranquil pride. I'm not annoyed with you for placing me in the position of having to prescribe it to you, but I beg you to lay to heart this undoubtedly clear and veracious résumé of our relation as my answer to your repeated indictments, and to make its substance yours ; which cannot possibly fall hard, or be distasteful to you. And so, dear Minna, cease tormenting *yourself*, and reflect that if you therewith torture *me* as well, it is only through its making me feel so concerned to see you still so agitated inwardly. As for myself, my mind is so clear on these points, and I have arrived at such deep inner calm, that I feel perfectly secure and justified in my every act in this regard ; for I may tell myself, I seek my *only* welfare now in no one's suffering any further for my sake.—Let that suffice you also for your peace of soul ; if you cannot represent the past to yourself in a conciliatory light, then put forth all your power to forget it, and abide by what I *am* to you.—

Soon more ; I shall write again tomorrow or the next day ! * Farewell ! Thanks for your letters.

Thy
RICHARD.

173.

LUCERNE, 30. May 1859.

MY POOR GOOD MUTZ,

Your having such thumping of the heart again is truly awful ! But how could you do me the dishonour of letting yourself be treated on my birthday to—Lössnitz champagne ? I trembled when I heard of that atrocious proposal in your last letter, and should have liked to stop it by telegraph, which I now greatly regret leaving undone. I should have thought we had both had sufficient experience of the abominable effects of that infamous drink (God forgive me my sin), and such an effect is accountable for my letter's having made so nasty

---

* Another missing letter ?—Tr.

an impression on you : with that stuff in your head,
I believe the big prize in the lottery might have been
notified you, and you would have deemed it a big loss.
If on the contrary you had honoured my birthday by
drinking a small bottle of *genuine* champagne to the
health of your husband at *your own* expense, firmly
believe me, my poor letter—which is supposed to have
wrought all the mischief—would have had a corresponding
effect on you. Do you imagine you're delighting me,
queer wife, to say nothing of making me friends with the
Sch., when you tell me she brought Lössnitzer into your
house upon my birthday? Am I to think you so shabby
that you can't stand something genuine out of your
own pocket on such a day? Indeed this faithful friend
Sch. becomes more and more fatal to me ; she reacts
on you, believe me, exactly like that Lössnitz, *lowering*
in the best event. However—you're fond of her : what
weigh *I* 'gainst such affection? I remain for you, as
ever, an object of suspicion ; I have had to perceive that
once more.

How my letter could *insult* you, remains downright
incomprehensible to me ! Do remember in general, that
between persons who are allied by true love there can
never be question of *insult ;* and whenever a thing wears
that appearance, nothing but confusion and misunder-
standing can have come into play.—Even at Venice I had
thrusts from you about that passage in my " Preface "
which offends you so ; I smiled at them, because I
saw you were involved in a passionate misunderstanding
of that remark, and—held my tongue. But when you
returned to the charge, and made me a distinct reproach,
I couldn't but believe you were wishful to hear my
defence. So I summarise the evolution of our reciprocal

relations, how true love gradually resulted from the
first violent inclination, and fancy I'm telling you something quite fine ; the more so, as I set forth all the
facts—which indeed it was very needful to allude to here
—according to your own account of them, and didn't
upbraid you in the slightest, but threw into relief the
trials of the human heart.   My, what it is to have to
do with women !   One may look out for anything then ;
the best meaning, the most honest intention, may be
twisted to the opposite, especially if Lössnitzer is fizzing
in the brain !—

This time, dear good Mutz, lay it all on the Sch. ;
you do *me* decided wrong !   Moreover, looked at calmly,
your rejoinder quite agrees with my account, only that
there's a shade more light and shadow here and there
than with me, which doesn't make much difference at
bottom.   Do be reasonable, and after all you *must* have
now become aware of in me, please tell yourself it can't
be my object to wound or provoke you in any way.   I
may be imprudent now and then in my remarks—often
better say nothing !—but precisely when I do unburden
myself at last, you surely ought to discern no object but
a good one !   And if you wish to avoid even that, dear
pet, don't keep commencing, and don't give me such
repeated digs and scratches on a certain spot that at
last I think I'm bound to answer you.   For that matter,
bad as it would be if it had seriously excited you again
now, no doubt it's also better that a clean slate should
finally be made regarding some things : it is bound
to have good consequences, if certain innuendoes etc.
are rendered hors de combat.   In this case, though, I
really didn't want to wound you ; that sort of thing, for
sure, is put behind me !

Nevertheless, you may have been right if you thought
I meant to rub it into you a trifle that your love
perhaps was not so altogether fireproof in those earliest
days (which I only meant to let suspected *mine* shine
all the brighter) ; there you've paid me soundly back
in my own coin, and I willingly believe you that I was a
wicked fellow.   Neither can I take it quite amiss, that
you give me that dear Bordeaux to smell at in return,
especially as you still had kept a secret from me which
has really set me in astonishment to learn.   So, someone
wrote you at the time, that I made my second journey to
Bordeaux [*cf.* letter 37] to abduct a young wife from her
husband ? ?   Now let me assure you, on my honour
and most sacred conscience, that such a *shameless lie*
and *calumny* was never yet invented against any man.   If
it might conduce to your honour and peace of mind,
I should gladly be prepared to give you every detail
of that episode, and you then would find I doubtless
acted *very stupidly* at that time, but certainly *not
evilly*, and that to *no one*.   Believe my word !   And
don't let any hairs turn grey about my sins ; that
I'm attending to already, poor grey-roan me !—See, dear
Mutz, I now can discuss my whole past so quietly
and unabashed, that I've nothing more to shun *for my
part*.   I willingly and openly admit where I have acted
hastily, absurdly or erroneously ; of *bad* actions I'm not
conscious.   Believe that too !   But above all—no more
Lössnitzer !

So much for this evening, in haste.   Tomorrow
more, I hope.   Be calm and afflict yourself with *nothing*
as regards

Thy
dear good Husband !

174.

LUCERNE, 31. *May* 1859.

MY GOOD MUTZ,

No, I can't yet get over your drinking Lössnitz champagne on my birthday ; I could poison the Sch. for it ! To my dying day I shan't forget how both of us once dropped to earth like lead through that stuff. But you're always playing me this kind of prank of false economy, as with your 3rd class on long railway journeys, and so on; the evil consequences of which *I* always have to share. The same again this time ! Do take my word for it, the letter wasn't nasty ; nor could it have stirred up bad blood in you, if that hadn't been poisoned before : 'twere as though I wrote the very opposite of what I meant to, and as I'm drinking neither Lössnitzer nor any other champagne, I should be at a loss to know how that could have happened to me. In reality, whoever reads that letter without bias, can only find in it a panegyric on yourself ; and if I also had a little fling at you, it was merely to shew that *I* was downright mad upon you, whilst *you* believed at the commencement you still might exercise a choice : in short, that I loved you more than you myself ; and that is really a reproach a wife may willingly put up with from her husband, since at bottom it contains a flattery. Further, my object with it was to answer you, and talk you out of all the stuff and nonsense you have got into your head about that passage in my " Preface." But where does it occur to me to try and make you any fresh *reproach ?* I made you a compliment, indeed I did ! Do I not take all the blame of that time on *myself ?* Do I not follow in everything *your own* account of your behaviour then ? Your own answer, in fact, is fresh proof to me that we strictly are quite in agreement. And what could alone have been the object of my letter? Why, simply to refute what had occasioned it, and those were the *repeated reproaches* you had made me concerning that (hackneyed) passage, that I meant it to deny my having married you for love.* I believed I could dissipate this haunting suspicion of yours no other way than by shewing you the true *sense* of that passage, viz. that I thereby said, on the contrary, that our precipitate—i.e. in such indigent circumstances etc., at any rate too early— marriage, with all its consequences of unrest and want, had originated in the very vehemence of my obstination ; which really can be only read as flattering to the object of my choice. Moreover, that you might thoroughly understand those words as well, I then shewed you how true love had finally evolved from that through sufferings and trials ; consequently the whole is one hymn to that [true love], and yet—you have felt compelled to "answer" me "with tears of blood" (! ! !)

Well, nobody could have made a greater mistake than I did this time, and as mistakes of that kind, springing from the best intention on my side, have so repeatedly occurred to me before, to avoid all further possibility thereof in future I most heartily beg you to be a little more careful yourself, and not keep dinning into me these constantly recurring innuendoes and reproaches about past events and utterances misunderstood to boot.   For, once again : it disquiets *me* purely for *your* sake, because I see it still fermenting in you. Then I ask myself : Shall I stay mum, Shall I enlighten her?   If I attempt

---

* This makes it look as if she had misread "*ich war verliebt*," "I was in love" (see the quotation, p. 500 *sup.*), as "*ich war geliebt*," "I was beloved."—Tr.

the latter, I always make bad worse, as this time ; say or explain what I will, you take it all as fresh upbraiding. If I'm silent, it returns once more, and still you do not pacify yourself ! Isn't that a thoroughly sad and stupid plight for me ? Couldn't you improve it radically, by giving up this constant harping on the same old strings ? How is it, for instance, that ever since [your stay in] Dresden you've kept reverting to that old passage in the " Preface " ? Must I not believe you're keeping idiotic company ; or is it *yourself* that takes a pleasure in always raking up the past ? How did you so much as get hold of the book ? I had ceased to possess it at Zurich myself ; have you procured it again for your private use ? O folly without end ! If I were *only* shrewd and prudent, I should *never* answer you another syllable to prods like these ; but indeed I'm far too fond of you, you make me so terribly *sorry* for your continually torturing yourself with such absurdities ; so I rack my brains to set about conveying you a different idea of our relation, and—commit a fresh folly forthwith. For of course I recognise (too late then) that *any* allusion to certain past times is bound to be painful to your still so ailing heart, and therefore had always better be averted and avoided. There now, you shan't lead me astray again in such a hurry, and if it ever should again be downright unavoidable (which God forbid !) I'll take care at least that you drink true Good-luck champagne first, no Lössnitz fusel. But the damage is done, and *you've* to pay for it again ! Oh ! Oh !—

For my own part I can swear to you that all this old lumber no longer exists for me, I call up reproaches against no one whatever, and least of all against yourself; and yet I am living so void of distraction, that it would

be more excusable in me if I took to worrying from time
to time. For *you*, in your present situation, that ought
to have been made still easier ; so mind you get away to
Schandau soon, and may the dear faithful Lössnitz-
champagne lady-friend not honour you quite too often
with her affecting attachment ! I stick to it : old maids
like her have *nothing* in the world at heart but scandal,
and scandal again, in one form or another ; what else
is left them, than to interfere in other people's business,
since they themselves have nobody whom they can call
their own ? And that applies to all of them, from the
dressmaker to the artist ; they all have something suspicious and suspecting about them, poke their nose into
everything, and know something about everyone that
isn't as it should be, and at which that nose must be
turned up. You'll contradict me,—no matter ! I know
them, all the same, and stick to it ; and they shan't have
an excessively good time in my vicinity. Amen.—

Lord, what a quantity of needless scribbling again !
If it goes on like this, I shan't even arrive at telling
you my delight about the lovely blotting-book ; and yet
I've daubed its inside terribly already, notwithstanding
your polite invitation to pack it up again at once and put
it by : with which you certainly succeeded in soundly
seasoning my first delight at its receipt, and so much so,
that I really couldn't thank you for the gift *straight off*.
Was that your object, Minna ? Did you only make me
a present of the blotting-book to cool a revenge on me ?
How you would be to be pitied ! After a little reflection, at any rate, I soon guessed what you wanted
to take revenge for, and told myself I had probably
offended you over that embroidery for the piano-stool—
2 years ago—only I was surprised at your not rather

repressing a thing like that in our present position, and leaving *me* to make myself reproaches about it; which surely must have given you greater satisfaction than *your* making them to me, when vengeance indeed is wrought, but not repentance. For your reassurance, however—as I see you still need reassurance even upon that—I will confess to you, a little late, that you really didn't hit my taste that time; for, as I first found out through that embroidery, I'm not particularly fond of glass-bead work, and even have a little loathing of it. I didn't let you notice it—in fact it was the first time you had made me a whole piece of bead-work—and proposed to have it put on the stool for my next birthday. Well, you know the sort of humour we were in last year, about this date; moreover, I forgot it : so don't be cross with me about it any longer, and seek for nothing worse behind that undoubtedly wounding neglect. All the more beautifully have you hit my taste with the blotting-book, exactly as if I had ordered it myself; only, the embroidery is almost a shade too coquettish and dainty : Lord, how do I match such elegance ! And the violet velvet, with the beautiful inner lining ! In short, indescribably splendid ! Accept my best thanks and a hearty kiss for the magnificent present !—I didn't get it till the 23rd, when, to my joy and relief, my box also arrived at last from Venice ; which really made me very glad, especially on account of the sketches for *Siegfried*, which otherwise would have been utterly lost. It all costs an awful amount of money, tho', and I shouldn't care to lead a vagrant life like this much longer.

A great improvement seems to be commencing in my health through the Kissinger water I've been drinking every morning since my birthday. Also, the morning

promenades attached thereto are doing me a heap of good ;
6 o'clock in the morning, be it day or night, off the roost
and on to the promenade, from which I don't get back
till 8. Really I feel surprisingly lighter and better since,
which no doubt is to some extent assisted by the weather,
as it doesn't rain *continuously* now, but only once a day,
either forenoon or evening ; without that much it can't
do, and true enough, I've not been up the Rigi yet, or
anywhere else. Unfortunately I have had to take to my
Venetian stiff stockings again ; my legs are again very
swollen, and the veins stand out from them like whip-
cord. That comes from so much sitting. Moreover, I
have really been tormented everywhere of late (except by
my wife !) : for I've contracted a bad finger (proud flesh,
they call it), and to crown it all, so severe an inflammation of the * * * * that I took cold hip-baths for it ; as
it got worse, however, I called in the doctor, and the
poor wretch had literally to inspect what was up. Then
it transpired that the cold hip-baths hadn't been the right
way of combating it, for it wasn't an ordinary hæmor-
rhoidal inflammation, but an abscess, which the doctor
lanced. So I had a fine time of it : I couldn't sit,
couldn't hold anything in my hand, elastic stockings on
my legs, and on my heart the old reproaches of my wife !
I asked the doctor where the Devil I had got the abscess
from, my living and diet were so terribly strict : he
replied that such a thing occurred to hæmorrhoidalists
at times, but Kissinger water would soon help me to
form better blood ; and in fact, as said, it seems to
suit me.

And now, good Minake, just see about your getting
on a better road yourself. Do take that nonsense which
oppresses you a little lighter : both of us take everything

much too seriously and heavily. For God's sake, a touch of frivolity!—that's all. But yes, that too will come: you were on the high road to it already; don't let yourself be turned aside too long. And if it eases you, why, go on thinking me a thoroughly bad lot; I'll put up with *everything*, and Devil a bit be enticed into fresh explanations, even if I get another abscess, which certainly can draw one into arrière-pensées. But don't come across or be told such an awful amount of disasters yourself; Lord knows where you fish up all the stuff from. So that poor beast X [E. Kietz] is supposed to have a Matratze? How he could contrive it, indeed I don't know. Only the other day, with the usual laments he wrote me from E[pernay], where he's still tied to the family's apron-strings, going to Paris very seldom. How he could contrive to keep a mistress in that very strait-laced house, in such a small nook, God only knows. But what's impossible to God himself is confided to you, and as it has been confided (by a person, of course, who never scandalises!), no doubt it must also be true. A deuced dog, that X!!

For the rest, I can tell you nothing more about the future yet. Nothing has occurred, all preserve silence, and my American hasn't shewn up. The best news is that my work is making progress, however slowly; and if I get into the swing at last, as I still hope, I shall stay glued here after all, subject to a little straitening, merely to get quite done without another interruption. To the present, the only possibility I still can see before me is *Paris*. Accustom yourself to the idea, dearest Minna; really there seems nothing else for it, and it's not at all a bad place to put up with, provided we've no other lack. Politics won't interfere with us. Only I must wait for

my American before I can decide on anything more
definite.—Perhaps a miracle will yet take place! God
knows what eccentricities may still arrive: Garibaldi is
close to Milan, and the King [of Saxony] has pardoned
Heubner: what more would one have? My situation
can't get any worse, and that's another consolation. Now
only let's both get supportably well, to live as happy as
the day is long when we do regain each other; that's
what I fondly wish.

Poor chap, I'm literally going to the dogs now; for
I've struck up no other acquaintances. On each of my
chief walks I now know certain dogs to whom I regularly
bow, and with whom I hold a scrap of conversation. On
my morning promenade I've quite a tiny little friend,
who always sits before his house: a small pug-dog with a
big pitch-plaster on his head, which makes him look most
comic. He wears it because of his eyes, which the poor
little chap has had quite blinded; but he's beginning to
see quite well again already, and whines as soon as I
approach him from the distance, in return for which
I very gently scratch his ears behind the plaster. So
innocent is the life I'm leading, that I shall turn in time
into a lambkin on the meadow, whilst my poor wife
regards me from afar as wolf in fox-skin. No, no: only
I'm sometimes an ass—, and that I was again the other
day! But nobody sheds tears of blood for that, dear
Mutz!—Adieu; be calm, and don't let anything disturb
you. "And yet he's a good husband!"—A thousand
greetings!

Thy
RICHARD.

175.

LUCERNE, 8. *June* 1859.

POOR DEAR MINNA,

How inconsolable I should be, if the fresh disturbance in your health had sprung from any wilful or
malicious intent of mine, as you appear, alas, to consider
yourself bound to believe ! Judge what my true intent
must have consisted in, when I assure you that even your
last letter awoke in me nothing but care for yourself, no
other feeling. You fancy I wanted to wound you anew,
and just because I again " had a mind to." No, Minna !
Rather, I was looking toward our speedy reunion with
the honest wish to end the present situation, and therefore
fain would see the last dispute between us resolve itself
to suavity and reconcilement. The good accounts of your
health deceived me as to your inner condition ; I believed
I had only to dispel a few more clouds : but to my horror
I lit on a whole thunderstorm oppressing your heart. I
therefore was very imprudent, by all means, as I quite
see *now*, and oughtn't to have touched those subjects in
any way, not even with the best intent. It never shall,
nor can occur again ; be sure of that ! Compose yourself
accordingly, and however badly you may think about
me in the past, please think better of me in the present
and future.

Naturally there can be nothing to reply to your last
letter itself ; it would be unworthy both of you and
me, to linger in this evil region any longer. Here the
sole course is Oblivion : may it succeed with you as
well ! On the whole I candidly admit all blame attach-
ing to me, and in particular deplore the sternness in
sundry of my [past] remarks to you : on sundry points,
upon the contrary, my conscience speaks me free, and

above all I regret the resentfulness and want of modera-
tion in your expressions thereanent. But these are no
matters for argument ; it is certain that you're suffering
greatly, and that's enough to make me feel my fault.
For your own sake, though, I beg you not to represent
to yourself that fault as greater than it is. Recognise
this time also, that no hostile object lay at bottom of my
last attempts to come to understanding with you, but
my fault lies more in my mistake about you, and my
incautious handling of you. Fear no repetition even of
that, however ; this last experience will always be a
warning and instructive memory to me. In fact you
may venture on it with me again in the future : the last
result shall not recur. Through angry statements, accordingly, you'll alter naught in *my* intentions ; for those
have honestly no other aim than to make up to you,
to the best of my power, for all you have endured,
and at hand of the experience of riper years to do you
as much good as I can ; thus at last to reach with you
a level looking back from which you may see in our
joint past the points of light emerging brighter, and the
darker points quite disappearing in the end. In spite of
all and everything, I shall not cease to nurse that hope,
or to strive for the attainment of my wish reposed thereon :—and first of all, I beg of you to give me the delight
of telling me full soon of your remove to Schandau ; I
shall judge from that itself that you've already somewhat
calmed. For the rest—forget and forgive ! 'Tis what
beseems good people !—

I also have to fear, though, that you may have taken
my last jocular letters amiss again. In your present
suffering mood, perhaps they may have made too garish
an impression ; which would again have been a total

failure of my aim.   Reassure me on this point as well.

Otherwise I have absolutely nothing to report to you from my extremely monotonous life.   I'm working, as much as my cure will allow me ; but *no* other news has reached me whatsoever.—I was on the *Rigi* yesterday (at last !), awoken by the alp-horn, but also, alas, by the rushing of torrents of rain.   I wouldn't force things, and came back again.   You may well believe how much my mind was occupied with memories of you, on this ascent ; what particularly grieved me, was my having then [1850 ?] exposed you to the hardships of an ascent on foot, and to my great reproach I recollect the fearful thumping of your heart on the last climb to the Kulm !   How deeply and keenly my wish is strengthened at such moments, to be able yet to shew you many a pleasant reward !

Farewell, and be quite calm about me !   A thousand hearty greetings !

Thy
R.

176.

LUCERNE, 12. *June* 1859.

DEAR MINNA,

Last week I wrote you still to Dresden.   You left orders, I hope, for letters to be sent after you ?

You have given me great joy, and a very pleasant surprise, with the news of your removal to Schandau. Going by steamer was certainly the best thing you could do ; I was also pleased to hear that N. remains with you. I hope you won't be too severe upon me for my remark about Charlotte's illness * : I grant that, if her condition

---

* In some missing letter.—Tr.

is really dangerous, it isn't to be excused ; for which reason I shouldn't wish to appear too heartless to you, and you will judge it less sternly if you remember how you wrote me last winter from Chemnitz, in not exactly reverent terms, of Ch.'s "fat, in which she would presently choke." It wasn't right of me, to remember those remarks of your own at the very moment I heard of the serious crisis in her illness, and I'm truly sorry I did so ; but you ought to have known me well enough, not to take a somewhat loose and random word so strictly. So I beg you to inform me about Ch.'s condition.—To make a thorough clean breast, I have only further to acquaint you that I burnt unread the letter you lately enclosed to me [*cf.* p. 509 *sup.* ?], as you knew everything and wished for no more explanation from myself. May the same thing happen to all remembrances from dismal days !

From my side, dear Minna—shall I say " alas " ?— I have nothing whatever to tell you ; neither a letter, nor any other piece of news has reached me from anywhere. For a long time past you've been the only one through whom I learn anything of the world outside. The only thing I have to say to you, is that I have determined for my work's sake to endure here till it's finished. It can be managed now with this hotel : true, I shall have to restrict myself in space from next month forward, but even then I hope to preserve the needful tranquillity. The landlord is most obliging to me, and the chief con- tributory circumstance is their expecting no great influx of visitors this warlike summer. Of course I'm living very dear, tho', and for every consideration the wish to take up a fixed residence with an abiding home again is strong and active in me. Where that will be at

last, is still the knotty question.   Naturally I should
like Germany best, after all ; but I suppose I must more
and more abandon every hope of that.   Nevertheless
I almost shouldn't care to decide quite definitely on Paris
yet, as I still think my visit to Carlsruhe—which remains
certain for the production of Tristan—in combination
with the effect of that production, and through my
personal acquaintance with the Grand Duke, may lead to
a favourable turn yet, and perhaps determine the Grand
Duke not to let me go away again.   In any case, however,
I shall have another look at Paris first : if I can pluck
up courage to regard a settling-down there as agreeable
alike for my own self and yours, that certainly remains
the safest.—

My work is going forward, but slowly.   Unfortunately
the weather doesn't help me a bit ; it rains regularly once
a day, and I read your report with great envy, how you
had only had a few brief showers since the 18th April.
Switzerland, when all's said, is a cloud-trap, and—I
candidly confess—I am heartily longing to get out of
it again ; really I've had about enough of it, and
one oughtn't to have the imposingness it offers one
too long before him all the time.   If I were allowed,
I'd very gladly come to friendly Schandau.   So there
seem to be plenty of animals there, and just as Rüpel
made such a gallant assault on the tortoise, I hope Fipps
will have been no less energetic in confronting the
lizards.   Howbeit, you have done very right to exchange
that too lively apartment ; you know how I wished
you to engage a better one before, because I couldn't
conceive that anything nice and unobjectionable would
be obtained at so low a rent, with present prices.   Now
let every good power give its blessing, that this stay may

thoroughly heal you poor tormented, sorely harassed wife ! Believe me, I long for nothing in life more devoutly, than to close it in peace, tranquillity and comfort with yourself. Our still so easily misunderstanding one another will improve in time, and each of us contribute to the other's peace. If I fall into my random mood again, just you take nothing too seriously, even when I run the Schiffner down : you really might have learnt this one thing, that my tongue is often looser than my heart, and even toward the Schiffner I believe I've hitherto behaved quite bearably. However, that will all come back to you, once you have seen me again and can go by the tone of my voice.

I am getting very satisfied with my composition : *what* I end by making, turns out well ; and I admit I'm looking forward with great hope and pleasure to the performance of this music, which is certain to surprise everyone greatly, and of whose transporting effect I am sure. I shall write to *Schubert* about Lohengrin in a day or two, so as to have someone to rely on in the band. Otherwise I think the Dresden representation will be quite good, even *very* good : the *Ney*, after what I've heard of her from you, is most welcome. As this will be your first opportunity of making thorough acquaintance with the opera, please see it twice running ; that is a great assistance, and the whole thing has rather skimmed past you heretofore. While hearing it, remember me !—Believe me, I need strong courage and an almost unheard-of mental energy, to endure my situation— toward my works—and still go on creating in face of the most hopeless prospects !—

Now farewell for to-day. Afford me the pleasure of giving me frequent reports on your health, which

I really hope is on the mend again. Good times are sure
to come ere long, the last storms will disperse, and a pair
of *good* people at last prove themselves such to one
another. Greet N., and go on conserving the beasties so
well ; I am denying myself any, and remain without dog.
So farewell ; take care of yourself, and—hope !

Thy

RICHARD.

177.

LUCERNE, 21. June 1859.

I have nothing of importance to tell you, dear
Minna ; yet I'll answer you at once, and see what this
bad-weather humour will bring forth. Really, my
patience is put to a severe test by this weather-disease ;
I shan't forget this last Swiss visit. For 3 months the
weather has grown no better, but steadily worse ; now it
has been raining incessantly again for days, enough to
make me despair. And yet—were I to suddenly break
off, and go to Paris ? So soon as I had turned my back,
fine weather would appear, and I should arrive in Paris
together with the fiercest heat ; whilst the main affair—
my work—would be interrupted afresh. So I mean to
hold out still. But once I've finished with this work, I
won't write *another note* until I get into a different
style of living, at the least have presented my Tristan,
and feel a little refreshed and encouraged to life again.
The last note of Tristan will be the *utmost* one can rap
out in *my* position. Then *nothing* more : or things must
alter first.—

Anyhow I shall need some distraction myself then,
a rest from this eternal brain-consuming, grinding labour.
I ardently long for that time ; my life is growing ever

harder,—from no one in the world can I hear anything. They've held a music-festival at Leipzig, given the prelude to Tristan without asking my leave [June 1], and not a soul has written me a word about it. No news from Paris for a whole quarter. From Newyork nothing. Nothing from anywhere! I'm completely dropped. Well, one must comfort oneself that if only the weather turned fine, the rest would follow. But that's my worst chicane. Moreover, I feel that my constant malaise will not even yield to fine weather before I lay my work entirely aside ; which also is the opinion of my doctor. But I couldn't bring myself to take a decent outing now, even with fine weather, so violent is my longing to get done and then be free. I hope it will not be too late then ! The Kissinger water acted quite agreeably so long as I drank it, but has not effected any great improvement ; neither can that be at present, my head is too much occupied.

My little doctor tries his best to tide me over, and has recommended *riding* now. The landlord has good horses, one of which is very gentle and an easy goer ; he lets me have it very cheap for an hour's ride each day, from 6 to 7 in the morning. That really seems to be something quite capital, and I am expecting good results from it pending completion of my work. It's going off quite well ; the first morning I took the groom by my side, but ride alone since then. It really is the only thing that gives me a little pleasure now. As I have no dog, horse company takes its place ; and that is something quite unique. It doesn't only go beside one ; it goes *with* one, bears and moves me. One has to be constantly on the alert with it ; comes an unaccustomed noise, a startling sight, it winces, shies a little ; then the rider needs

to grip it tighter and say something to it : at once
it's quiet, and merely pricks its ears.   It really affords
very much entertainment ; I look forward to my ride
each time, and can scarcely wait for it.   And then the
motion is so beneficial : much walking or running simply
tires the legs, and doesn't stir the liver ; after a ride, on
the contrary, one detects no fatigue, whereas the liver
is duly shaken up, and the stagnant blood disperses.
My only equestrianism, as you are aware, dates from
Riga ; but I soon felt at home on horse-back, ride
English, rising in the saddle (*mit Balance*), and—it goes
quite passably.   For the last two days, however, I've
been debarred from my ride by the rain ; tomorrow
morning again, let's hope.

I would beg you to insist upon their sending my
letter on to you from Dresden ; it was dated the 8th inst.
—I believe—will please you, and you oughtn't to miss
it.—Now mind that the cure sets you thoroughly up ;
I am glad to hear of the chalybeate baths, and delighted
that Pusinelli allows you them already : that's a good
sign.   You must always present your right ear when
people want to tell you nasty things about your husband ;
when I'm back with you myself it shall soon hear as
well as the other, especially if I make thorough fine
music.   Poor woman, you, still half deaf !   But that will
soon pass off again ; the whole trouble with you is simply
nervous, and once a radical composure of the nerves sets
in, the majority of these symptoms will vanish, whereas
with other constitutions they would prove organic lesions.
I am not very timid about them ; you'll still recover all
your powers quite tolerably.   I have come to know you
pretty well now, and hope to be quite clear about your
treatment upon my side also.   Don't you have any more

fear ; everything will come right, and is so in the main already, do believe me !

I wrote to Devrient lately that we'll fix the production of Tristan for about October ; it couldn't be at the beginning of September without great rush and risk.   I am glad I've got *so* far.   I have no fear of the war, and with me doubtless every perspicacious person.   The South German *Reich* cry, proceeding from the Catholic Austrian party, will be put a sensible stop to by Prussia ; never, never can *she* declare war against France to save Lombardy to Austria : that's sheer impossible, and our brilliant German Unity (O Papa Fischer !) has already dissolved into smoke.   That cry quite made me ill. To resume—I think the war won't interfere with us, and so let *us* hold fast to our own peace.   If it must be, I shall join the Cavalry, unless they can find any use for me among the Engineers.*   For yourself, please quit the Lazaretto soon ; and to enable you to do so, take as much care of yourself at present as if you had composed the Tristan ; then I shall.—

Keep Nette with you ; tell her *mille choses* from me. Squeeze Fipps's paw, and tell Jacquot he's a sheep's-head ! As for you, just keep delighting me by return with good accounts of your cure.   Probably I shan't write to Schubert myself, but send him word through Tichatscheck.   It is understood that you're to put up at the *Hôtel Bellevue* [for Dresden *Lohengrin*].   And so farewell, and hold dear

Thy
RICHARD.

(Enclosed the card of a new Zurich beer-host.)

---

* " *Genie* " = also "genius" ; the same pun occurs in the letter to Frau Wesendonck of May 23.—Tr.

You still have the Rheingold full score, have you not? Mind you take good care of it ! !

178.

LUCERNE, 28. *June* 1859.

I am expecting a letter from you tomorrow, dear Minna, it's true ; but I want just to bid you Good-morning to-day.   Your letter—the answer to my last but one, detained in Dresden—amused me very much by its descriptions of the Schandau Royal shoot with concert ; still greater was my delight at Fipps's hare-hunt : I'm always glad to hear of our good beasties.   As I wrote you once before, myself I'm keeping company with almost none but animals here, and my out-door friends are now augmented by a cat who plays magnificently with a young black poodle—so that everybody stops to look—and finally by a—donkey.   The latter is penned on the hill for grazing, seems to feel lonely, and comes towards me whenever he sees me ; then he stretches out his head to me, and I scratch him behind the ears a little, which seems to do him a world of good.   As soon as I pass on, he always starts a hideous howling ; to scold him out of it I couldn't well call him an " Ass," as to him that would have been no opprobrium, so I've had to say : Donkey, don't play the goat !—

For the rest, the fine weather now set in at last is doing me much good.   How beneficial the effect of this air is, with the *bise* that's always blowing now, I feel to my complete surprise.   It has made my mood quite excellent ; the Kissinger too, which I still drink at intervals, may be shewing its good effect now ; and in particular the riding seems also to contribute very much to my improvement.   I've seldom felt so merry, as of late ; this greatly helps my work, and in its turn the progress of my work contributes to my general good humour. So I hope for certain to have finished Tristan entirely by the end of August, and what contributes the most to my cheerful mood is the prospect of rest and recreation then, which I may well—indeed, must accord myself after such a marvellous piece of work. Consequently I am looking forward with extraordinary joy to next winter, when I mean to unharness thoroughly for once, and distract myself at ease. I fancy Paris will be the very thing for that ; in tiny holes one is thrown back on almost nothing save one's work. On the other hand, I remember how much we strictly neglected in Paris ; whilst we can also take a trip some day to London, where I likewise saw next to nothing. In short, I'm hoping for a very pleasant, entertaining and diverting winter, and already have a presentiment of the benefit that will be to me, and how much good it will also do yourself again. Even if I don't make any American earnings at present (I hear nothing more from there whatever) my new opera will help for a good long while, and it is appearing at the nick of time for acquirement by many theatres for this winter itself. Tannh. and Lohengrin, too, continue to yield something to live on, especially through Berlin ; and indeed I cannot grumble at the abundant way my operas are helping us out. Last year really cost a fearful amount of money, and yet there was always some when wanted, so that I didn't need to run into a *farthing* of debt. Tristan will be of great use to me : it is a very long time since people have learnt anything new of me, and no doubt the world almost regards me already as a man from whom there's nothing more to expect. This work, then, will greatly revive the interest in me ; its

music is bound to make an incredible effect, as has been
the case already—so I read—with the orchestral prelude
at Leipzig.

I wrote to Tichatscheck yesterday.   If you are going
to Lohengrin, please order yourself a thoroughly well-
situated room at the hotel in advance.   I do hope the
opera may turn out well at Dresden ; but there, you'll
tell me all about it.—

I no longer think of any larger excursions now, despite
the lovely weather, work chains me so.   By the bye, I
owe that lovely weather to the priests.   A week ago
le bon Dieu walked the streets in person : it was Corpus
Christi day ; the evening before, when the right wind had
already come to stay, the priests drove the children into
the churches to pray for fine weather, which accordingly
succeeded in the amplest measure.   That padre who was
always up at Seelisberg, and paid his court to you, had
also clothed himself in a very beautiful lace shirt, and
gabbled away in the procession.—What pleased me better,
was a company of Tyrolese (splendidly handsome people)
who sang in the gardens here with wonderfully fine
voices, especially the women's.

Now mind you're soon able to send me as good
accounts of your health as I you of mine to-day.   I hope
for the best, only I should like just to give you one piece
of advice : if you wake up early and cannot get to sleep
again straight off, arise at once, put on your clothes, take
a short promenade, and then a thorough good rest after
breakfast instead ; the more tired you then feel all the
day, the earlier and better will you sleep at night.   I get
up regularly soon after 5 now, ride or walk, and—how
divine these early mornings in high summer are, can't be
extolled enough ; and what one loses if one passes them in

stuffy bed, is not to be deplored enough. In revenge, to
bed by 10. Just try it for once. In summer one can
hardly be out of doors at any other time, you see, than
very early. The air is so gloriously invigorating then,
that I'm always of a wellnigh irrepressible good-humour
at breakfast.

—So : early to rise !—And now—to dinner, which is
being served this instant. Farewell, be calm and cheerful. Everything will turn out quite splendid !

Thy

RICHARD.

Tell me, foolish woman, how ever did you come by
that woful idea that I meant to foist an organic defect of
the heart on you, with my allusion to its thumping on
the Rigi ? And yet you must have believed something
of the kind, or you wouldn't defend yourself against it so
stoutly ? No, that beats all !—It's getting time you met
me face to face again, or I shall be sporting Devil's horns
and hoofs in your eyes next ! ! !—

179.

LUCERNE, 29. *June* 1859.

See what a good husband I am, dear Minna ! I
wrote you yesterday, and to-day again I'm answering you
directly on receipt of your love-letter, for which I thank
you much. I've written at once to *Charnal*, Paris, about
Rienzi ; no one else there answers me. Really the thing
had occurred to myself before, only I've nobody reliable in
Paris ; Olliviers didn't answer me last time. The end of
August, however, I'll have a see there myself. By the
way, they've given the overture to Rienzi at *Florence.*—
We have no need to trouble over-much about the American
manager ; he hasn't made another sign. If it comes to

nothing, that will *quite* suit me also ; for I only grasp
a thing like that when it's absolutely thrust upon me and
I should have to reproach myself with the omission.   As
I wrote you yesterday, we shall be able to keep things
going without America ; which, for the matter of that,
may still come off another year.—From Leipzig I've
positively heard nothing from a *living soul;* merely from
the journal [*Neue Zeitschrift*].   Nice fellows, those !—

I'm almost sorry you still are thinking of my amnesty ;
it's surely better one should build no hopes on that.   If
you had read my letter to the Minister of Justice, you must
have shut up shop yourself after the reply received.   I
had expressly begged the Minister to lay my letter before
the King.—What the political situation may end in, God
only knows !   Thus much is certain : that unmatched
L. N[apoleon] knows what he wants, and prepares his
moves with an incredible tenacity, foresight and cunning.
None of the others can lift a finger against him ; all are
checked and hampered, England and Prussia, and I hardly
believe Prussia will get very far with her last step.   They're
all plunged deep in sin, not one of them has clean hands ;
and L. N. has laid his game of chess accordingly—which I
believe he may easily win, at least for a long time ahead.
Meanwhile Austria is doing badly, and may soon do much
worse ; but that sort of thing rather scares off the rest,
than emboldens them, and the game is always easy to the
victor.—I look on the course of events as on the wind and
weather : both depend on blind forces one cannot command ; wherefore one merely falls into step according
as the weather turns out good or bad.—Whether it might
lead to any result for *myself,* I must leave a very open
question !—Otherwise it's quite interesting to me that
I ran through Upper Italy such a short time previously :

it makes everything very present to me, and in particular I can also picture *Zezi* with a big tricolour sash.—

I wrote you yesterday about weather and health, and hope the latter pleased you. It's droll that I should have so recommended *morning* air to you precisely yesterday, and you the same to me at the selfsame time. There really must be something in it !—

As to riding English, it is this way : if a man hasn't a firm seat, that is to say, can't grip the horse tight with his thighs, at the trot he rides *balance*, i.e. maintains his equilibrium by balancing. To get a proper seat, I should have needed to take a regular course of riding lessons ; with good hacks that isn't necessary, however, and I come out of it quite famously, so that my trot mustn't look at all bad. If I had a vicious horse, I grant you, I shouldn't care to wager that he wouldn't throw me ; but my land-lord's horse is such a steady-goer that I have no fear. Only the silly creature cannot abide my straw hat, which I've been wearing the last few days ; as soon as he sees me coming, he lets fly with his hind legs, so that I can't help laughing every time. A lump of sugar, though, is accustoming him to the fatal hat now ; and when I'm on top of him, no doubt he imagines my hat is black, for he goes like a lamb then.—

You seem getting on quite tolerably again, dear Minna, don't you ? The remission suits my book as well. Only don't go exciting yourself again over the Dresden Lohengrin. I have great trust in your present place of residence and cure ; if the baths (the iron ones) agree with you, you'll soon feel as if reborn. Only be thoroughly lazy, let yourself be carried, and drive. How goes the appetite ? Unfortunately one's feeding suffers with this heat ; I'm also living like a bird just now.—

And now I won't forget what I've constantly been intending to ask you : did you duly receive the *opera-glasses* from Geneva that time ?—Then : have you the full score of Rheingold in safe keeping still ?   Mind you let none of it be performed at Schandau !—

Your lovely motto only caught my eye the other day, turning over the leaves of your blotting-book.   I have been learning it by heart since, and repeat it to myself each day :

> " Ueb' immer Treu' und Redlichkeit
> bis an Dein weiches Grab,
> und kühle keinen Tiger breit—" *

no, it wasn't quite that ; but I shall soon pick it up.

Have you quite given up scolding with Nette, then ? Has she passed through such a heavenly transformation all at once ?   That would be splendid !—Greet everybody.   So the Auerbachs have their cellar at Schandau now ?—My God, I really must-write to Pusinelli too !—

Farewell, good Madame.   Take care of yourself, get thoroughly well, and, for all *I* mind, stout.   But if you ride, don't put a white straw hat on.

Write again soon, and be good to

Thy
Husband.

---

* " Be faithful aye and honest, until thy tender grave, and cool no tiger feelings "—.   By a punning interchange of the roots " kühl " and " weich " in the second and third lines, and a conversion of " Finger " into " Tiger " (unless this latter is a mere misprint), Wagner has succeeded in parodying the old German equivalent of Dr. Watts : " Ueb' immer Treu' und Redlichkeit bis an Dein kühles Grab, und weiche keinen Finger breit von Gottes Wegen ab " (L. H. Ch. Hölty, 1748-76).   *Cf.* " Among all vaunted things, unfortunately, this 'honesty' has been turned into something risible for me ; and that springs perhaps from ' Ueb' immer Treu' und Redlichkeit,' which was the first little piece I learnt on the piano " (to Mathilde Wesendonck, May 29).—Tr.

180.

DEAREST MINNA,

You give me much anxiety whenever you keep me waiting too long for a letter. Thus I really was very uneasy already to-day ; the hot weather, in which you have never been well, gave me all kinds of misgivings that you might be feeling severely knocked up. Your letter, thank God, has reassured me again, and I willingly accept the pretext of " too many callers," providing the callers themselves were agreeable to you ; which seems to have quite been the case. So we'll pass it this time. —

It is natural that you shouldn't remark much effect from the cure yet ; in fact, it will fatigue you at first. Only keep nice and quiet, and take care of yourself, when you'll feel better by the autumn.—What you write about N. worries me most ; if her tantrums were to start again, it would be highly deplorable, for you require very placid and good-humoured company. If it doesn't tire you, please write me about it again soon, and perfectly candidly.

As for myself, ever since the good weather my humour has also kept good. And that was needed, to support my existence in general here ; for I had to shift a week ago, and that into the main building and a smaller and none so quiet room, where Joseph has regularly had to palisade me, to prevent my being too much disturbed by neighbours. Naturally I'm by no means so well off here as before, when I was all alone in the house, had a beautiful balcony and a big salon, and yet came off cheaper than now. In the fine lodgings, however, nearly always bad weather ; now fine weather, but—. Enough, tho' ! I am glad enough to have got what I have, and to be able to end my work without another break. Solely to be undisturbed in my work, speaking strictly, have I such hard-to-satisfy needs in respect of Abode. To satisfy those needs abroad, and in some sense as a traveller, is fearfully hard. In small towns it is only the inns, and the first of them, that can supply one what's needed ; pensions are impossible for me, since they're all merely reckoned for " company ", possess *none* but small rooms, apart from the coffee-room, and everybody is noisily huddled in everybody else's lap. As I didn't want to go to Paris yet, I could do no otherwise than what I have done. My work once completed, however, and if I take up nothing of the sort so soon again, the question of abode will be far more indifferent to me ; and for the first spell in Paris, as long as I'm alone, I shall jog along with little fuss.—

Tell me, dear Mutz, you very often still seem longing to return to Switzerland ? I cannot blame you, and shouldn't care to forsake it entirely myself; but merely for a periodic stay. When I depart I'll go viâ Inter-laken and Thun again, and take the opportunity of looking out for a nice little house one can rent for the summer, so that one may have something in view for the future. On the whole I am glad to be quitting the mountains now ; in spite of the glories of Nature, what I very much miss are—fine *forests*, or parks : here one gets nothing but panoramas. In that respect I have a sort of hope of *Fontainebleau*—not far from Paris ; its famous forest or park (many miles square) is said to be something unique. I confess, I can conceive nothing finer for summer, than to roam about among such lordly groups of ancient trees.—But, the future must wait !—

For the rest, we have a real message of peace to-day ; the two little emperors have provisionally concluded an armistice. I don't yet know what may come of it ; we soon shall see, though, and meantime it's permissible to hope for that speedy peace which will be quite extraordinarily welcome to myself. In every respect I could wish for it, alike for our stay in Paris, where everything will be at full tide after a triumphal treaty, and in particular for my little businesess, in which *everyone* is silent just now. (Get no more fads into your head about America : that seems to have quite blown over, and the manager to have altered his mind ; all the same to me !) Moreover, peace will come in capitally for Tristan ! Work's going nicely forward : Tristan waggled his jaw for the last time to-day ; by the end of the month, I think, Isolde will also be done for. This last act promises quite famously ; I drew profit for it even from my Rigi excursion. At 4 in the morning we were roused by the boots with the alp-horn ; I jumped up, saw it was raining, and returned to bed to try to sleep ; but the droll call went droning round my head, and out of it arose a very lusty melody which the Herdsman now blows outside to signal Isolde's ship, making a surprisingly merry and naive effect.—

To change the subject, my riding suits me admirably. In this heat I really can't walk out till very late, half past 7 [P.M.], and then I perspire immediately I attempt much of a promenade ; besides, a little hour on horseback is better, in respect of its effect, than 3 hours' walking. Only this horse already isn't mettled enough for me : I trot quite famously now, and don't fall off ; but my young steed is 20 yearlets old and always has to get a wee bit warm before he'll break into a trot. Otherwise it's a very handsome beast, only it isn't *I* who have *it* for riding on, but *it* has *me* for scaring flies. You know my compassion for animals : presently I shall have to mount it with a fly-whisk in lieu of a riding-crop : it will look quite splendid, when I sally forth like that.—

Otherwise I neither see nor hear a creature, beyond Joseph and Vreneli ; but Herwegh fired me the other day. I enclose you his poem [" *Gruss zum Eidgenössischen Schützenfest* "] ; really it is very *fine*, and it did me such good to hear a thing like that from the man, that I congratulated him upon it very cordially and invited him to pay me a visit. That's just my way !—

Now give the hare-hunter my kindest regards ; in Switzerland at any rate he never saw a hare run. And *Mr.* Jacquot !—But don't greet Nette if she's in her tantrums ; Ksch ! Ksch !—And write me nice and punctually, do you hear ? I fret each time a letter's overdue. Think of nothing else at present than your cure and health. Let bon Dieu take all thought for the future now ; things will all come right ! Very best of greetings ! Fare well and in good humour !

Thy

RiRaRichard.

181.

Lucerne, 17. July 1859.

I shall be unable to write you much to-day, dearest Minna, since, to speak candidly, I'm a little pulled down by my work—to which I'm now sticking with the most passionate zeal—and incapable of any effort after table. Moreover, I have next to no occurrence to relate, as usual. The solitary thing to tell is just my happy perseverance with my work, and that I now may expect to have quite finished it as early as mid-August. You know how I get seized with an almost extravagant eagerness when a thing's once in full swing and approaching its end ; then I've all but no mind left for anything else.

Your letter, poor dear harassed and buffeted Wife, touched me deeply, and I could really curse my fate, at my present ripe age to be still incapable of offering you true peace of life. I can appreciate your desire for rest, indeed I can ! Believe me, if I'm more indifferent thereto myself, it is half desperation at the abominable way in which I'm treated by my fatherland. But I'll briefly jot you down to-day my plan for the immediate future. Mid-August I hope to be able to leave here and go to Paris. I have also written direct to the Paris director concerning Rienzi ; if anything comes of it for this winter, so much the better ! In any event I shall devote my immediate visit to a study whether and where I can find us the most suitable dwelling ; if I can persuade myself that it would please us both to be in Paris, I suppose I shall have to embrace that, for I can see nothing better in front of me. Nevertheless I shall try to keep another door still open, and in case nothing comes of the Rienzi, perhaps only think of a provisional *logis garni* for us, still to leave a choice for the Carlsruhe possibility. For I still think that, once I am there, the Grand Duke may resolve on an extremity, and not permit me to depart again.

So I would beg of *you*, when you have quite finished with Schandau and want to get out of it, to start with Nette, dog and bird, direct for *Carlsruhe*. I shall ask Devrient to engage a small furnished apartment beforehand, where you may await me in comfort until I can come too and alight in your quarters straight off. I do hope that everything will have got that length by the end of October. Then—if not sooner—it shall be definitely

decided whether we can remain in Germany or not.   In
the latter event we shall travel thence to Paris.   If I
were to find a very suitable abode in Paris first, tho', and
especially if Rienzi were set down for this winter, then
we should hold to Paris in advance for either case, just
to be completely safe.—That's my provisional plan; what
do *you* think of it??—

By the way, America is on the haunt again.   A
German *Opera* will *not* come off there, but they want to
engage me for 3 months' *concerts* on the terms discussed.
Well, we'll wait and see; in the meantime I do not set
much store by it.—

As regards my tantièmes it appears to go with you as
with many others in Germany, who look at them through
magnifying-glasses.   You wrote me of two performances
at the beginning of April; *Ander* sang Lohengrin twice
at Berlin in May: which makes 4 performances.   Then
hoped for perhaps a 5th—even a Tannhäuser perf. in
addition—and made out for myself quite a nice little bill.
Instead of that, exactly 3 perfs. have been notified to me—
2 with Ander, and only *one* before.   It came to 158 thr.,
as another 50 thr. was struck off for the advance.   I owed
precisely this amount to Bülow, who had had to raise
me money on my tantièmes last winter when I required
it, and to whom I couldn't pay it back before; consequently—nothing for me this time.   But—be easy; it
will all come right, once this *fearfully* dear hotel-life
stops.   In Paris I mean to draw in my horns to begin
with.—

And now I really must break off; don't be cross with
me, good Minna, my head is quite dizzy.—I enclose a
few lines for the Ney.   Friend T. appears to be a raga-
muffin!—

The weather continues splendid, and for the last week a strong breeze has been blowing, which keeps the air fresh.   This does me an extraordinary amount of good ! May I only hear good news of yourself very soon ; I know how much you always suffer from the heat.   For that matter, if you want to take a drive oftener, surely a little chaise must stand at your command ?   Please drive—along the valley to the Kuhstall,—don't look too close at money, I'll see to more if it runs out.   The main affair is that you poor good wife should thrive for me !—

So pluck up courage, pluck up hope !   Something delightful is sure to arrive soon.   Congratulate me also on the approaching termination of my work ; I build great hopes on it !—

Now a thousand heartfelt greetings !   Farewell and ever think kindly of

Thy
RICHARD.

182.
LUCERNE, 25. July 1859.

Best thanks, dear Minna, for your letter of to-day. Don't be afraid of boring me with insignificant items ; I enjoy everything you write to me when I see by its whole tone that you are calm and in good spirits ; then I con- clude that things are going tolerably with you and you're feeling better.   And that really is the most important news a letter from yourself can tell me ; whereas I know quite well that no great marvels can be taking place around you.

For the last 3 days I've had incessant rainy weather, which has made me feel bad all at once : I do so need clear skies and buoyant air ; I know how to protect

myself against the heat at a pinch.   Still, it's to be hoped
you will also have profited by some of this rain ; and in
that hope I'll willingly put up with it.   Only don't speak
about your journey yet ; you shall embark on it whenever
you feel equal to doing so ; at any rate the approaching
autumn will do you good.   But I am glad you approve
of my plan as regards Carlsruhe ; that will facilitate
everything.   This last 19th I finished the composition
entirely [orchestral sketch], and in a fortnight at latest I shall
have polished off the last page of the full score as well.
Then I perhaps shall make a small excursion up Pilatus,
prepare for my departure, and expect to reach Paris
mid-August.   If I only took count of the temperature, I
should by all means stay in Switzerland a little longer ;
but I'm really craving for a cheaper life now, than is
possible to me with this continual hotel-existence, and
above all I want to procure myself swift certainty about
the future.   I want to know how I stand as regards Paris
in every respect, and in particular how things will prove
with a suitable dwelling ; for which I need ample time
to have a good look at everything on the spot, weigh all
the pros and cons.   It would be lovely if we could live
out by the Champs-Elysées ; we must keep an eye upon
a handy promenade etc.   But, about all that from Paris.—

I will write to Moudon in N.'s behalf.   On the whole
I am bound to agree with you ; nevertheless the plan
has many drawbacks.   I am afraid N. is already too
old for this proposal ; one doesn't first go to school at
her age ; and that is what it comes to.   What a thousand
pities !   As we are childless, she would have been just
cut out for looking after you, keeping you company,
managing the house, and so on ; it would have been
the best chance alike for her and for yourself !   And yet

I am obliged to recognise your ground for questioning her aptitude for that once more ; I can—advance nothing against it, and must endorse your wish to let no wretched misrelation rise again. So, if you have otherwise been pleased with her of late, and she has been of use to you, I gladly will shew myself grateful to her, and— although I can't hope very much from it—I'll willingly do all I can towards supporting her desire, however late, to get herself trained for a governess.—

Your inspired effusion on father Geyer has rather puzzled me. Can Luise [Brockhaus, his eldest sister] have persuaded herself to leave you in the delusion under which you're labouring with regard to that picture? Incomprehensible ! That painting, dear Minna, is really nothing but a *copy*, and that from *Raphael*, which my father once did as a study to perfect his use of oil-colours. Moreover, Geyer *only* painted portraits.—I'm quite grieved to have to snatch you from the illusion that this picture was an original painting by my father ; for you're perfectly right, whoever invents and executes a work like that can never be forgotten.—

There really is nothing more—singular, than the way in which I'm again and again told of remarks of the King's that he can't pardon me if I do not present myself. As if I hadn't most plainly set forth to the Minister, as previously to Lüttichau, how unpractical, impossible and inadmissible it would be, to ask me after 10 long years to undergo examination touching things which merely float before me as dim shadows now, and with the best of will I often should only be able to give a vague account of. Naturally, they do not answer such a plea at all ; it's spoken to the wind, and they keep returning and returning to the old, old phrase. I don't

10

know what to do with such people ; moreover their whole behaviour to me is so humiliating, that I beg everybody to spare me hearing any more about them. Many a one has had to repent his stubbornness of late ; it may be the turn of others next. If I cannot see my situation improved *in despite of* those gentry, I suppose I must submit to it at last, and safely leave posterity to judge my fate.—The best of it is, that my spirit isn't broken yet, and it will need but a little enlivenment to brisk me up again from time to time. Under pressure of the most cross-grained and forlorn position I again have completed a new work which is bound to bring me fame and honour. Already—besides the Nibelungen —I have another *two* works in my head, and if I spoke of a pause in my work for the present, it was not that I'm at any loss for matter, but because I do not wish to overtax myself, and need recreation, not impulsion. Between now and November I could easily turn out the last act of Siegfried also, and that would make the *fourth* big work all spick and span within *six* years. Whoever compares my present works with those of others, must admit that such a productivity of mind is well-nigh incomprehensible,—and thus equipped I mean to snap my fingers at my fate, and calmly leave the King of Saxony to his opinion of me ! It will do me no harm.—

As to the Dresden production of Lohengrin, I read in the mus. journal that it had been set down for the 5th of August, true enough, but would probably be postponed to the middle of the month. Just as God wills !

I have no other news. The American manager will call on me in Paris ; remains to be seen ! I cannot help thinking we both shall live cheaper in Paris than has been the case this last year. With or without America we shall make ends meet ; only it is well for me to keep such a chance open. Over our present decisions, however, it shall exert no influence.

What did you think of the other company at Luise's ? Please send me an atom of gossip thereon : it amuses me.—I'm glad to have a good opportunity of taking my revenge on Mad. Erard now ; I shall dedicate to her the new engraved edition of the score of Tannhäuser. The piano continues to be my grande passion ; it does me good as soon as ever I touch it.

And now goodbye for to-day. Greet the whole Bad Schandau, and get the Kuhstall made a little larger when you visit it again. Go on feeling better ! The news of the departure of your deafness gave me great delight. So will many another ill depart, and we shall both be hale and young again for our Silver Wedding [1861].

Hearty greetings from   Thy
                                        R.

Here you also have a letter " *in Zierig* " !—Luckily the Post doesn't know it's from your sister. For that matter, it might also be from my lamented Mama.—

183.

LUCERNE, 2. *August* 1859.

DEAREST MINNA,

Only 2 words to-day : I'm in the last throes of my work now, and expect to have finished by Saturday [6th].—

Yesterday I laughed like a goblin for the first time for ever so long. *Boom* is here on a visit, also Herr *Dräseke*, a young composer who wrote from Coburg begging my permission to visit me. Neither of them is allowed to come until 6 P.M., after my meal, and

yesterday I took them somewhat late in the evening for a
long walk through a mountain wood——: Boom wheedled
wine from a peasant, and wasn't to be stirred from the
spot ; so it became a case of finding our way home in
the dark.   A madder vagary I've never gone through : a
thicket of trees, not a glimmer of light, criss-cross paths,
many of them very steep *à la* Uetli.   What a shouting
and swearing !   At one point Dräseke called out, to the
left of me : I was leading them all wrong, that couldn't
be the way ; to my right Boom cried the same.   A match
had to be struck——: when, behold you, *I* was on quite
a good and level path, but Dräseke stuck sideways in
a swamp, and Boom kicking his heels above both of our
heads on a bush-clad slope.   It was too funny !——

I just wanted to report you this adventure quick ;
it still sets me laughing whenever I think of it.—Boom
sends you his very best regards ; he is *very well !*

Child, I won't hear of your going to Petersburg [to
another married sister ?—see last postscript] ; on that another day.
Only patience, we are sure to manage without Russia
yet.—My head is reeling, and how I shall feel by next
Sunday I know not ; between this and then I'll write
again and properly.   Sunday week I expect to be in
Paris ; but about all that next time.   For to-day merely
a charmant salute and best thanks for your letter.   May
bon Dieu present you with the rain I've had here off and
on !   Otherwise you seem doing tolerably, don't you ?
Be of good cheer, and trust in better times !   Farewell,
dearest old woman !   Kind regards to the beasties and
Nette.

Thy
over-diligent
Husband.

184.

DEAREST MINNA,

I'm writing you another couple of hurried lines ere breaking up ; until to-day I shouldn't have known what to tell you. My pass hasn't come back from the French embassy yet, so I absolutely don't know where to lay my head. I am very depressed and put out, and a great bitterness is taking possession of me. Moreover, the terrible drain on my pocket here really robs me of all heart ; after $4\frac{1}{2}$ months of it, I am glad to be clearing out of this hotel, where tips and general dearness almost ruin one. And then all my fearful amount of luggage, piano, etc., and even yet no actual prospect of a thorough solution of all these problems. You may well believe that, in these circumstances, and as it alters absolutely *nothing*, even your accounts of the Lohengrin have made no great impression on me ; though I thank you very much for them, and for your sake they were highly acceptable. But I also know that everything will remain as it was, notwithstanding, and none of all those my work delights again will seriously raise their voices for me.—

To restore myself a little, I now intend to seek the higher mountain air, and—as I telegraphed to you an hour ago—to stay awhile at Rigi-Kaltbad, and at the same time wait and see whether and when I get my pass. I have no farther trip in view now, and shall be only too glad if I feel a little fresher again.

In my present plight I consequently am left no other joy than the welcome assurance I glean from your latest letters, especially from that with the description of your outing, that your health is improving. I assure you,

that indeed has rejoiced and consoled me ; for all the
rest is really transitory, and subject to a change which
also may conduct to better things.   So I simply beg you
constantly to bear in mind that my last care upon this
earth remains your restoration and your prospering ; keep
that itself in constant view, and do your utmost to lighten
this care for me. —

I had arranged a rendezvous at Strassburg with Ed.
Devrient ; unfortunately I have had to cancel it by telegraph already, since the unadjusted pass affair, as said,
still blocks my setting foot in France.   However, I must
be getting an answer on that point as well soon, and am
not afraid it will prove unfavourable.   I'll write you
again before I definitely depart ; I'm also hoping for a
letter from yourself in answer to my despatch of to-day,
to be sent after me from Lucerne to the Rigi in case
I do not fetch it here myself.   To-day I have waited in
vain for a letter.

Now farewell ; give me good news of yourself, which
will be the best contribution to an improvement in my
own condition.

A thousand heartfelt greetings !   Thy

RICHARD.

185.

LUCERNE, 16. *August* 1859.

Thanks for yesterday's letter, dear Minna, which I
found awaiting me on my return from Pilatus this
morning.   In the first place I inform you that I've just
packed up *twenty Napoleons d'or* for you, which I shall
hand to the Post with this letter, but not send *in* the
letter itself, since money-packets (as I know from experience) always arrive several days late, and I wish my
letter not to be so long delayed, in order that you not

only may have news of me (which seems to be very seriously disquieting you already, according to your letter of to-day !) but also may learn in advance that money is on its way to you.—

As you will have gathered from my last letter, I have been very undetermined about my steps of late, the immediate cause of which has lain in this passport delay. They issued me another pass at Zurich, as I had succeeded through Hagenbuch in renewing the validity of my habitation there ; so that the only hindrance resides in the French visé. As I already have told you,* the envoy informed me he would have to report to his government in Paris first ; that was a fortnight ago, since when I've neither had an answer nor my pass back How much this fresh chicane in my position puts me out again, I have told you before, and I really am resolved to take no further step at present, and in particular not to approach the Grand Duke of Weimar again for intervention, since he has behaved most backwardly to me in every respect, and I am heartily sick of all this begging. If I find at last that there's no other course for me, I'd rather write to L. Napoleon direct : meanwhile, however, nothing presses me to give myself at all away in that direction. Paris is said to be very unhealthy to stay in just now ; already they're talking of cholera. Olliviers don't return there for another 3 months. I have been answered concerning Rienzi, that under the latest political constellations this subject is completely impossible again ; otherwise I get hardly any answers at all from there, and in any case my conscience tells me I am not the man to carry anything

---

* A letter missing ?—if so, probably between nos. 183 & 184.—Tr.

through in Paris unless I'm met half-way. Consequently the only value Paris retains in my eyes, regarded calmly, is that, supposing Germany stays closed to me, I there may hope to live the most conveniently and comfortably with you, both quietly and yet with some distraction. The finding of an abode was therefore my chief consideration, since I cannot reckon much on any other Paris prospects now. But I won't conceal the fact that at bottom I shudder at the thought of our settling down in Paris for all time ; and so I still cleave to the hopeful possibility that my visit to Carlsruhe may, in fact must have results which perhaps might relieve us from all necessity of setting up our home in Paris. The consequences of a success of Tristan and my personal intercourse with the Grand Duke are at any rate incalculable. How if I were to declare, for instance, that I refused to quit Baden again : would the Grand Duke have me expelled or extradited ?—Those are mere ideas, of course ; but I set great and decisive hopes thereon [Carlsruhe].—The approaching death of the King of Prussia, who hitherto has much checked the Prince Regent in this sort of matter, may also be of moment to me.

All these are considerations which determine me calmly to await God's judgment, and before all to see if I obtain my passport visé. In addition, I gave you to understand last time that I have had unexpectedly heavy expenses again of late ; consequently I am obliged to wait for a reinforcement of my finances, which make my Paris project almost impossible for the moment. Do not let that disturb you afresh, though, but go on getting all the comforts you require ; you shall never lack before our meeting, when further provision shall already be made.

It was quite impossible for me to stay at Kaltbad; these pensions are really not for me, and this one least of all. In fairly bad spirits I resolved to await further developments at the Schweizerhof again, where I can live the quietest and most sans gêne. I have only taken one small room; as I don't want to unpack the piano again, I can manage with that. I was compelled to decide on a definite abode again, were it only because the proofs of the full score of Tristan are very urgent now, and I had to let Härtels know at last exactly where to send me them. So I am seated here again for an indefinite period, and gladly would wait in perfect peace for dear God to send me something pleasant for a change, as my every effort stays so futile.—

That your visit to Dresden should have so greatly upset you again through the amount of talking, is quite conceivable, and again has made me very anxious. Keep thoroughly quiet now, and repeat with me: Who leaves the issue in the hands of God! Don't fash yourself for anything except your health.—A Herr Séroff, who likewise attended the first two performances of Lohengrin, has come to Lucerne expressly to call on me. His accounts (he is a connoisseur, and very intelligent) agree with yours on many points. He is enraptured with Tichatscheck and Mitterwurzer, but refuses to hear of the X [Ney]: she fits the part of Elsa as the fist the eye, her appearance is coarse and common, her face wears a singular look of mischief all the time, her acting is quite absurd. Dearest Minna, that chimes only too closely with my own experience of this singer [in London], and even through your praise of her performance there peeps the great constraint you put upon yourself—for good reasons—to gloss over her many defects. Consequently I believe Dresden still owes me an Elsa ; which is saying no little.

Regarding the band, Séroff tells me the wind-instruments were excellent, but the strings, on the contrary, played flat and without energy ; which agrees with what Dräseke also had told me of the Kapelle's present form. The tempi are said to have often been very false, and the cuts I've been told of, as at the close of the first act and in the duet in the 3rd, are so stupid and outrageous that it comes very hard to me to write to Tichatscheck as yet, since I don't like to repay his otherwise so fine performance by promptly lecturing him for having approved of such cuts, or perhaps even suggested them. What you write me about Mitterwurzer [" Telramund "], on the other hand, indeed refreshes me ; for I consider him the most genuinely talented and nearest me of all the singers I know. I intend to write to Tich. and Mitterw. tomorrow ; I should like the younger Fischer to get a line too. (Tich. himself has written me nothing yet, however —beyond his telegram.)

To the King of Saxony, dearest Minna, I cannot write again ; after the way in which all my letters have been received—down even to Lüttichau—I should only have to prepare myself for a fresh humiliation. Whoever it is that so warmly advises me to do so, first should give me at least a speck of guarantee that my letter would bear some kind of favourable fruit : if Lüttichau, for instance, could assure me that, it would be something different. I shall wait, however, for the document of which you write me.

Just now I again have a time, and a very prolonged one, when nothing prospers with me and I meet obstructions everywhere. Thus I had written to *Moudon* for N., and first to *M. Page*, as you wanted ; after a long wait, the other day I at last got the answer that every vacancy was filled till Easter, and moreover the sister-in-law, who hitherto taught English at the institute, had gone away from Moudon, so that no more English lessons could be given at their place. Now I will write to the second address, and see if I can obtain any better reply.

Nothing remains, then, but to hope that things may soon grow better ! I really think it ought to come to that at last, and many people on this earth might have occasion enough in what I offer them to tender me joy and uplifting for once. The impression you derived from Lohengrin yourself has much rejoiced me, and more than that ; for indeed I have to bear in mind that, as set-off for the many hardships and sorrows of life which have been caused you through your union with myself, the gifts of my art are the only compensations possible to me : accept in that light the exalting impressions of which you tell me, and reflect that a man who produces what I produce, in the main can recompense others for their sacrifices in no other way than with those products. Therefore be fond of my Lohengrin too ; it belongs to all I have to offer you !—

And now farewell for to-day ; tell me if you receive the money safely ; confide in me, as in our destiny ; avoid any over-exertion ! Pay another visit to *Lohengrin*, but to *nobody* else, that you may not needlessly excite yourself : quite alone ; don't tell a soul you're there !—

And now, God keep you !

Thy
RICHARD.

A request :—

> Please send me the *Rheingold* score at once. Declare value 10 *thaler*.

186.
LUCERNE, 24. *August* 1859.

But, dearest old girl, what has put it into your head to raise such a lamento over my having sent you some money ? I long since knew you couldn't manage with the last for ever, and in my own person—believe me—I am best experiencing that the life we're leading now is infamously dear ; and if it has come heavy to myself, owing to my needing quiet and convenience for my work, on the other hand your cure and health involved considerations I've been urging on you all along. Believe me, you would only have distressed me if you had denied yourself a single comfort, to say nothing of a necessity, for the sake of saving. For Heaven's sake be easy on that point, and don't let *that* care worry you at all, at all. On the contrary, I'm delighted that you should have notified me so simply, and without any fuss, of the approaching end of your resources. I am in no sort of difficulty myself, as I've really no idea of travelling within the next few days, were it only since it's much too hot for me. Moreover I'm already seeing to the needful ; a man who has such a beautiful new opera in his pocket, may be sure he will not want. But *you're* not to worry about it at all : merely make yourself quite comfortable at Schandau—which certainly is better than Spandau— and leave me to look out for more money.

It annoys me to have to confess to you that I've just been ill again. It seems I brought back a fine cold with me from Pilatus ; I developed a catarrhal fever which kept me three whole days in bed (my visitor, Dräseke, nursed me). I am recovering already now, only I mayn't exert myself in any way ; which I tell you chiefly to excuse me for not writing you at any length to-day,

as I've already had to work off several duty letters—
among others, to Tichatscheck a moment back.—Neither
has anything happened, excepting that I received my pass
back yesterday, with *visé*, which at least has made a free
man of me. I must still abide here for the present,
though, as I'm in very active proof-correcting correspondence with Härtels—whom I'm pressing hard—and don't
want to interrupt it until all is finished. Otherwise
my *laziness* now is a perfect disgrace ; I loll, stretch
myself, and yawn that one can hear it through every
room in the place. Just do the same yourself !—

For the rest, you do very wrong to blow up N. ; she
acted very cleverly, and has pledged me to especial
thanks, as I otherwise shouldn't have at all known what
to send you from *here* for your birthday. Now that
you have got to the back of the secret, however, just tell
Nette to present herself at Fr. Tänzer's ; the great trifle
of money, which she is to devote to a small present for
you, must have arrived there by now. But that's merely
to rank as half a joke ; we'll keep your birthday this
time on our *wedding-day :* in any case we shall celebrate
that together, and then I'll bring you half Paris city as
a present.—

Pretty secrets !—

Oh, lest I forget it—please write me out that *second*
Moudon address again at once. Lord knows, I can't find
your memorandum anywhere. It was to Mr. *Fage* I
did write ; but what's the name of the other pension ?—

Na, lazy, lazy fellow me, I must let this suffice for to-
day ! May even these few untidy lines tell you that
you're to be of good courage, take great care of yourself,
and by no means excite yourself again ; moreover, that
things are standing tolerably with me, and I'm greatly

looking forward to soon arriving at a regulated home, whether here or there, with a healthy, gentle wife, good merry house-pets, and other of God's blessings ! So be of good cheer ! Things are bound to go ! Best and most charmant greetings and other *mille choses* from

Thy most faithful

LAZY-BONES.

187.

LUCERNE, 1. *Septbr*. 1859.

MY GOOD MINNA,

Best thanks for your letter received yesterday. Your humour delighted me greatly, only I am worried at your still complaining of such severe thumping of the heart. I'm sure the last Dresden excitements are to blame for it, especially that amount of lively talking, since you called upon so many persons. Why will you keep forgetting yourself like that, and not take due thought for yourself and what you need ? I shall have to keep a sharp look-out on you when we do come together again. And mind you thoroughly obey me then ! You shall have plenty to hear and to see ; but much talking I shall not allow you.——

Fipps's revengeful deed is astounding ; lucky you were by, to rescue the poor tormented foe : he had never been so barbarous except with cats ! Nevertheless I'm looking greatly forward to the comfortable sense of having those surroundings also. How much I feel the lack of any living creature near me ; my only consolation is the knowledge that you're not suffering it. However, all that will soon come to an end now, and Carlsruhe will act as bridge, even if it bears us across the Rhine and we have to remain there. Two months more, and we shall know for certain where we are.——

FROM LUCERNE 557

Nothing has happened to me since. Dräseke has left, and I'm all alone again. Yet I've had a deal of occupation ; the proof-correcting keeps me hard at work.—

Why didn't I go to Brunnen ? Child, if you had arrived here at the end of March, with the weather we have had, you would certainly yourself have rather thought of anything than settling there, with its only outlook on the desolate lake with its roaring Föhn-wind, and all the rest of that threadbare existence. Besides, like yourself, I have none but sleepless memories of Herr Aufdermauer's hotel, and still less could I dream of his pension (without stoves), since even here I learnt how early all these pensions are filled up with Basle folk and their fellows. On the contrary, I found genuine convenience here, excellent attendance, the most perfect non-disturbance till the end of June, warmable rooms, and even now real quiet in the big hotel, as the hotel-guests only arrive in the evening, go to bed tired, and make off again early next morning. Indeed one can lodge quietly nowhere but in one of these big roomy hotels, where one hears nothing of kitchen or service, all which makes sound enough in smaller ones. And pensions, forsooth : catch *me* in one of them ! Believe me, under the circumstances,—it was the only course left to me. And in general if one's not between his own four stakes, believe me, let him make straight for the best hotel ; the prices don't differ perceptibly from those at inns of second rank, but the difference in everything else is enormous. Not that I mean to say, I should care to lead this life much longer ; I'm merely waiting for a few more answers, to go to Paris after all, where I shall live cheaper in a *garni*, under any conditions, than here,

What I am most curious about, is whether I shall take a fancy to any dwelling for the pair of us,—which would settle much ; but in the worst event, and if my fortunes do not alter through the Carlsruhe production, in Paris we both can take a cosy *garni* to begin with, when the other thing will soon be found. My new opera is the main affair : that's finished, thank God, and will soon begin to be rehearsed at Carlsruhe.—

That brings me back to Lohengrin. Tichatscheck has explained to me how the one shameful skip in the duet of the 3rd act came to pass : the X (who has to sing alone there) declared the passage didn't suit the compass of her voice (!) ; on T.'s expostulating that it really wasn't permissible to plump out the second question so un-prepared, she replied that she, the singer, must be the best judge of what to leave out, the composer had no voice in it.—Well—*stupid* enough the good lady appears to be, an arrant song-singer ; and a mischief-loving face she also has, you can't deny : but in itself that cut is so revolting to me, that she has forfeited thereby alone all claim to my acknowledgment. And with that, Goodbye to her : I can do nothing with persons of this sort— unless they come and paris.—

T. wrote me that last Monday was the 6th performance to houses constantly sold out. What do you mean, then, by keeping on telling me of the audience shaking its head at this music ? I should have imagined that what the totally corrupted Viennese immediately accepted with enthusiasm, could scarcely have caused the Dresdeners such mighty brain-rack : unless, that is, the execution was unclear in nuancing and tempo ; which under Krebs must certainly be very much the case. The Vienna Kapellmeister came to me, you see, and got instructed !

The result is manifest : at Vienna a swift and sure effect ; at Dresden picking holes, it seems. But there, you mustn't let yourself be led astray by the reporters : in such cases they have hardly ever concurred with the public, which at least is always free from bias. And what sort of chaps these Dresden scribes are, I again have witnessed in the C. Bank [critique] sent me : it perfectly disgusts and sickens me, even to regard such stuff at arm's length. You mustn't dream of worrying about a thing like that, but never read it. In return, on my side I won't read what's written in my praise. *Good, intelligent performances :* that's what gratifies me ; nothing else.—

I found the second Moudon address in the long run, and wrote at once. But the gentry there all seem to need a lot of meditation first : the answer is desperately late in coming ; I'm waiting still. In the worst event, couldn't enquiries be made again of an institute in Dresden ?—

Thanks also for the [*Rheingold*] score ; it arrived quite safe. I am much annoyed at not being able to telegraph to you on your birthday ; these asses declare they can only accept for Dresden, and I've learnt before how late it reaches you from there. You are right, however, we'll concentrate our forces this time on the wedding-day ; I fancy we shall have abundant occasion by then to celebrate it heartily and in good spirits. So another fond farewell for to-day, my good Minna ! If I've forgotten anything, I'll retrieve it in the next few days. Be cheerful and calm, and hold right dear

Thy

R.

188.

LUCERNE, 3. *September* 1859.

MY DEAR GOOD MINNA,

I hope these lines will duly reach you on your birthday, and so I offer you with fervent heart my profound congratulations on this birthday whose returns we certainly shan't celebrate apart again. It will be the second you have passed in succession without me ; but to-day, for sure, you're thinking of me with other sentiments than was still the case a year ago. For sure that doubt about me and my attitude to you has vanished altogether from your heart, and you know you've no more cause to fret about me. This, then, is the gain an otherwise so trying year has brought : hold fast to it, and let to-day's birthday give you this contentment for your poor tortured heart !

So—what do I wish you ?—That, just as your mind is now at rest, your bodily heart may also lull itself ! Health ! ! Everything else lies in our moral power ; even Luck at last will grant its blessing, be sure of it ! So keep you this day as a day of rest, of deep inward repose !—

I shall soon be able to inform you of—my departure ; all now depends on naught save one more letter.

Farewell, good Minna ! Accept the best salutes and kisses of

Thy

RICHARD-MAN.

189.

LUCERNE, 6. *September* 1859.

Well, dearest Minna, I am writing you for the last time from Lucerne. I expect to start away tomorrow, perhaps take another brief trip across the mountains, visit Sulzer at Winterthur, and attend to whatever there is to be seen to at Zurich, Kölliker, Kaufhaus etc., without exactly letting myself be seen much ; then make for Strassburg, where I still count on a rendezvous with Devrient. At the same time I propose to arrange with the latter for his finding us a suite of rooms for you to await me in ; so I beg of you to write me quick to Strassburg, *poste restante*, about what time you think of setting forth. Of course, until I get to Strassburg I can't give you any closer date for the production, as also for my arrival at Carlsruhe ; only it is my opinion that you shouldn't settle down again in Dresden first, even if you have to wait a few days at the hotel for another performance of Lohengrin. However, no doubt you will remain that long at Schandau, and take additional advantage of those autumn days which are always the more beneficial to you ; whilst I hope in any case to be summoned to Carlsruhe in the second half of October, and consequently you will doubtless have arrived there by its middle. Preciser information on that, though, after my interview with Devrient.

I shall send you some more money as soon as I get to Paris, that my good Mutz may want for nothing. I have struck a good bargain,* which provides us ample money to go on with, and above all ensures us a comfortable start in Paris. On that by mouth, which won't be very far off now. A great deal depends on my finding a dwelling that affords me hopes of acceptable sojourn.

For the rest, our immediate plans remain at what I have repeatedly outlined to you as my wishes, hopes and prospects. An immense deal will depend on my Carlsruhe visit : nevertheless we'll still consider Paris

---

* Mortgage of the *Ring* scores to Otto Wesendonck ; see No. 192, also letter to O. W. of August 28.—Tr.

as our chosen habitation; and so I intend doing my best to bring that Rienzi business to a definite conclusion there; which I really can only do in person now, as no sort of reliance was to be placed even on X.

I have been in pretty frequent correspondence with Tichatscheck of late. He besought me to draw up a fresh petition to H.M. for pardon, and hand it him for presentation through Privy Councillor *Behr*. I replied that *I* knew nothing fresh to tell the King, and as everything I had already said, or got said to him, had had no other effect than contemptuous silence, neither could I believe that the King expected any fresh communication from me; whatever there might further be to say in my favour, not *I*, but only a third person could say it about me: if it could then be intimated to me that H.M. really required nothing beyond a fresh petition from me, to declare his will, I should be prepared [to present one]; but that must be assured me first.— Dear child, Herr X [Lüttichau] would now have had a very good occasion, after Lohengrin, were it only to make amends for the unseemly supercilious fashion in which he replied with his snub to my so exhaustive, nay, hearty epistle from Venice; but it doesn't occur to him. So I have at least reminded him through Tichatscheck that the fee for Lohengrin should certainly, and according to my own desire, be struck off from that unliquidated big advance to me; only that in common courtesy he ought to come to an understanding with myself as to the *amount* of said fee, since I was no longer in his service and it was for *me* to assess the value of my works, and so on.—But these people continue to behave so disdainfully and disrespectfully to me, that I really no longer care to take the slightest notice of them apart from my rights. The —— take them all ! Pack of curs ! I know no other name for them.—

But let's leave all that, and think of something better to wind up with ! Unfortunately we had very bad weather here yesterday for your birthday, and I a little chill again, so I passed it quietly in my own small room. I thought of you with all my heart, however, and drank your health in a cup of most excellent tea. It did me good to be able to look calmly and cheerfully into the future ; firm trust in a peaceful and honoured life's-evening gives me good courage : may I be able to impart it to yourself ! And so farewell. A finis to Lucerne ; your next lines I shall read at Strassburg !

A thousand good greetings from

RICH.

190.

PARIS, 12. *Septr.* 1859.

DEAREST MINNA,

I'm writing you in greatest haste (in the midst of removal) merely to give you my present address. It is

Monsieur R. W.

4. *Avenue de Matignon*

Champs Elysées

Paris.

I have just taken this very nice and quiet furnished *logis* for a month. I'll write you particulars tomorrow or the next day. I received your letter of the 6th September, and was highly delighted with it. I couldn't wait for your expected letter at Strassburg, as Devrient was prevented from coming, and I therefore travelled on to Paris without further halt.—So—Adieu for to-day— soon more from

Thy

dear Husband.

191.

PARIS, 19. *September* 1859.*
4. *Avenue de Matignon*
Champs Elysées.

MY GOOD MUTZ,

So everything is taking clearer shape at last, and I am getting my fortunes more firmly in hand again. Accustom yourself to the idea of going on with me from Carlsruhe to Paris, where, as I see more and more plainly, we positively must reside for at least a few years, to reap weighty results for our whole future that are to be won me in this way alone. Thus much is certain, to wit, that it now only needs a longish and unbroken stay in Paris, upon my side, to bring my operas shortly out here. The théâtre lyrique is as if ordained by Providence to pave my way to that : they give Mozart's and Weber's operas there with great success, before a public d'élite, and the true Parisian charlatanry is all but wholly absent. The director is a cultured, pleasant *gentleman*, quite independent, and has only been waiting for my arrival to bring everything to a serious and definite conclusion with me. For a start he talks of Tannhäuser, and quite right too : spectacular operas like Rienzi belong to the *Grand* Opera, and as soon as *one* success is won, that other is sure to follow altogether of itself. All the French who have travelled in Germany know of nothing but Tannhäuser, dote on it because it's something so new and unusual, and whenever anybody breathes my name in Paris now, it always is synonymous with "Tannhäuser." Moreover, there still are great difficulties in the way of Rienzi, which could only be removed in consequence of a success with Tannhäuser. Myself, too, I'd rather fix

---

* The letter promised a week earlier is evidently missing.—Tr.

on Tannhäuser; I very well remember how, when I
fancied I could force things better with Rienzi at Berlin,
12 years ago, the reproach was most properly made me by
Franck and several others, that I ought to have insisted
on Tannh., as this work is in fact more original and
shews me at once as a distinct entity, whereas Rienzi
doesn't duly correspond to the peculiar expectations raised
about me. —

So I have taken the furnishing of a good translation
in hand before all else. I see it will cause me incredible
labour : a Frenchman really can't do such a thing alone ;
and nobody has truly helped me hitherto, but all my
commissions have either been badly attended to, or more
often not at all. Reliance is to be placed on no one,
unless I strike in energetically myself; wherefore it now
means : Stay in Paris, for some years at least. So I have
ordered my translator to my rooms each morning, to grind
out line by line with him : the only way to bring it off.
This translation is quite the most important business to
begin with ; for not until it has succeeded, can the rest
be fitly taken up. Nevertheless, the matter stands in
this way : that I may hope for the production this winter
itself; within the next few days I shall have a conclusive
interview with the director. —

Having thus explained to you, dear Minna, that it
will be needful to decide on our residing in Paris for the
present, it is agreeable to me also to be able to put you in
heart for it. The neighbourhood in which I'm lodging
shews me Paris from a wholly new side : splendid walks
within a stone's throw, beautiful pure air, repose and
quietness, yet life ; the *bois de Boulogne*, which has really
been quite magically improved, close by ; for distraction,
if one wants it, such a remarkable city at the back of one,

with its heavenly Conservatoire orchestra, its admirable quartets, etc. : I confess I don't know what I could desire better for the next few years, or offer more agreeable to yourself.   Besides, we can live as secluded as ever we wish ; Fipps will be on an open promenade in a trice, and can dance and run to his heart's delight.   Then the certain prospect of *considerable* money-takings.   And all this merely for us to make up our minds to.   I have the best hopes of an agreeable dwelling ; only I mean to have another good look round first, before determining.   All my acquaintances are in the country, even Monsieur Kietz. Only the grandmother Herold was at home, an uncommonly kind, good old lady : they are to lend me a hand, particularly in finding a female servant.   I went to the abode of Herold the son : it was completely new, had fine big rooms looking directly on to the garden of the Luxembourg, albeit 3 flights up.   It costs 2,500 *fr.* ; consequently I expect to get all I want for 3000 *fr.* at the outside.   About that soon, tho', next time.

Under such circumstances, dear Minna, you will quite perceive I don't feel driven to address a fresh petition to the King of Saxony unless he should expressly ask me for it, and under promise of the amnesty.   In any case it doesn't press just now at least, and consequently I shall leave this question in abeyance till I've had a last definitive discussion of it with my friends, the Grand Duke, and yourself at Carlsruhe.   That's not a long time off, you see ; and, having waited until now, the thing can surely stay at rest till then.—

I have been considering what to do, supposing you had an insuperable dislike for Paris.   In that case, if the Grand Duke offered me enduring refuge in his capital, perhaps I should have to contemplate our setting up there, and *my* coming to Paris alone for some months whenever needful. Doubtless that could also be arranged ; but what should we gain by it ?

I received your Strassburg letter on the very day I wrote to you ; for its welcome to French soil I still have to thank you : let's hope 'twill be fulfilled. I am expecting fresh tidings from you soon, which are certain to tell me good news of your condition, aren't they ? As with all my changes of address, I have still to write an awful quantity of letters, but am expecting an answer already from Berne about N. Only, in that case you must see to procuring yourself an agreeable feminine companion and attendant. I assure you, there shall be no lack of means for a liberal life, else I would never have offered you Paris. So farewell again, good old wife ! Take care of yourself yet, and hope for the best in every direction. Adieu ! A thousand heartfelt greetings from

RICHARD.

I gave Frau Cl. Stockar a kiss, she touched and affected me so by the care she continues devoting to the grave of our poor Peps. A lovely fenced bed above the grave, with a constantly fresh pot of flowers in the middle ! Really most touching.—

I am expecting preciser news from Devrient in a day or two, about the date as well ; you at once shall hear it all.—

Apropos : if you don't want to go to Kaskel's yourself, it will be sufficient, as he *knows* you, simply to write him to send you the money consigned you by myself through Rothschild.

192.

PARIS, 25. *September* 1859.
4. *Avenue de Matignon.*
Champs Elysées.

DEAR MINNA,

I should have written you again before this, since receipt of your last letter, if severe indisposition hadn't this time prevented me. On the whole I have regained great confidence in my health since last year ; I feel better in many ways than before, and in particular my Kissinger-water cure, combined with the riding, seems to have been of great benefit to my liver. Only, I still am very sensitive and easily put out ; most of my illnesses come from that cause. About 4 days ago, then, exactly at my lunch I received a letter of Tichatscheck's informing me of fresh piggishnesses of my Dresden publisher-set touching the full score of Rienzi ; the vexation caused me by these dirty tricks came into conflict with my digestion, and so sensitive am I, that I forthwith detected a fatal alteration in my state of health, which also made me susceptible to a chill I caught that evening. Instead of a simple cold, there developed a fever ; and, together with the catarrh, this has been plaguing me ever since without cease, making me quite weak on the slightest exertion. Well, that's passing off now ; but it really is my nature, and without this great susceptibility I could never be so vividly sentient and creative an artist. Consequently we shall both, dearest Minna, have to pay quite a number of kind and affectionate considerations to one another.

In any case *you* need them in far fuller measure than I, and it therefore rejoices me to feel so easy on the whole about my own health, that I may count on ample strength to execute the task my heart and mind dictate to me. In any case you're more in need of sparing and indulgence than myself, since you are at once more suffering and your health is more acutely threatened ; wherefore I wish for nothing more from you, than that you should pay just so much heed to my susceptibility as is needed to allow me to remain at all times master of myself. In this sense, then, I make *one* claim on you before all else : You must unconditionally commit yourself to my care and treatment ; for it is my duty to bestow that mental and corporeal care on you, poor Wife, with faithfulest affection. And that amounts to this : you must let a great change take place in your previous uncommonly active household management, which now exhausts you so. It would be inexcusable of me, to plant you once more in a manner of living to which, with the best will, you can no longer prove equal. *I* require no nursing, merely peace around me ; but you require more. Ere deciding on Paris, I therefore took mature thought for the means of keeping up a pleasant home here. Concerning the transaction of which I speak, as I have pledged my word of honour on it, I can tell you no more than roughly its subject. You assure me you are not inquisitive, it's true ; nevertheless I may remind you that in the matter of publishing the Nibelungen Härtels would never consent to fix an honorarium, but merely offered to divide the future profit with me. Well, I have now found somebody (his name he strictly wishes told to no one) who, in return for assignment of that prospective profit up to the height of the sum advanced, has paid me a small fee in advance for the completed pieces ; so that as soon as the Tristan [score] is out I can let the [engraving of the] Nibelungen be commenced, whilst I have enough money for the present to cover the great expenses of removal and refurnishing, and also to live for some time longer without encroaching on my receipts to be anticipated from Tristan. Consequently, as according to my latest arrangements the Paris production of Tannhäuser will take place this very winter, I'm looking forward with the greatest calm to handsome and continuous returns, and therefore can also offer you what is indispensable for our renewed life in common.   So :—

Once and for all, you are to have nothing more to do with household drudgery.   You will be the mistress of the house, you will keep the purse, and everything will and shall go according to your wish ; but yourself, you shall exert yourself no more : all you shall do, is to command.   Therefore I *demand* of you, as an irremissible duty which I impose upon you, that you engage for yourself a *companion :* by which I mean an agreeable young lady to your own liking who is to fill the place of a younger relative (unfortunately denied us *).   It isn't absolutely necessary that she should speak French ; for she is only to be here for *yourself,* for no one else. It would really be woful if you couldn't find such a girl, as *I* can't possibly engage you a young lady, who mightn't please you in the end.   Surely it only needs your advertising your requirements in this sense repeatedly and plainly, nay, strikingly, in the Tageblatt, or indeed in various newspapers.   I don't ask if she can perform any other domestic work, but simply and solely that you shall have a nice sort of daughter about you with whom you can chat, who will read aloud to you, and above all, tend you.   I shirk no cost for it, and

---

* " Die uns leider abgeht,"—the whole question of Nette's relationship is thus obscured once more.—Tr.

authorise you in case of need to offer the same terms
as an English family would.   Our future years cannot
cost us more than this last one, believe me ; and yet
I have come out all right, and shall do, better and
better.   So—obey me, and don't contradict !   It must
be !—

I certainly should never have thought of Therese for
Paris, as she can't speak French : which really is indispensable for a *cook*.   However, she's a clever girl, and
perhaps will soon learn her way about here ; if she'll
accept, *I'm* quite agreeable.   Write to her quickly, or
else I must procure a cook through the Herold.   For
my own person I perhaps may succeed in securing a
servant who has taken my fancy immensely ; and a man
of *my* choice would be a great comfort to me, especially
on journeys (which might happen pretty often later on,
into Germany.)   A person like that is a real need to me ;
besides which he could make himself very useful in the
house, dusting, sweeping and furniture-cleaning (which
the cook never does here, but solely the housemaid or
garçon), waiting at table, running errands, and so forth.
If I can only secure him !   He would please you very
much as well ; he's a native of Berne, speaks German
and French.   If I don't get *him*, I shall wait awhile ;
for I shall only take a man-servant, as said, if he pleases
me much and has my full confidence.   But taken all
together, this won't cost me so much as the attendance
and tips of the past year.   With *my* mode of life a valet
is the best economy.

—For the rest, I think of leaving our equipment, all
the furniture, exactly as at Zurich, and only adding
what is absolutely necessary ; consequently I hope our
outlay on our setting up won't amount to much more than

the expenses of transport.—I haven't hired a *logis* yet, but don't doubt I shall find one to suit ; I have meant to wait for Mad. Herold first. — By the way, don't fret about your French : what you learn without troubling, is all very well ; but no one will force you to it.   Moreover, I expect to go on living as simply as ever, and shall mostly spend my evenings alone with you indoors, unless Kietz or that sort of friend should drop in on us. You must and shall have *rest :* rest and coddling ! All else is subsidiary.

I shall be unable to add much more to-day, as I still have a good deal of fever, which is increased by exertion ; so only a few more remarks.   If Frau X told you she found me gone from Lucerne on the 5th of September, she *lied :* also, it is impossible for anybody to have told her that I left as early as the 3rd.   I left the evening of the 6th, as a sum of money I had been expecting luckily arrived that very afternoon.   So rectify that, and place no doubt—if you please !—in *my* statements.—I further hear [from you ?] that Willh. Heim and the Grand Duke of Baden himself had a hunt for me at Zurich, [whilst] the Grand Duke spoke very enthusiastically about me to *Heim* (who serenaded him).   [More canards ?—]   I have no answer from Devrient yet ; naturally he will have to wait for the Grand Duke's return to go definitively into everything, especially my demands in respect of the band's reinforcement.—I'm much needed here at present for the translation of Tannhäuser and the adaptation of the full score, which I have engaged to supply by the end of October.   I must combine all this with Carlsruhe as best I can, and in any case I see plenty of work in front of me.—

Frau Pauline has stuffed you up a bit with that

theatre-director from Florence. It was a young Swiss tradesman, who lives in Florence, is an enthusiast of mine, and entertains the remote possibility of giving the Florentines a work of mine to hear some day ; I recommended him to hear Rienzi at Dresden, and wrote to that effect to Tichatscheck. That's how you mix things up—you chatterboxes !—

And now farewell, good Mutz. I'm glad Alwine has been to see you again, and found you for once *without* the Schiffner ; may she have had a composing effect on you ! I shall write you soon again, and send you true love to-day,

Thy

RICH.

The distress you are feeling in your body comes from nervous excitement ; I know it myself ! Only be at ease, about our future also ; believe me, I know what I'm doing if I am preparing for our reunion ! So just follow me, too, and rely on my good intention ; with me you'll soon feel easier.

193.

PARIS, 2. *October* 1859.
4. *Avenue de Matignon.*
Champs Elysées.

I was prevented from writing you yesterday, dearest Minna. To-day, as I have this moment received Profess. Fröhlich's answer, I can discuss that affair with you also, and mean to start off with it. The enclosed letter will shew you that on my side I have left nothing undone to meet your wishes in respect of N. ; I leave it to your-self to decide what's to do at this juncture. According to Fr.'s calculation, board and instruction will amount to 636 *fr.* a year ; if to that I add travelling expenses, pocket-money and outfit, no doubt 800 *fr.* will scarcely cover it. I cannot assume that *one* year will see the end of it, and N. get an engagement directly thereafter; so I should at any rate have to be prepared for 2 years. Meantime it is indispensable according to my own determination, cost what it may, that you should engage yourself a companion and attendant. How ill these two things fit, and how nearly it embitters me against N., I leave yourself to judge; but I may tell you quite candidly that in my opinion *nothing* will have been gained for N.'s future even by this sacrifice. To take up such a thing at her age, one ought to have an energetic character and somewhat more thorough rudiments of knowledge; but intercourse with children seems to her the pleasantest simply because she has no idea of what an English family, for instance, expects from a governess, and that even if her attainments should be raised to the requisite level, her slack and apathetic character would never please folk. Should the attempt be ventured at her time of life, however, I could only give it my full approval if that attempt (for I absolutely can regard it in no other light) could be made under lighter conditions. To a girl of energetic character, in spite of her maturing age, I unconditionally should say: To Berne by all means! systematic, thorough, and the best! With N.'s nature, on the contrary, I ask you to reflect if it wouldn't be preferable to make that attempt nearer home. An opportunity *must* be discoverable in Dresden, where surely there exist establishments for training governesses. Even if 3 years were named as term (from which something might surely be knocked off under circumstances and if one explained things), the Dresden attempt would come cheaper, and from my own point of view more convenient, as even at Berne I should have to reckon on *two* years at the least (piano-playing and English are not learnt over-night). Consequently I would beg you to try all you can again with Dresden first ; as to which I take for granted, though, that you are not to give *yourself* excessive trouble, but it would be just the occasion for exercise of the Schiffner's so very staunch friendship. If you should positively consider it the only good expedient to send N. to Berne under this condition, out of regard for yourself and your instant desire I gladly consent to assume the needful obligations, and—let it turn out as it will—you shall never hear a word of reproach from me on that head.—I promised N., if she looked after you to your complete satisfaction, I would shew myself correspondingly grateful to her ; though she doesn't appear to have fully answered my wishes, nevertheless I have made up my mind to support her for the future in any event, and am prepared to allow her fifty thaler regularly every year. I should have thought that with such a contribution, which in case of poverty might even have been raised a little, I had given her sufficient in hand to make her way. I even have thought of *Meck's* family [Minna's Russian-married sister Amalie]: are none but *strangers* ever sought there, and one's own kith and kin compelled to take foreign persons into their house? The Mecks have children, too : please let her have a try there, where they no doubt will not be so particular, and her present attainments would quite suffice ; with my annual contribution she wouldn't be a burden to them, but might even prove very welcome. Forgive me, if I can see almost nothing but childish obstinacy in N.'s contrary wish. But bring this affair to a conclusion after your own best judgment ; for my part I have placed free choice in your hands for everything and any event, only I deemed it advisable in all respects to speak out my frank opinion of the thing to you.—

Another topic.   Best Minna, I think I now have reached an age when one really would like to enjoy to some extent the fruits of a long life of labours.   By which I mean nothing else than household comfort and convenience,—and what I can provide myself on that side has this value to me, that repose and comfort tune me to productiveness, whereas with a certain constant untranquil discomfort I lose an uncommon amount both of time and good humour.   Moreover, not only out of regard for yourself—whom I would so gladly make quite comfortable—but in particular for my own sensitive and fastidious nature, I find it less easy than some persons to satisfy my needs in an agreeably calming fashion.   Simply the point of Abode, for instance : what strict precautions I have to take to ensure my being undisturbed, hearing no tiresome noise, and particularly no piano-playing. Imagine how difficult it is to protect oneself entirely against that here in Paris.   At last, after incredible efforts, I have succeeded in finding a dwelling which answers my every requirement ; at the sacrifice of 1000 *fr.* more per annum, I admit, than another dwelling would have cost *without* these guarantees.   I signed the agreement yesterday, and to gratify your curiosity, will tell you at least so much about it : it is situated a few 100 feet from the Arch of triumph, off the *Avenue des Champs Elysées*, in a completely new quarter and a side street thereof, very pleasant, with splendid pure air.   More building will be going on in the neighbourhood, to be sure, as new boulevards are to be pierced towards the *Arc de triomphe ;* but that sort of thing is done very quickly in Paris, and one notices but little of it, especially

with the favourable position of our abode.* For yourself,
dear Mutz, I have taken full consideration with it in all
respects ; you, too, will be able to live very quietly and
to yourself, and have a nice view into the bargain. The
rooms are small, as everywhere in Paris, but well distributed and quite sufficient. I will just tell you what
you'll have to yourself : a pretty, very cosy little bedroom ; adjoining it a small but quite sufficiently com-
modious boudoir with 2 windows, entirely to yourself
(only I think of breakfasting in your domain) ; in direct
connection a room with cupboards, for your companion ;
and then the maid's small room for wardrobe. You are
certain to be quite pleased with it, as it's all very snug.
I likewise have all the accommodation I need, and beyond
that there's a *Salle à manger*, a reception-room which you
can always sit in if you want to, and finally a cabinet for
the man-servant. Let me tell you nothing more about it
now, and grant me the small surprise I am thereby preparing for you. Fippsel will be uncommonly happy.
There are *most glorious* walks quite close, and the whole
situation has the purest air.

I was obliged to sign a contract for 3 years, and
to pay up the final term's rent in advance. In any
case, though, I intend devoting those 3 years to Paris and
my undertakings here ; in spite of all dearness of living,
I may hope to leave here with some profit then, and if
Germany by then stands once more open to me, to plant
myself with my old Mutz wherever we please for our
last resting-place. And those 3 years we'll pass agreeably ; so there's no hurry about my pardoning till then,
and I therefore beg you not to let the persuasions of

---

* With his usual luck, the piercing of one of those " new boulevards "
rendered his little house quite uninhabitable within a twelvemonth.—Tr.

‘others mislead you into pressing me in that respect just now.

I have no answer yet from Carlsruhe ; which is ex-plicable enough to me.   For I had to insist on conducting the first performances myself ; consequently the Grand Duke must set all that in order first.   Moreover, they want to defer the production till the Grand Duchess's birthday,* if possible, and as I am up to my eyes in prepara-tions for the Tannhäuser here, I've no particular cause to hurry them.   At any rate, then, commence your very needful grape-cure : don't disregard Pusinelli's advice. The beginning of November, at latest, I hope to meet you at Carlsruhe in any case ; so turn the additional month to your health's good profit.   Let me also know how much more money you may need.   Don't disturb your mind about the fashions here ; I see people wearing everything, and there'll be opportunity enough for some-thing new once you are on the spot.   So a thousand kind and hearty greetings for to-day.   To our speedy glad meeting !

Thy

Old man.

I fancy Tannhäuser will come out here about the 15th January ; soon more on that point.   I believe I may count upon a great success.

194.

PARIS, 9. *October* 1859.

MY GOOD MINNA,

I received your last letter from Schandau last evening.   Meantime Pusinelli had written me, and given

---

* The German edition says " des Grossherz.," but the " des " *must* be a misreading for " der," as the Grand Duke's birthday was only just past (Sept. 9), whereas the Grand Duchess's fell on Dec. 3.—Tr.

me another full account of your condition : he considers
your health improved on the whole, only you continue
so excitable on the smallest occasion, and your heart
causes you so much trouble upon any emotion, even that
of joy, that he has grave doubts about giving his prompt
consent to your journey to me in Paris, where there
would be so many excitements again for you.   I replied
to him thereon at once, and tried to remove his mistake
as to the influence which Paris and our own reunion
might have upon you.   I hope to have sufficiently proved
to him that, with me in Paris, you were embarking on
a more soothing and beneficial mode of life than you
had been leading in Dresden ; which latter I couldn't
think the least adapted to afford you the needful rest and
comfort, were it only for reason of your numerous
acquaintances, mostly consisting of women, alas, among
whom one might seek in vain for common sense : I
instanced Frau P., who has repeatedly made thoughtless
and agitating communications to you (only the other day,
again, about my Pardon business).   Further, the misfortune that you were thrown entirely on your own
resources there, and had no reasonable, affectionate and
truly considerate husband at your side to restrain you, for
example, from too much talking, too much company—
for instance on the occasion of performances of my operas.
Then you had the peculiar vanity of always forcing yourself to appear to people as if there were nothing whatever
the matter with you, which simply upset you the more.
In brief, I told him I considered it a great good fortune
that you had come under his medical treatment, but
a misfortune that this should be in *Dresden*—if only
because of your many acquaintances.   I couldn't leave
you there any longer, and if there were *one* human being,

apart from the Doctor, who still might exercise a
beneficial influence on your mind and your whole system,
that person was myself—your husband : on *me* depended
all your weal and woe, and therefore it was *I* who had
to care and decide for you now.   In Paris there would be
nothing lacking to make your life agreeable and comfortable, whilst *I* should certainly attend to quiet, soothing
company, congenialities etc., as I also needed them
myself.   In the first place you would be living with
me in a very quiet, most comfortable little house, among
the familiar surroundings of our own old furniture ;
you would have a pleasant young lady of good education
always about you, who was to act as your reader, take
care of you, and obey your every nod ; and you were
to select this girl entirely after your own fancy.   Then
you were to live at peace and undisturbed, do no kind of
house-work any more, but merely issue orders.   I should
know how to keep all intrusive visitors at arm's length
from you ; only a few intimate, cordial friends from days
of old should come to us ; nowhere would I drag you
against your will, but every day you should be able
to take a 2 hours' drive, and only go into the noisy
city at your pleasure or infrequent need.   The abode was
situated high and in pure air, in a new and most agreeable
quarter, where there were splendid promenades close
by.   Distraction would be at your command by the
handful whenever you required it ; but alongside of it
such a repose as you couldn't easily find anywhere else,
since there would stand at your side a most sensible
husband made wise by experience, who had no other
thought in your regard than for your welfare, your
fostering and thriving.   But according to my inmost
conviction, this assurance and your untroubled residence

with me alone could supplement and complete all that which his own medical treatment had laid the foundations of, and brought about. Neither was he to fear that the performance of my older operas in Paris would usurp my attention to such a point that I should be unable to bestow on yourself the needful tranquillising treatment ; that would simply interest and entertain us, and finally afford us joy.—It would undoubtedly be otherwise with an entirely new work, just completed, which I intended to produce for the first time and in by no means quite adequate circumstances. Myself I could only look forward with a shudder to that time at Carlsruhe when I should have to go through all the agitations of such a *first* production, which I must necessarily conduct myself ; of late I had been plainly picturing to myself all the annoyances, the half-despair, success and failure, and their consequences on my irritability : as for myself, why, *I* was bound to take the plunge,—but to drag *you*, dear Minna, into that kind of vortex for our very first re-meeting, at a time when the whole of Weimar and all my German acquaintances will be conspiring to inflame my brain—this, I certainly must perceive, would be downright insanity and absolutely inexcusable ! And therefore, after due deliberation, I have simply concluded with Pusinelli : To Paris ?—*Yes !* and that *as soon as possible*. To Carlsruhe ?—No ! in no case.—

Give ear to this decree, dear Mutz, as a thoroughly sensible woman, and with perfect trust that it's merely in *your* interest. Since *I* am now taking your cure into *my* hands with full responsibility, as the physician to whom your welfare is entrusted I simply order you to strike out *Carlsruhe* entirely, and come to *Paris* instead *the sooner the better*. It must be so ; it would be inexcusable of me to

allow it to be otherwise.   But first let me inform you that
Carlsruhe is giving me great anxiety already, which I
perhaps do wrong even in imparting to you.   In the first
place, Devrient is very pedantic and wooden ; it can't be
drummed into his head that this is a question of an *extraordinary* performance ; on the contrary, nothing lies at his
heart except the even tenour of his theatre.   I am to
content myself with *his* female singers, just as they are ;
no other than the voiceless Garrigues for Isolde.   Neither
is even the latter point quite settled yet ; much [of the
music] lies too low for her, as she can only make herself
audible in her top notes now.   Of the Grand Duke, too,
I still can learn nothing ; Devrient hasn't seen him for
5 months.   At any rate, then, everything there stands in
by no means such immediate prospect, and—quite between
ourselves—under the rose I'm already looking out for
other chances.   I have written this very day to Tichatscheck, also, in this sense.—

So—let *us* leave Carlsruhe entirely out of our plans
for the present, but hold all the firmer to *Paris*.   And so
I'm of opinion that you should unconditionally follow
Pusinelli's advice of a grape-cure now ; but I recommend
you to come direct to me in Paris as soon as that cure is
ended ; which I fancy may be in about 3 or 4 weeks.
All the rest shan't worry us at all ; you'll be with me
then, and—my coddling of you, rest assured, is bound to
suit you.   But you must assist me in it, i.e. you must
accord me full authority and unconditionally comply with
my wishes ; since those wishes have no other object than
to prepare for you good oft-tested wife an agreeable,
tranquil, cheerful and unconcerned existence, in reward
for your many trials.   To this end, dear Minna, I forbid
you in the very first place to bother in the slightest about

the furnishing and all the concomitant upset.   All these petty cares must now be absolutely non-existent for you (at least for as long as you still are so ailing) ; and if I were still in the position to have to burden you with them, I should regard it as my bounden duty rather to keep you still away from me.   Thanks to the great repute I've won (!) however, I can relieve you of all that now. You shall enter your house only to find comfort and rest there, not to worry and upset yourself again at once.   So you must accustom yourself in advance to an entirely new order of things in this respect ; you're only to be the convalescent now, the coddled, and thereby alone can you react composingly in turn upon myself.   It will cost me no sort of exertion ; all my measures are taken already.

I promise you that whatever may have to be procured afresh shan't be luxurious, but simply sufficient, neither silk upholstery nor damask curtains ; set your mind at rest on that.   Moreover, everything is so easy to get here, and will be well and easily attended to.   I am expecting the furniture soon, and must beg you to forward me the *keys at once :* everything will have to be opened at the Customs here ; but for all that, I shan't go rummaging in your belongings.   Regarding Therese, I ought to be able to count on a definite answer soon : let her plead illness of her parents, and come quick.   If I only had her address ! I ought to know about this *soon*, and wish I could have saved you that trouble also.   Unfortunately I have been unable to get my Berne lackey, but I have been recommended quite a smart young fellow here instead, likewise a Swiss (from Fribourg), whom I mean to take on trial for the present ; which is very easy here, as one can give a week's notice and discharge.   He is to enter my service on the 15th inst., and I hope he will answer, also not displease yourself. As I must vacate my present furnished lodging, I shall move into the new abode as early as the 15th ; in case our furniture doesn't stand at my disposal by then, I shall simply hire the few articles I need for a week (*à la* Herwegh !). How I should like Therese to come soon, then ; but I can manage in the meantime with my man.

Yes, my good Mutz, that's how things stand, and how you're being disposed of. Does it strike you as comic ? Well, get accustomed to it, and imagine it's a fairy-tale : in any case you shall enjoy it. But have no fear at all about finances ; we shall live quietly and modestly, without any waste, but we *must* be quiet and well-served. At all events this style of life *cannot* cost more than, if as much as, the past 14 months ; and I pulled off that in the end, you see, even without Paris. But Paris now is coming on, and undeniably great successes stand before me here, provided I remain here. As to that, only thus much : I am run after, people come to my house, I don't have to go and seek them ; the whole of my operas are displayed in the music-shops. The bringing out of Tannhäuser this winter depends on nothing but its translation, and for that itself I have the best offers [of assistance]. So far I've mixed with none but Frenchmen ; when I have expressed myself as still indifferent to the undertaking, they've answered me, " But do you realise that it's a matter of an annual income of 60,000 *fr.* for you ? " And even if one discounts that a little, so much is certain, Mutz : we shall pull along, and probably also be able to lay something by. So courage and trust ! and—obedience to your good husband, to whose care you are now to entrust yourself !——

In conclusion, a word about N. Your decision,

equally with N.'s letter, affected me. Once again I
deplore her not having been able, of all people, to prevail
on herself to be a faithful, genial nurse to you for ever ;
but it's a question here of qualities of temperament which
plainly are not to be changed. The Berne project
annoyed me in particular because of the special and
expensive *pension ;* such pensions, moreover, are really
only meant for inexperienced young girls. Then, why
on earth to Switzerland, when exactly the same thing
as is learnt there may also be learnt anywhere else from a
middle-aged person of sense ? So let N. adhere to her
wish to get trained for a governess ; but let her gratify
it at home. I should be sorry if, for mere sake of the
small cost of living, she re-entered the crude milieu of
Zwickau ; you found it repellent, dear Minna, yourself.
Consequently I wish N. to remain in Dresden and take
a room at the Schiffner's, or near her, when she must
arrange with the Schiffner for board. Then let her look
about her for good tuition : for geography and other
elementary instruction she should hunt up some good
school ; she must learn French properly at last, and take
lessons in English ; beyond which, thorough pianoforte
lessons, hiring a piano for her room. All this she must
try and get as cheap as possible, but not too cheap
for the instruction to be of any value : for the piano I
recommend Blassmann. *Whatever all this costs*, I will
defray it, and that until N. gets a situation to maintain
her completely. Consequently she is *in any event* to
devote a few years now to learning something thorough ;
it will be of benefit to her entire future, and raise her
to a better lot. Should an opportunity of marriage
present itself, and the marriage appear impossible for
simple reason of her poverty, I hereby pledge myself

not only to provide her with a good trousseau, but also to allow N. 200 thaler [£30] a year for life, which ought to suffice a decent husband for her dowry.

Consequently from this day forth I assume all care for N., so she may know that she's fully provided for and has to depend on no one any longer in this world except myself.

At your departure from Dresden I shall also remit you what N. will require to begin with, whilst I shall shortly expect the preciser account of what she'll need according to my plan.

So my greeting to N., and tell her to make her mind easy.

And so farewell, my good Minna. May this letter, too, have none but a reassuring effect on you. Don't let yourself be influenced by anything, by any further care, than that to reassure myself; and that you'll do if you vouchsafe me unconditional trust, worry yourself about nothing, and unquestioningly conform to my advice and wishes, which aim at nothing save your greatest welfare, such as should indeed be granted you after so many hardships !

Farewell, and take a thousand salutations from Thy
RICHARD.

So :

16. *Rue Newton*
Avenue des Champs Elysées
Paris.

195.

PARIS, 17. *October* 1859.

Even to-day I can only make you scant answer, good Minna, to your letter received the day before yesterday ;

I have only a bare hour's time left. Our things have arrived, and have given me a deal to do the last few days, to get everything in place. Unfortunately with the frequent lading and unlading of the cases, some of which are very heavy, there has been a fair amount of damage ; and perhaps it would have been better to have packed the books, etc. separately, as they made the cupboards and drawers unnecessarily heavy. All that can be repaired, however ; only it means a lot to do still, and I thank God that you're not in it. *You* had the awful time, when you attended to the packing up ; I still reproach myself for that, and think it a very mild recompense that I should relieve you of the unpacking, which in itself is far more pleasant. Moreover, I am admirably assisted. In the first place my valet (from Canton Wallis) is shaping very well ; he appears to be an entirely uncorrupted good sort, extremely good-natured and indefatigable, so that I believe I may be quite satisfied with him. Then in the concierge of my late lodgings I've found a perfect jewel of a woman, who takes the Devil's own interest in me, has always given me very good and reasonable directions, and now is lending an uncommonly expert and zealous hand in getting me straight. So have no care about me and the toil ; it is all going right, and will soon be got over.

Therese's coming so late is most inconvenient to me. I have sent orders to Zurich for her to try and get away sooner on the plea of her parents' illness.—

Among the furniture I miss my green work-fauteuil, also the two red-velvet fauteuils : why did you sell precisely those ? In fact you might have been more sparing with the sale in general. Where so much was to be carried, the dining-table and the sofa-table might easily have found their place, also the better bedsteads ; we surely should have saved that way. Did you sell all the mattresses? In general, tho', please tell me what you may have with you now. What are you bringing in the way of bedding ? Are your blankets, etc. still in good condition and worth the carriage? These are just the sort of things not dear to buy here. Have you the table silver with you ? Please answer, and I'll then direct you how to pass it in. In short, supply me with a list of everything you're bringing with you.

And now for the main affair. I'm highly delighted you took my last letter so well ; now only let yourself be treated by me, and obey me : I really am the only one who can have a thorough good influence on your whole condition, and I have good hope. I am sorry everything is growing so late ; I had hoped you'd have started your [grape-] cure the beginning of October, and assumed you were in Dresden long ago : all that has been greatly delayed, and I'm afraid the long postponement of your coming hither will give rise to a collision [with Carlsruhe]. However, the chief thing remains that the grape-cure (which I also deem most advantageous and needful) should do you real good, and that you shouldn't overtax yourself thereafter with the preparations for your journey ; for the smallest over-exertion would be more detrimental than the few days' gain of time were worth. Bear that in mind as well.——

Whether I shall come out to meet you, or await you here, I must determine later. On the whole I'm *against* a first meeting and talk in a railway-carriage, and prefer receiving you in the tranquillity of one's own hearth. On that another time, though.——

Now for N. I have well and maturely considered it,

and believe it my most bounden duty to be dead *against* N.'s coming to Paris too. Our experiences of your mutual incompatibility are so utterly deterrent, that I should judge myself greatly to blame if I risked another attempt in your present state of health. The last attempt has just been made again at Dresden, and from your own letters I've repeatedly gathered that you two can't hit it off for long. On the other hand I recognise in your last change of mind the selfsame weakness you displayed 4 years ago, when we corresponded between Zurich and Mornex on this point and you suddenly declared yourself once more for N.'s remaining. The results thereof I then experienced in that unseemly scene which finally accelerated N.'s removal ; a scene which, just as it should never have occurred, must also be kept at arm's length from our house in future. I'm not at feud with N. for that, however, and what I promised her in my last letter shall be adhered to. Tell me how much more money you believe you'll need, to leave N. something like 30 thaler behind to go on with.

But I beg you *the more insistently* to use your most earnest endeavour to engage such a young person as I wish for you. In any case please advertise repeatedly in the Tageblatt : " Wanted a young lady, aged 18 to 30, as companion to a married lady ; one who can speak French preferred." Through public announcement one can find what one wants just as well, indeed easier (as it gets known far and wide) than by personal enquiries ; and then one always has a choice, and doesn't need to bind oneself until one thinks one's suited. For instance, a man-servant was personally selected for me by the M. [for the Asyl] : well, if that creature hadn't been engaged already, his travelling money paid and so on,

I should never have taken him ; so I forced myself to put up with him, though my feeling was always against the Saxon * * * *.——Wouldn't you care to go and see Uhlich's eldest daughter ?   You absolutely require a trusty *educated* girl about you.   If you can give me no hope of it soon, I shall make enquiries myself ; in fact I've no doubt one could find just the thing here in Paris itself, where there are so many German families.——

Now farewell for to-day.   Write me nicely how you're getting on ; be calm in every way, overtax yourself with nothing, and above all attend to your health !

Adieu, dear good Mutz !

Thy
R.

196.

PARIS, 24. October 1859.
16. Rue Newton
Champs Elysées.

MY GOOD MINNA,

Let us merely run through the most urgent points to-day.   Really my time is very much taken up, what with the necessary purchases and answering letters,——and the most urgent is quite enough, in fact, now we so soon can talk everything over again.

So, lest I should forget anything :

Your muff and fur-collar are here !

That was the most important ; now for the rest.

Everything named on the list has duly arrived.   A little crockery is broken ; not much, though.   Pictures and mirrors unharmed.   Only the furniture was very much damaged, but has already been repaired again.   Everything fits in very well, and I already have bought what was needed.   Carpets and curtains were a job : additions

were necessary ; but nothing has been left unused, and
you'll find all old acquaintances.—Please send Jacquot's
cage, with the bedding, etc. *at once*, and consign it to
the "*petite vitesse*," which takes longer, but costs considerably less ; whereas "*grande vitesse*," i.e. "to be
despatched with great rapidity," costs considerably more.
For this one package, however, perhaps one might run
to "*grande vitesse*" ; in any case consign it soon, that
Jacquot may find everything ready.

(*Enquire how long it takes.*)

Your wanting to come viâ Augsburg has quite amazed
me.   Has somebody really advised that ?   I don't know
all about the German routes to Paris, but I do know that
one can get here from Berlin (viâ Cologne and Brussels)
in 24 hours ; please enquire if you wouldn't have a shorter
journey by taking this route.   I must tell you in confidence, that I am having strong pressure applied at
Zurich to get Therese here earlier.   Which brings me
to your travelling companionship.   Someone must travel
with you, it goes without saying ; on the other hand
your last letter shews me that you really are clinging to
N., and would like to have her with you.   Dear child,
when I committed you to her care a year gone by, I
indeed had nothing else in mind than the hope that one
after all could get on with her ; but you dashed that hope
of mine yourself.   Now, how is one to take you women ?
Were you right then, or are you now ?   Is it merely the
thought of parting, that is making you tender—or do you
really believe N. might please you better than another
girl ?   What am I to say to it, who have my eye on
nothing but to make life easy for you, and to keep every
occasion of anger as remote from you as possible ?   Of
course it would be the most natural, if one could manage

with N. ; provided it were offered her, N. could have no other choice whatever, than to attend to you and share our home.   In the case supposed, that is her plainly-destined natural vocation, from which she at utmost could escape through marriage ; but God knows what is best here !   I leave it entirely to yourself : you must know what you've to expect from her now ; if you want to hazard it, and would even prefer it, I'm quite agreeable, bring her with you.—It is self-understood that *I* would have forced no girl upon you ; neither had I exactly a picture of beauty in mind, but just such an agreeable young person as one can be without precisely being pretty, and which rather consists in a neatness of nature and good education.—Well, do what seems the pleasantest to yourself; but someone you *must* have.—

My servant is a splendid chap, quite uncorrupted still, very good-tempered, full of zeal, untiring ; he remembers everything, has a really bad time of it at present, but shifts for himself and never complains ; he's after people like the Devil, and had already learnt a thing or two in his only previous place.   He is very droll, and will amuse you much.   He speaks Valais German, and pulls through passably with French.   Added to which, he has quite a good appearance, and is only longing for the wife's arrival.—Without him I couldn't manage at all ; he makes my bed, does the room, boils me eggs, *etc.*— I am keeping fine house with one teaspoon as solitary table-gear (apart from knife and fork).   I'll write you again about the silver.—

And now for something else.   Carlsruhe is—off. Devrient wrote me yesterday that the Garrigues also cannot trust herself to sing the music of Isolde, and—I must admit—I'm glad that *she* declines, or *I* should have had

to decline her.   The Hewitz had declined before, as the
part lay too low for her : they must be pretty squeakers !—
For the present I'm really pleased it has come to this
pass.   So it's true that Devrient had done absolutely
nothing to procure the needful female singer through a
fresh engagement, as I originally arranged with him : he
positively thinks the Garrigues the greatest woman artist
in Germany.   Good : I should have said No thank you
to a voiceless Isolde for the first performance of my
work.—So we'll see what else to do with this new
work : I should prefer giving it first with Tichatscheck
and the Ney ; there I at least know what I've got.   If
it came off at Dresden, I could fairly stomach the delay ;
on the contrary, I'm even glad of it, as I should have
found it most difficult to get away from Paris this winter.
There's work to be done here, best Mutz.   Not until
yesterday could I come to an arrangement with Roger.
I went to see him at his country-seat (you know that
the poor fellow lost his right arm a little while ago) ; I
brought the pianoforte score of Tannhäuser with me, but
he not only possessed it already, but had even translated
the first scene, which he sang us in French very finely.
So it's all settled : I am invited to go out to him as
often as possible, and preferably to take up my abode in
his château so as to be able to help him with the work
each day.   That I mean to do, so far as possible, to push
the thing ahead ; for the only point remaining now is
the finishing of the translation.   In the next few days,
accordingly, I shall fix up everything with the director ;
consequently I must belong exclusively to Paris this
winter, and the Tristan would simply have gêned me.
On Paris, though, depends my whole financial welfare.

—And *thus* you also have no need to *hurry* over-

much.   When I urged you last, I was afraid I should
only be able to welcome you here for a very few days,
and then have to set out again for Carlsruhe.   But we
thus shall stay snugly together, and celebrate the wedding-day at leisure.   So—everything is straightening :
keep quite calm, take your time over your preparations,
and arrive in good trim !   Farewell, good Minna.   A
thousand greetings !

Thy
R.

197.

PARIS, 31. *October* 1859.

DEAREST MINNA,

This moment I receive your latest letter just as
I was about to dress and be off to the station, having
announced myself for a visit to Roger to-day.   I had
nearly seized the necessary reply to you as pretext for
not going, and at the first instant was heartily glad of
having found that pretext (with such gusto do I go
there !), when I remembered that Roger's carriage would
be waiting in vain at the station at Villiers, besides which
I must really bite my sour apple if I want the so needful
translation brought off.   Imagine my laughter, then,
when I read your strange insinuation that I might find
myself so well off at Roger's château (as I'm so easily
dazzled, you know) that I might repent having taken and
furnished a dwelling here for the sake of reunion with
you !   I should have almost exclaimed, How little you
know me ! if I didn't recognise at once that this time
you had let yourself be deluded by my brief remarks on
Roger's country-seat and so forth.—But let us drop that ;
you'll soon learn different, and I shall make you **no**

reproach about your curious apprehension. Merely thus much : these excursions cost me great, great self-restraint, but to bring the thing off I absolutely have to spur the somewhat lazy creature, who much prefers playing dominoes, to serious work.

I wrote to Fischer at once, as you will have learnt by now. I confess that this eternal grief and trouble around you fills me with positive horror, and I shall be heartily glad when I have you safe with me again ; everything seems combining to give you sad and gloomy impressions. My poor dear Fischer, he has moved me deeply ! I hope my letter will have a good, invigorating effect on him, and—after all he'll rally once again.—

I never want to see anything more of all the loose music etc. you've sent me a list of : it's a sheer encumbrance ; throw it away as you please. What surprises me, is your saying nothing of the two Tannhäuser scores, originally presents to Boom and A. Müller of Zurich, which I reclaimed from them a short while back. Those two copies have *not* been used (at least I have given no order for it), and as the engraved full score will soon be out, I hereby request that those two copies be returned to their original owners, addressed to Alexander Müller. I shall thus get clear of the resulting obligations.—

What occupies my thoughts the most now, as you well may imagine, is your journey hither. Acting on the surest information, I had planned you out the following itinerary as the best and most convenient :—

1st day.   From DRESDEN to MAGDEBURG.
          Depart 2.45 afternoon
          Arrive 9.39 evening.

2nd day.   From MAGDEBURG to COLOGNE.
Depart 10.33 morning
Arrive 10.15 evening.

3rd day.   From COLOGNE to PARIS.
Depart 9.15 morning
Arrive 9.0 evening.

This plan has the great advantage that you always have convenient hours of departure and arrival, travel express all the way, and in particular do not reach Paris at quite too late an hour. For the Strassburg and Metz train doesn't arrive till 11 at night ; which, with the cere- monies over luggage etc. meaning another full hour before we got to our abode, would make it exactly midnight ! That I should like to avoid. Then, I had of late been firmly reckoning on your having N. for companion the whole of your journey, and since I really greatly need Therese, I wrote Therese the other day to come at once, as you would be travelling *another* way and she therefore wouldn't join you. Now I must wait and see if she complies with my request and really gets here in the next few days ; but as you have just written that you are *not* bringing N. with you, and also have found no other companion, consequently are definitely counting upon picking up Therese en route, it places me in great perplexity. However, I'll arrange it *thus :* Either—Therese obeys *my* orders, and comes to Paris in the next few days, when she shall first help me get things into order so that you may find no exertion awaiting you, and, as soon as you write me to do so, I'll send you Therese from here to *Cologne* (*or* to Frankfort, if you're absolutely bent on travelling viâ Metz) ; as far as *Cologne* (or Frankfort) you would get yourself accompanied by N. in any case, for you mustn't travel a *single stage* alone.   *Or*—Therese obeys *your* orders, and remains at Zurich till *you* bid her join you ; which would be pretty much as first arranged, only that I should urge you nevertheless to travel by Cologne (according to my plan above), and *you* would then order Therese to *Cologne*, to which distance N. would have accompanied you in any case.   Once more I most earnestly recommend you the journey by *Cologne*, firstly for the advantage in the hour of arrival at Paris (9 o'clock), secondly because you would be travelling express *the whole way*, which is an inestimable convenience (believe me), whereas the route from Metz to Paris is one of the most circuitous and disconnected, with frequent change of carriage.—So follow my advice, and we shall soon know all about Therese.   In any event she shall receive you at Cologne (or Frankfort).—

I am extremely sorry you have found no companion ; we must try and get one here.   With your next letter I'm expecting a fixed estimate of how much money you think you will need still ; I would send you some at once, if I didn't want to wait and hear whether the Wiesbadeners have despatched the Rienzi fee to Tichatscheck (for you).   In any case I shan't omit to.—

And now bear up bravely, good Minna !   If I no longer wished to *press* you (after the falling through of the Carlsruhe undertaking), it was simply to let you start at leisure, and not set you in a flurry with it.   Otherwise, the sooner you come, the better I shall like it : rest assured of that !   I'm longing heartily for household order, and looking forward to the capability of being something to you poor tormented wife again.   Everything

will come right, and you soon shall thrive with me!
Adieu!

Thy
RICH.

If you haven't sent the bird-cage off *already*, please
send it by *grande vitesse* now, as the *petite vitesse* takes
at least 3 weeks. Do as I say!

198.

PARIS, 7. *November* 1859.

Tell me, good Mutz, what ever prompts you to such
curious letters as this last of yours again to-day? Whilst
I am nothing save concern for you and delight at soon
having you with me again, you charge me with all
kinds of preposterous things! Luckily I see it can
repose on nothing but misunderstandings, which I may
soon and easily clear up for you by mouth. Thus, that
good, perpetually excited and exaggerating A. may have
recently put something in your head again—with the best
intention, of course, but not at any rate with due regard
to your excitability. Nor have I truly anything against
the P., and I am firmly convinced she means well by
you ; but she certainly has not understood how to keep
useless excitement aloof from you : I simply go by the
last letter you imparted to me, for instance, in which she
entreated you to entreat *myself* to entreat the King, in
turn, and so on. *You*, foolish woman, say *that doesn't*
excite you : but what, then, is keeping you in that
eternal unrest which Pusinelli has so sorely complained
of again to me?—And was not that unsettlement, for
instance, altogether futile?—But let that be, and see
no ill in my doubt of your present surroundings in

Dresden—though with that itself I already am saying too much—and badly as you may think of men, and in particular of your husband's want of character, yet a little masculine society will do you good, and mine, please believe me, for certain.—

Tichatscheck's announcing to me Lüttichau's payment of the fee [for Lohengrin?] was imperative, because I should otherwise have seen myself obliged to send you more money from here. How can you misinterpret that?—

Now to the point. Frau Heim has written me at last, confirming Therese's inability to leave her place before the 11th inst. Consequently it abides by your wish, and you'll order Therese to meet you. I give it you to ponder once again, however, whether you wouldn't do better to follow my wish and travel by Cologne : whether Therese comes to Frankfort or Cologne, makes no great difference ; but an express goes from Cologne to Paris, with every compartment first class, consequently Therese could sit with you and take care of our animals. The fastness of this train is much to be recommended. For that matter, if I prefer your reaching here at 9, instead of 11 o'clock, dear Minna, I am by no means studying *my* convenience (it isn't nice of you to make me such an imputation !) but rather your own, or in general our mutual interest not to spoil our first re-welcome by a too protracted sleepless night, which necessarily draws after it a day of some malaise. On the whole I'm sleeping well now, and one night sacrificed is a bagatelle to me ; but after such a tiring journey it seemed to me a point to be considered for *yourself,* and your having seen nothing but a consulting of *my own* convenience in this forethoughtful sparing of you—

which even the blindest might recognise—simply shews me how needful it is that you are coming to me soon. Moreover, in my wanting not to meet you at the frontier, but to receive you here instead, you also seem to detect nothing but my own convenience. This time I stick to it, however, that I shouldn't care to pass the earliest day of our reunion in a railway-carriage, in company with every chance fellow-traveller; for every reason that concerns our Wiedersehen I prefer escorting you direct from the station to your own abode, where you at once will find rest and home-comfort, and both of us no interruption.—

Give way to my wish, or adhere to your will, i.e. travel viâ Cologne or by Strassburg (please not viâ Metz: that's a vile train!), in either case you now can call Therese to your side and I shall know you're well looked after. I shall meet you at the station here, and take my steps to have your luggage cleared as quick as possible. At any rate I shall get one more letter from you, in addition to which I beg you to telegraph to me en route, either from Cologne or from Strassburg, the exact time of your arrival.—

Beyond that I have nothing of urgence to tell you; I wrote you about a few other things the day before yesterday.*—

Dear old Fischer's death has deeply grieved me; but I will not tell you how I'm shattered by these constant sad and doleful tidings: nothing whatever encouraging appears to happen now. The more reason for your trusting me, that in our mutual trust we both may find the strength to bear life's griefs and burdens steadfastly

---

* A missing letter,—Tr,

together. For the rest, I implore you, at this our re-meeting itself please avoid all exciting emotions, even that of joy : let us strive to preserve calm and composure ; let us gladly accept the good that is unravelling for us from our tangled life, but simply rejoice in this reunion as though it were a Wiedersehen after a long journey by one or other of us. By letter we have uninterruptedly told each other everything, and consequently never ceased living together ; therefore we shall have absolutely nothing more of weight or moment to say by mouth, but merely many less important details to fill in, which get neglected in a letter, but find their proper place by word of mouth when one is much together. Consequently we shall have much to tell each other, much to narrate, but nothing of very particular moment, the latter having been promptly disposed of all along between us ; so we shall have much to talk of, much to chatter, but may hold all agitating things at arm's length with good conscience and without dissimulation. So arrive here in thoroughly good heart, serene and confident : you'll find plenty still to see to, but nothing fatiguing will await you. All gloom has now dispersed behind our backs : then let us look towards a bright and cloudless gloaming.

I will attend to the Homage to Fischer, and hope to set about it tomorrow.

Farewell, be good and calm !

Thy

RICHARD-MAN

(alas, no woman).

199.

PARIS, 10. *November* 1859.

Here, dear Minna, is the Homage to Fischer.* Hand it to Heine, and tell him to look upon it as a letter to himself. Let him preface its publication with a few words explaining how this *Nachruf*, albeit destined also for publicity, was originally intended as a communication to a mutual friend of Fischer's. Let him preserve the date ; unfortunately I've been so interrupted, that I couldn't undertake the copy till to-day. And greet our dear Heine most heartily ; from my lines he will gather how dear my friends are to me, and how I cherish their memory, even though my correspondence should often remain intermittent.—

Your mind will be at rest about Therese by now, and providing you have duly notified her, she will not fail to be at Frankfort. I suppose I may look for a telegram from there.

Certainly I had my fears lest the next day after your arrival might be too early for you to see the young person recommended to you ; but I never dreamed you would perceive in that a more serious ground for uneasiness, to say nothing of an attack on your independence. My trouble was our not having a creature in the house who can really speak French, for even the man-servant only scrapes along with it ; so I wanted to have somebody who could at once assist Therese through her earliest stage, conduct her to the market and on other shopping expeditions, and quickly ground her in the first

---

* " *Nachruf an L. Spohr und Chordirektor W. Fischer* " (see *R. W.'s Prose*, vol. III.), originally published in the Dresden *Constitutionelle Zeitung*, Nov. 25, then in the *Neue Zeitschrift*, Dec. 2, '59, under the title " Dem Andenken meines theuren Fischer."—Tr.

essentials of the language. Further, I thought it would be nice to get this point itself soon *settled* to your satisfaction. However, that's easy enough to countermand, and you shan't see the person before you wish to yourself. For that matter, dear Minna, you will remember that after every dispute I have done my best to concede you the point : henceforth I shall concede it you *before* a difference of opinion, and confidently hope to obviate disputes themselves for ever that way.

One thing I commend to you : do acknowledge my good will !

To give you no cause for excitement, then, I'll not even surprise you with anything upon your arrival, but rather tell you at once that I really have taken a small house to ourselves. It was a great rarity to find such a thing in Paris, and I'm paying 1000 fr. *more* for it than I should have had to for another suitable abode (as I couldn't go into a very high étage—were it only for your own sake). I didn't decide on it until after I had seen that *otherwise* I couldn't possibly think of our settling down in Paris, as no flat afforded me a guarantee against being surrounded with piano-players some day. If I hadn't closed with it, I couldn't have offered you a point of reunion as yet ; on the other hand, my need of household rest and permanence was great. Finally, I reckoned up what our last mode of living had cost us both, and found that if we meant to continue it, it would come far dearer to me than an agreeable settlement in Paris ; so I seized the latter, and now beseech you not to make it hard for me in any way. With 4 mouths already, the companion's fifth will be easily fed, and the pay's a mere nothing compared with the advantage. If we do require the sum you've named, even so we shall scarcely be requiring as much as it has cost me this last year : consider that. And I afforded that, and shall afford it still more easily now, in far more favourable circumstances. If the worst came to the worst, a trip to America would redress the balance ; but even that will not be needed.

Fond as you are of mocking me for this as well, once more I bid you : *Set your mind at rest!* And I bid you that with serious, kindly calm myself.—Make it easy for me, ever to stand calmly and affectionately at your side ; don't accuse me of what is chargeable to Fate ; and tax me with no frivolous whim, if I simply bow alike to the demands of my position and my needs. If I have tried to relieve you of all that is possible on your arrival, I have done it both with insight and with good intention, not to circumvent you, but to make things easier for you, and finally to have order in the house myself as soon as possible.—

So—jeer as you will—I repeat : Be calm, and don't let yourself be agitated by every mistaken notion !

Farewell, my good Mutz ; write once again, and give me friendly reassurances.

Thy
R.

I suppose I'm to blame for the death of R[eissiger —Nov. 7] ; I said to myself on Fischer's death : To think that such a man must die, and such a —— remain alive ! So far as I'm concerned, however, he might have gone on eating dumplings many a day.

Should Heine think it out of place for me to couple *Spohr* with Fischer, I beg him carefully to cut the part respecting Spohr.

[*Minna arriving a few days later, the next occasion for correspondence was her husband's trip to Brussels, there to repeat by request those concerts which had had so great an artistic success, though a financial failure, in Paris Jan.–Feb.* 1860. — *Tr.*]

200.

BRUSSELS, *Thursday evening*
(22. *March* 1860.)

Heidideldumm ! Juchhe !

Ah, what good luck I do have !—

Surely it must delight you to hear I'm so well off, most charmante Mutz ?—

The day all but came to an end without my getting a chance of writing to you ; you know what it is, to hold concert-rehearsals of this sort ! And indeed it isn't easier here than in Paris : there I plunged into all kinds of expenses, to have it *good ;* here I certainly save those expenses, but—whether it will go *well*, remains to be seen.—However, with the little I have time to write you I won't indulge in lamentations, but simply tell you that I'm still alive, and moreover would much prefer getting back home to Paris tomorrow.

The journey was miserable, the arrival miserable ; then trundled about the whole day, calls upon calls paid. To-day I was really glad to see Giacomelli [Paris agent] again ; it seemed quite home-like. On my leaving the rehearsal, too, young *Trabody* ran after me (you remember him, perhaps, one of those young Russians who fiddled with me at times in Zurich). The rehearsal didn't much entrance me ; the orchestra is miserably placed, and that must be altered or nothing will come of it. Chorus miserable—yesterday and to-day I've had to hold extra chorus-rehearsals. Oh ! Oh ! what an ass am I ! ! !—

Well, don't take it amiss that you haven't a more

sensible husband ; it shall have been my last stupidity.—

I'll write you properly tomorrow, if—God wills !
Don't be cross with me for its not happening to-day,
but I'm all tumbling to pieces again. And hoarse ! ! !
—Na, greet Fipsel and Jacquot. Amuse yourself, and
enjoy the tranquillity ! Think a little of your stupid
husband, too. Fare nice and well for to-day, and love
Thy

faithful partner

RICHEL.

201.

BRUSSELS, *Friday*. (23. *March* 1860.)

Very good day, good MUTZ !—
>   Tho' tired and half broken,
>   I let you hear by this token
>   that my health isn't bad,
>   and things aren't so sad.
>   At this morning's rehearsal
>   the band tusched me a morsel :
>   it is being better placed,
>   too, to humour my taste,
>   and to earn what I need
>   in a world full of greed.
>   Now yourself write me soon,
>   that I may not be woon-
>   d'ring if you're not ill-used
>   and Fips is amused.
>   Tomorrow morning more rehearsing,
>   then my garments reimbursing ;
>   to the concert off then quick,
>   curiosity to prick.

Eke from Antwerp and from Ghent
shoals of offers have been sent
to me, concerts there to give,
or they really cannot live.
But I shall nicely keep away,
save my person for another day ;
it's already much fatigued,—
see these rhymes that I have rigged.
Now fare you right *wohl*,
and don't eat too much cole,
lest it make your tummie hard :
the advice of your Richard.
And if you go to Frau Szemere,
don't forget your Herr Jemere,
how he freezes here and sweats,
and conducts with all his wits—
just as if it were for honey,
whilst it merely is for money.
Now preserve you the dear God,
else He won't be worth a nod !
But may me His mercy bless
with this concert's great success ;
and Therese with her doughing,
and Josephine with her sewing !
And just think in all your woes
of your own dear loving spose
Herr Wilhelm Richard Wagner,
your arm-and-leg-bruised pardner !

PIMPERLEKEF ! ! !

202.

BRUSSELS, *Sunday* (25. *March* 1860.)

DEAREST MUTZ—

Merely 2 words in the greatest fatigue and prostration :

no more concerts!

After the fearful exertion of yesterday I couldn't sleep last night for over-excitement, and am feeling awful. The thing went very well, the success *exactly as in Paris* over again—*notwithstanding* the colder Flemish blood.

But a mass of extra expenses once more, no very big takings, hardly any profit.—That seems to be the settled fate of all such concert enterprises.   I really have no fancy for a second concert, and therefore beg you to prepare your mind for having to welcome me home again soon.—Tomorrow you shall hear more details ; for to-day—be sorry for your poor husband, and thanked for your beautiful verses.

A fine Good morning !

To our speedy meeting !

Thy R.

203.

BRUSSELS, *Monday* (26. *March* 1860.)

BEST MUTZ,

Yesterday I really had a good mind to leave the second concert here in the air and be off to Paris to-day ; the fearful labour for such a small reward annoys me hugely.   To-day I've quieted a bit, and as the concert is already announced and advertised for Wednesday, I am really afraid of the scandal my abrupt departure might possibly—or rather, certainly—occasion.   It might have looked as if the success hadn't come up to my wish, and that would have been very incorrect. Everybody is surprised at the fire of this Flemish audience, which really has espoused my cause with the selfsame jubilation as the Parisian. Moreover, all the best seats were well filled, especially in the first circle ; only the upper galleries were empty : but the prices are' very low and won't yield much, particularly as I have had to bear the cost of reinforcing the chorus and orchestra. However, I've had the director informed now, that he must share those expenses with me. Anyhow I shall give this second concert too—for honour's sake ; but after that— never, *never* again such concert-givings ! For I now see that no profit can ever be drawn from them, and nothing but the artistic success can be kept in eye. True, people tell me *this* itself is not to be made light of this time, since I have suddenly become very popular in Belgium, and thus ensured the giving of my opera here as soon as ever it has been given in Paris. Really that isn't to be despised, for Belgium alone has nearly as many big cities with theatres as France itself, and they are all bound by treaty with France to pay full tantièmes also. Brussels will in any case be getting up Tannhäuser concurrently with Paris ; Antwerp, Ghent, Liège, the Hague, also wish to bring it out the same winter. That would considerably augment the Paris tantièmes, you see, and consequently I should have to look for good fruits from my present exertions quite soon.

The theatre here is remarkably fine, exactly like the Berlin opera-house. People tell me that without these concerts I should have remained a stranger even with my operas here for years.—Well, we shall reap all that benefit next year.

This evening I'm to dine with Count Orloff—the

Emperor of Russia's right hand, and an intimate of Napoleon's—at Klindworth's uncle's, an eminent diplomatist ; so you see, I can't get away from diplomacy. Lord knows what all these high enthusiasts will bring to pass for me some day ; in Paris they really have effected much for me this way already.—Well, well ! I have had callers all this morning ; now I mean to go and pay my return calls on M. Fétis (who is quite raving about me) and several other musical notabilities. Tomorrow I shall make a little trip to Madame Lohengrin, née Elsa—at Antwerp ; then sweat and overtax myself once more on Wednesday. Then I shall return to Paris *Thursday* evening between 8 and 9 ; before which you shall have heard from me again.

Now—a thousand good wishes ; hearty regret for the hurricane, which has been raging here as well, and the promise that all that shall be altered : without fail !—

So fare nice and well, and hold dear

Thy

GOOD RICHARD.

[*Some three months after the above, Minna went to Soden for several weeks, by Dr. Pusinelli's orders ; but at present we possess no letters to her from that interval. During her absence Wagner at last obtained his partial civic freedom, largely through the influence of Louis Napoleon, and made his first trip to Germany since 12 full years to fetch her home to Paris. Soon afterwards came the removal from Rue Newton to cheaper apartments, the fiasco of* Tannhäuser *in March '61, and the necessity of seeking another sphere of operations. Minna is still in the Rue d'Aumale at the time of the immediately succeeding letters.*—Tr.]

204.

CARLSRUHE, 19. *April* 1861.

My, Minna, it's quite nice here ! Splendid drinking-water, excellent butter, and kind cheery people : what more would you have ?

But the Envoy in Paris is without a peer. The first thing I learn on my arrival yesterday is that the Grand Duke had gone woodcock-shooting! I refused to believe it possible; but indeed it was so. He doesn't return till this evening; so I shall have to practise a little patience. The delay is no harm inasmuch as I see that it's just as well for me to come to some sort of understanding with *Devrient* first. The man is not to be eluded in the long run, and one might easily find him an obstruction.

So I am turning my time to fair advantage, and getting the thing as ship-shape as possible before I have the last word with the Grand Duke. Man proposes, God disposes.—

I couldn't sleep on the journey at all, and was much knocked up; this morning a cock awoke me: another new experience!—The cheapness here quite does one's heart good.—Na—in short, we'll see, but not reckon on anything!—

So—a very good morning to you! Greet Fipps and Jacquot. Take a thorough good rest, and be a good woman!—

(Kalliwoda, that kind good fellow—has this instant come.)

Fare a bit well!

Thy
entirely good
HUSBAND.
(At the Erbprinz.)

I expect to get back about Monday or Tuesday.—

[*The next week he returned to Paris, after arranging with the Grand Duke of Baden for a "model performance" of* Tristan *at Carlsruhe in September, special singers for which he was himself to select from other theatres. With this intent he leaves Paris again May 7 or 8 for Vienna, where he is to be offered his* first *hearing of* Lohengrin, 13 *years after that work's completion.*—Tr.]

205.

VIENNA, 13. *May* 1861.

MY GOOD MUTZ,

The performance of Lohengrin won't be till Wednesday ; Frau Ortrud has had a small mishap. This delay really suits me, for the excitement of the performance would have followed too swiftly on the emotion into which the rehearsal plunged me. That rehearsal took place last Saturday [11th] : I sat on the stage, and never stirred from my chair, yet could scarcely stand on my legs when it was over. That rehearsal far exceeded *all* my expectations, and for the first time in my thorny life as artist did I reap a full enjoyment atoning for everything. Words cannot express the deep, completely unalloyed delight I felt. Orchestra, singers, chorus—all admirable, incredibly fine ! Possibly the reverential mood of all who were to represent my work to me for the first time contributed much to the quite incomparably tender, noble and vibrant warmth of their achievement : everything proceeded with the utmost regularity, and yet without any constraint ; there was something touchingly hearty about it. I sat quite still, without moving a muscle ; merely one tear chased another down my cheek. Then the dear creatures came and silently embraced me ; only the band and chorus broke into loud cheers at last. You may imagine the style in which I thanked them all ! But it was good Kapellmeister Esser to whom I gave the greatest joy : the poor man had been in dire anxiety beforehand whether I should be satisfied, and not want a great deal

altered ; so he was quite taken aback, and stood dumb
as a pillar when I declared to him that upon receipt
of such a heavenly boon as this performance one lost
all thought of criticising : it was all so excellent, that
I felt nothing but emotion, thanks, delight.   And indeed
every word of that came literally from my heart ; never
have I so ogled anybody, as this honest good Kapellmeister at his desk.—

In short, dearest Mutz, it's a heavenly Opera here :
a mass of glorious voices, one finer than the other,—
chorus—orchestra—transporting !   Ander—the tenor—
quite perfect ; his voice, too, not merely sufficient, but
of brilliant energy where needed ; and with it all, a
conscious artist through and through, admirable in
delivery, altogether penetrated with the thing, full of
life and fire.   Frau Dustmann, with a heavenly soulful
voice which *nothing* comes amiss to, but everything fits
like a glove, has an excellent dramatic delivery ; she
brings out every nuance so naturally and distinctly,
so moving and so true, that I shouldn't have a hint to
give her.—With these two—not a doubt of Tristan and
Isolde !—

My God, how it warms the cockles of my heart for
once !—

Beyond the above, best Madame, I can report nothing
further to-day.   Whether I shall be able to decoy these
little people for August and September, I strongly
doubt ; I fear it's quite impossible.   To-day—just now—
I have been presented to Count Lanckoronski, *Court-*
Intendant of the Imperial theatres : he is said to take
an interest in the smallest stage detail, and with a
good conscience I could only tell him the most flattering
things ; for my own part also, *I* had the advantage

with him of being an enthusiastically admired composer here. So we parted, I fancy, quite excellent friends. He has placed his theatre at my disposal for all my operas ; and I am told he doesn't trifle, but literally means and keeps his word.—

At any rate I cut a comic figure in my own eyes now with my laborious Carlsruhe model-performance, for which I've got to beat up everybody first; and I almost believe I shall have to lay hold where I find *everything, everything* ready to hand, and an enthusiastically attached big public at my back into the bargain. —On the contrary I still adhere to our Carlsruhe plan for a residence. Soon more and preciser on that, my good Minna ! In any case a favourable and lasting change is coming over our prospects ; Heaven grant us calm deliberation, to hit the best choice to give security and permanence at last !—

And now farewell for to-day ! Unfortunately I'm quite beleaguered here already, and feel somewhat fatigued the whole time : Tausig and—Cornelius are here as well ! That confounded youngster amuses me as much as ever.—

But enough now !—I'm hoping for news from you soon, and hope it will be good ! Kindest regards to our friends, and all sorts of endearments to our tiny house-mates ! Adieu. Be quite well and of good cheer !

Thy R.

206.

VIENNA, 16. May 1861.

BEST MUTZ,

It is getting difficult for me to bring off a letter to you to-day. People have been coming to me since

8 in the morning, and it still goes on ; moreover I have
really much run down. Last night was something
positively *incredible!*   And everybody assures me that
such a thing had never been experienced with this
public : it was an ovation the like of which had probably
never been offered to any composer before.   I had a
box in the 2nd tier, to get a thorough good hearing
and view of the performance.   Naturally I was observed
at once, and after the prelude, which was rendered in
heavenly fashion, the whole audience turned towards
my box with a never-ceasing tempest of applause, so
that I was obliged to stand up 5 times over and make
bows without end.   Precisely the same thing took place
after the principal pieces in every act ; after the close
of each act, however, I had to appear on the stage,
always *thrice*, and at the final close as many as 5 times.
But what was most striking, was the incredible unanimity
of the *whole* audience : a shout of delight as from 1000
trombones, and of a duration I absolutely couldn't
comprehend, so that I feared they all must burst.   Consequently I had also to say a few words at the end,
which naturally came straight from my heart, and were
received with cheers beyond description.   The Director
—an extremely good-natured Italian—turned quite pale :
he had never witnessed such a thing, he said.—I can
believe him !   Moreover, I don't mean to evoke it
again.   Saturday we're to have the Flying Dutchman,
which is said to be very well given : in any case I
intend to be supposed to have departed, and to attend
the performance in hiding ; for such a thing mustn't, and
shan't be repeated.

  Good God, how I should have liked *you* to be present
this time ; it would have made you also forget your dis-

gusting Parisian experiences. But something similar is surely in reserve for you as well! Rejoice that it has at least occurred to *me* for once ; that must be your indemnification for the present.—Under such impressions as mine here, you may easily imagine that your account of the fresh annoyance you have undergone has affected me very disagreeably. Luckily, nothing much depends on our friendly relations with X, and so far as I remember, we have good reason to disclaim in toto whatever is alleged to have been said, and to let the whole bother alone.—Please don't take it at all to heart.—

I shall write you again in a day or two, with something more definite about the [our ?] departure and the next step to take. For the present I'm still entirely absorbed with the reception I have had in Vienna ; I am so full of the affection shewn me, and the splendid artistic means here, that I must re-focus my wits a little first on what I propose for the future. Meanwhile I will merely repeat that I firmly abide by the plan of our settling at Carlsruhe : everything shall be made certain ere the end of the month.—

Give my best remembrances to Liszt. Was I really not destined to meet him in Paris, then ? How strange ! *
—Greet our friends and the animals, about whom I'm telling many tales here—among others to the Laubes, with whom I've dined, and who send you kind regards. They have 5 dogs.—

So, good courage, dear Minna ! Forget your momen-

---

* Liszt arrived in Paris the evening of the very day on which Wagner left for Vienna ; in the event he did remain, however, until after the latter's return.—Tr.

tary vexation in the lovely amends now prepared for your husband.

Farewell and be good to me !

Thy

RICHARD.

I must really keep steady : they're devising honours and ovations for me here on every side. The *glorious* band is to give me a banquet ! The big University choral society wants to serenade me solemnly after the Holländer, and so on.—Messrs Aulic Councillors, too, are laying their heads together for what's to be done with me.—There's so much heartiness about it all, that I can't well decline anything !—

207.

VIENNA, 2C. *May* 1861.

DEAREST MINNA,

People begin coming to me at 8 in the morning, Lord knows ! I can't stir, and am merely jerking off a couple of lines to you now while three visitors are talking together in my room.

Saturday we had *fliegender Holländer.* Quite irreproachable, superb performance ! Public exactly as at Lohengrin again. I had buried myself in a parquet box, not to be seen ; but that availed me nothing. After the overture I was compelled to ascend the stage to bow my thanks ; 3 times after every act, 5 or 6 times after the last, when I was obliged to say something again. An incredibly hearty, sprightly folk ; Princes and Counts in the boxes, too, all shouting and applauding with the rest.—Well, I really have something to crow over !

They wanted to give me Tannhäuser the day after tomorrow—the 22nd—but I have declined that : firstly, the Wolfram isn't well cast—just now ; then, Esser isn't conducting ; I'm afraid of not having such a satisfactory performance, and—I don't want to challenge the public to a similar demonstration again.   On the other hand, a fête is to be given me by *Strauss ;* probably I shall refuse that also.   So soon as everything's settled about Tristan, I think of starting back at once, presumably tomorrow evening, so that I shall be en route on my birthday.—

Tristan is be given here the 1st October ; I shall arrive here the 15th August.—All are heaven-appointed for it !   Nowhere shall I find similar means.

Now don't be vexed with me, good Minna, if I break off short : the disturbance is too great.   I shall be back with you a week from to-day, in any case.   I must bring everything to a head at Carlsruhe also ; I shall write you thence again.

Adieu, be of good cheer !   Best greetings to our friends and the house !

Ever thy good

RICHARD.

[*After a night at the Wesendoncks' villa en route for Carlsruhe, Wagner returned to Minna and Paris May* 26 *; by the date of his next letter she has already left him, primarily for another course of baths at Soden : they were never to dwell together again for more than a few days.   What had happened in their domestic life meanwhile, we do not definitely know, but he writes Frau Wesendonck the* 15th June *: "Perhaps I might describe my condition as a preservation of patience . . . A life I have no longer.   Perhaps I shall somewhat pluck up heart again—particularly for work—when I have got away from here . . . I am going away alone"; and the* 12th July *: " My household goods have been packed again, and stowed in the depôt here : where they will get unpacked, God knows ; in all probability I shall never see them more.   I am wanting my wife to settle down in Dresden, and take them to herself there; for my part, I can think of no more settling down.   This the upshot of a last hard, infinitely miserable experience ! . . . To Carlsruhe I therefore am* not *going ! !—From this indication of results you may infer the latest happenings in my life, both inner and outer"; and on the 25th to Malwida von Meysenbug, who had seen a good deal of both husband and wife in Paris during the* Tannhäuser *period, " I will not dwell upon the history of my last month ; that sort of thing is only fit to be forgotten . . . Two precious years have been clean squandered, and I feel extraordinarily weary; but what I have lost for my art, perhaps I have won for life, a last and deeply-graven lesson : not to try and force what will not fit."*—Tr.]

208.

PARIS, 16. *July* 1861.

DEAR MINNA,

I had already been greatly expecting a letter from you. Your having let yourself be carried off to Kreuznach first, explains the whole delay. So I will answer you at once, and make use of your own blue ink for it.

It will be a week tomorrow since you left here, and we again were obliged to abandon a hearth and home. I have been in a mood of great depression, through this constant repetition of the same unrestful fate ; I hadn't believed that not one inviting sign of life would come to me from elsewhere before my departure from Paris. I cannot help confessing that I am in a very hopeless frame of mind and bitterly dismiss each flattering fancy, at least to spare myself and you this eternal repentance. Therefore I mean for once to wait for Fortune to declare her favour with no doubtful voice ! That must be—and let patience help !

I cannot sufficiently extol the Pourtalès' ; in every way I am regarded as one of the family, and treated with great and kind consideration. Only my being able *thus* to pass the little time I have still to hold out here, could help to make it endurable to me. It is almost like the country here, and when I open my big window of

a morning, and look out across the garden and the Seine
to the Garden of the Tuileries, I'm often taken with a
pleasant sense of ease.   I am served with great attentiveness, and lack nothing in the way of convenience.
All of which tends to lessen the bitterness of my farewell
to Paris.——

Nevertheless I feel that one sole thing can altogether
wean my mind now from the untowardness of all my last
experiences of life,—a serious engrossment with my art !
Not before I'm in my own true element again, shall I
also conquer the great sadness now possessing me.

From *Vienna* they're entreating me not to delay any
longer, but to come myself as soon as possible : everyone
is in need of my animating presence, they say, to begin
the study [of *Tristan*].   In particular, the Director
himself is urgently begging me.   So I'm resolved to
restrict my stay here to the briefest length, and then
go direct to Vienna—without stopping at Weimar.   I
shall see Nuitter to-day, and set him a definite limit for
termination of our present labours [French ed. of *Holländer*] ;
otherwise they'll drag on for an eternity.   If it is
possible, I think of leaving here the end of next week,
when I shall likewise travel by Cologne, only visit *you*
at Soden, and then make direct for Vienna.   Here I
strictly am sitting on thorns.——

Of other news I haven't much to tell.   I've only
seen Therese once, the day after your departure, when
she brought me the tea-service and I also wrote her a
character.   Last Sunday I looked in there, but didn't
catch Therese, as she had just gone for a walk with her
female friend.   Otherwise, the concierge assured me, she
never went out at all, but sat knitting herself stockings
all day in her lodge down below ; nothing had been

heard yet of a situation for her. On Thursday she will come and see me again.

I have received a very satisfactory answer from Volz about the furniture ; he believes he can keep it on his premises as long as ever I wish.

Only to-day can I settle my account with the packer ; moreover, the good man charged more than was agreed. The amount of money that takes wing is awful ! Ah, how prudent all this sad experience makes one in the end.

And now, dear Minna, think of nothing for the present but your health and utmost possible convenience. For God's sake, think of nothing further now, and take everything calmly and quietly !— Think of nothing but your restoration ; these two Parisian years again are weighing on my conscience like a dreadful nightmare ! Indeed I meant well ; but once more my good will precipitated me into the greatest rashness. I can only tell you that I marvel at the way in which you have survived this terrible, incessantly obnoxious time again ; I almost deem it a good omen for your health, since I can but think that with a quieter existence, freer from care, you may even get quite well at last. For sure you shall not lack for anything ; rely on that : my immediate life will cost *me* little.—

Well, we shall see each other soon : may you have somewhat rested by then ; and then we'll also have a quiet talk, and agree on what's most sensible. Farewell, good Minna ! Sleep well soon, and pluck up heart for life's last round !

Thy

RICHARD.

Seebach has hopes of [my] speedy amnestying in Saxony !

209.

PARIS, 25. *July* 1861.

DEAR MINNA,

Best thanks for your tidings. There will be some confusion now with the small sum of money sent you from Berlin : I wrote there as soon as I learnt your address ; so just give orders at your former lodgings to forward that money-letter to your present ones. I place this first, not to forget it later.

Everything with myself is now revolving round the question of my journey. I wrote you last, I should like to go direct from Soden to Vienna, but I learn that Liszt would be beside himself if I didn't go to his performance [*Faust* symphony etc., at second "Tonkünstler" meeting] ; consequently there is nothing left for me but to get through this Weimar visit also before Vienna. So I'm sitting on hot coals here now, and anxious to be off, for all the kindness of my hosts. The Countess, who had been waiting for the visit of her father, Minister Bethmann-Hollweg, went away with him to the seaside last Tuesday ; so I am alone with the Count and Hatzfeld : but all sorts of diplomatic guests are constantly at table, when there is always a very good spread.

That might be all very well : nevertheless I've nothing more to do here, and—without my nice apartment I couldn't have stood it another week. Monsieur Truinet [Nuitter] is as charming as ever, also doing his job very well, but at times lets three days pass in succession without assisting me ; with which I have had to put up. I've now declared to him, however, that I shall start on *Monday* [29th] and he *must* have got finished by then. I mean that seriously moreover, and accordingly should arrive at Soden *Tuesday*. I'm not

quite sure yet, whether I also shall come by Cologne, or direct viâ Metz ; that will depend upon weather and whim. Should anything still alter in respect of my journey, I will let you know in good time. But I shall be unable to stay with you long, as you may easily imagine.

Well, I suppose Mathilde is with you again, to drop her money on the gambling-boards as fast as possible ?— With myself, for all ambassadries, things are going pretty monotonously.

Herr Volz is behaving very well ; he at once undertook to bring the packer to reason, and so I probably shall get off for the original price. He declares he will let the boxes remain at his place as long as ever I wish. He's an admirer of mine :—what more would one have !—

Gasperini has returned, and looked me up : he sends you heartiest greetings ; we spent last evening together. That absurd Dr Schuster also has given me no peace ; I've had to dine with him once at the restaurant.—

I have dined once at Ollivier's also ; after which we drove to the *bois de Boulogne*. With the Pourtalès's I've been twice to the theatre.—That's about all that has occurred to me !—

God knows what will turn up for next winter. I intend shewing myself very cautious and chary on all sides, so as to reap something quite solid and fully meeting my wishes at last. I am horrified when I look back upon the past ! !

Daily have I to recognise that my not having hurried with Carlsruhe was a very good move : intolerable things have reached my ears about Devrient again.—However, even that may still right itself : only they must be shewn I've no need to go hawking myself at any price ; they must learn that they can *have* me, but must offer me something like.——

But we won't let that worry us just yet ; diversion will do both you and me a heap of good. Let us wait, and—not look beyond tomorrow for the present. For your part, before all look after your health, to make good the damage once more done you by this unhappy Paris spell. I should need an energetic cure myself now ; my ailments have developed to a pitch I never knew before. Schuster very much wanted me to go to Wiesbaden :—for this year, impossible ! So I shall have to see how I can pull through the winter !——

Enough now ; we shall soon meet again, and on everything else by mouth !

The very best and kindest wishes ! !

Thy

RICHARD.

[*Leaving Paris about the* 30*th, Wagner appears to have spent a couple of days with his wife at Soden, and reached Weimar Aug.* 2 *or* 3 *for the first time since his flight from Germany in May* 1849.—Tr.]

210.

WEIMAR, 5. *August* 1861.

MY GOOD MINNA,

I think about you more—believe me !—than is good. Which means : I cannot break myself of continually occupying my mind with plans for our fresh habitation, and taking one possibility after another more seriously and definitely in eye. Only, I believe I am always catching myself on the high road to rashness again, and it costs me a violent wrench to retain that full prudence and patience which must guide me, this time, to prevent my taking any step that—after such woful experiences—

so easily might become a fresh source of unnumbered disasters and sorrows. Rest assured, however, that it comes very hard to me to force myself to wait at present with the utmost caution for the right course, nevermore to be repented, to present *itself*. My only consolation is the hope that even that will not delay too long !—

For the moment everything is happening that could serve to make me forget in a measure the last sad times. The only misfortune is that I can be far too little by myself, the whole Altenburg is so full of guests ; luckily, however, they're not the dreaded counts and princes, but simply Liszt's pupils, who lead a fairly jolly life here. Liszt himself is perfectly charming, and pleases me uncommonly again. I'm quite magnificently lodged, and can retire at any instant ; of which unluckily I get but very little chance. The Grand Ducals will only come to town for the performances, and I still hope to get away from here unnoticed by them. Liszt is giving up the Altenburg definitively,* and will never return to it. His own future remains quite uncertain.

—Since [I saw you] I have received more letters from Vienna, inviting me urgently. Unfortunately I had made a miscalculation with this festival, however ; I must remain till Wednesday evening, and no doubt cannot leave before Thursday.

So I shall probably write you once again from here— if possible—and then—let us hope !—a trifle more, and with less disturbance. (For you may easily imagine how I'm taken possession of here by all the musicians from Germany—the *Panther*, too, who sends you his compliments !—) But I think a letter from yourself will catch

* A few days later ; Princess Carolyne had left in May 1860.—Tr.

me here, so I would most heartily beg you to give me a little account of yourself with all speed.

As soon as you have settled anything preciser about your next movements, please tell me at once ; I hope (and above all, wish) that our plans upon both sides may soon coincide again. Meanwhile don't let it worry you, however : this temporary laisser-aller—how and whither—has its recreative uses for our run-down nerves ; at least I'm beginning to remark that in myself, and I noticed it in you as well. Should you prefer a prompt fixture, tho'—entirely according to your choice—rest assured that *I* by no means make a point of Dresden.

Weimar might perhaps receive a glance from you as well, but do pay a visit also to the land of Baden ; have a look at Carlsruhe for yourself. If the choice of domicile proceeds from *you*, it can be small and modest to begin with ; and that will relieve me of a certain burden of responsibility, which—before I obtain a good and warranting occasion for re-settlement—indeed I horribly dread.— So, be you the mistress of our fate for once ; I believe I shall feel justified in saying Yes to everything !—

Soon more, and more at peace, tho' !

For to-day, good Minna, another thousand hearty greetings ! Console and take care of yourself ; enjoy the time when it at least is granted you not to suffer directly under my singular fate. Then—Hope !

Adieu ! Greet Mathilde and Jacquot !

Thy

RICHARD.

[*He leaves Weimar Aug.* 9, *accompanied by the Olliviers for a great part of his journey—see p.* 632—*and reaches Vienna alone three or four days before the next letter.*—Tr.]

211.
VIENNA, 16. *August* 1861.
Seilerstätte 806, *3rd storey.*

Not until to-day, good Minna, have I had a chance
of writing you. Things have gone confusedly enough
since my arrival in Vienna, and various disagreeables set
me in a fairly melancholy mood to begin with. Even
to-day I can't yet write with true tranquillity ; you
may readily conceive that I have many calls to make
at first, and many acquaintances to renew, but the worst I
could have heard on my arrival was of *Ander's* continued
hoarseness. Only the day before, he had had a medical
consultation, as a result of which he has had to apply
for several weeks' extension of his leave. He caught cold
last June, while visiting the Emperors' Tombs at Speier,
and hasn't recovered his voice even yet. I was quite
aghast at this. Yesterday, however, I managed at last to
call on him at Mödling, near Vienna, and at any rate
my mind is much easier now, as he has considerably
improved already, and—after a thorough rest—may count
on being completely restored soon ; it is more of a nervous
affection, which suddenly may vanish over-night, especially when this heat diminishes. Otherwise he was quite
well and eager for the fray, so that I had to keep begging
him not to disturb himself, not to dream of studying
his part, and not to fash himself on my account. Consequently I'm merely faced at present with a *delay* in
the rehearsing of my opera. Of course the first question
I asked myself was, of what good I could be here meanwhile ; but I found (alas !) that I was neglecting nothing
elsewhere, as I really have nothing in prospect whatever
beyond this Vienna production. To go away would
be highly unadvisable, and my constant presence is

needed under any circumstances to keep people up to the scratch ; for they had already begun to doubt my really coming (! !).

I had another shock with my lodgings. Good Kolat-scheck lives in a frightfully distant suburb, so that I promptly recognised I couldn't stay there, as my cab-fares alone would have cost more than my lodgings. Moreover, it was very uninviting otherwise, and I was on the point of hunting for fresh lodgings when *Dr. Standhardtner*, my highly enthusiastic Viennese friend (a kind of Dr. Schuster), luckily intervened, offering to house me in his roomy abode for as long as his family is away—till about the middle of September. This lies in the heart of the city, and I'm getting to feel quite at ease in it ; the only thing I have to procure for myself is dinner. At least so far as lodging is concerned, then, I can quietly wait now and see if anyone else will invite me thereafter, or if I must look out for a furnished *logis* for myself, which indeed is what would suit me least. For—now comes the other melancholy item in my communications, which will make it comprehensible to you that I'm not exactly in a cheerful mood !—

At Weimar, to wit, the last scales were completely removed from my eyes. On no *prince* can I rely *for anything* whatever ! You don't make me the proper reproach in respect of the Grand Duke of Weimar : it wasn't I who avoided him, but he me. The reason for all this shy demeanour resides in my Dresden bearings. How things are still standing there, you may infer from the following. *Liszt* (naturally without telling me a word of it) had set his heart on inducing the Grand Duke to confer on me his Order. The latter made enquiries about it in Dresden, whither he had dealt out half a dozen of his orders a year ago, and received the answer that, if he wanted to give *me* his order also, they at once would send him back all those he had bestowed at Dresden. Thereupon (still without letting me know of it) Liszt tried to get the Grand Duke to invite me to dinner at Court with him alone ; which also the Grand Duke pronounced impossible. On the other hand, he drove to Liszt's one day to pay a call and take the opportunity of seeing me as well ; but we were at rehearsal that very moment. From this you may judge how far the Grand Duke of Baden (in any case the best of the bunch) already went when he repeatedly received me in audience : even *he* couldn't invite me to table, out of regard for his own courtiers, consequently can do nothing at all striking for me ; * the utmost he can do, is to tolerate my settling quite *privatim* in his capital. Without any sort of official appointment to provide him the means, however, neither can he support me from his pocket, as otherwise he isn't rich. So—my good Mutz ! —no illusions on that side, please. This kind of thing can't change at all until I'm fully amnestied in Saxony. Consequently I mean to wait and see what Seebach can bring off yet ; but, with this pitiful disposition at Dresden, I really nurse small hope, and am accustoming myself to lay all further plans of life without reckoning on the aid of German princes, and be only too glad that I've attained so much as the ability to reside in Germany itself unscathed.

At any rate these *last* experiences have this immediate

---

* To make sense of this clause : " Einladen konnte · auch *er* mich wohl, und zwar aus Rücksicht auf seinen eigenen Hofadel," I have been obliged to assume that its " wohl" either is a misreading of "nicht " or was mentally intended to be followed by that privative."—Tr.

result : I naturally *withdraw entirely* from my advice to
you to settle down in *Dresden.*—In your last letter you
wrote me that you meant to go from Soden to Weimar
for the present, didn't you ?   Good : but I assume you'll
visit Baden and *Carlsruhe* first.   As I *very* much wish
you to decide on a domicile *soon*, I still give most preference to Carlsruhe.   If I put my trust in anyone, it still is
greatest in the Badener : [whilst] Carlsruhe is very cheap,
agreeable, and cheery.   You do wrong to fret about the
gossip that has happened : if *I* could find no dwelling
to my mind straight off, it's quite another matter if *you*
now take yourself a humbler dwelling while I am away
on account of my opera-performances, and if I come to
you [from time to time] because you are unable to travel
with me everywhere and it is easier for me to be put
up *alone* by strangers.   Thus your small abode will
become the actual focus of our broken home-life for the
present, and I should always be returning to it when
in need of rest.   Such a modest establishment will produce a very good effect, and if my circumstances do not
alter *very notably*, then—in truth !—let it remain so all our
life, and I shall have to think that nothing more was
destined me !   But nowhere can even this *modest* menage
turn out better or more agreeably than at Carlsruhe, just
because of the cheapness there, so that we can always
have things much pleasanter for little money than anywhere else.—Please give that due thought !   Weimar is
really detestable compared with friendly Carlsruhe ; everything on a smaller and more beggarly scale. —

You see, dear Minna, how, even under the most
unfavourable circumstances (for my financial prospects,
alas, are very shaky), I am making it my first concern
to bring about the possibility of a speedy habitation :

only those horrible last Paris troubles (*Beschwerden*) have given me a positive terror of any fresh step that might plunge me into similar sad experiences. Wherefore, now that I know that I can count on nothing sure just yet, I definitely withdraw my first proposal ; but on the other hand, I feel how absolutely necessary it is for *you*, at least, to come to rest soon. If *I* go roaming round awhile, that in fact has its necessity in my vocation, to promote and supervise productions of my works, make acquaintance with the various theatres, and provide for a more distant future. With *you* it's quite another matter : you can't and mustn't roam about like that, and in particular, I seriously intend you to *become a burden on nobody*. Therefore I mean to be as thrifty as possible myself, to keep you supplied with the needful ; and as for repose, you shall also precede me in that. So soon as I know you're settled somewhere with our household chattels, I shall also know where I'm at home once more ; and— believe me—that is a great need to me, a mighty re- assurance. I who am so used to domestic surroundings, already I often feel profound dislike and actual sorrow at having to make shift in this way as a stranger, to be nowhere at home. The most brilliant hospitality can't shut my eyes to my dependence, and many a tear do I shed —believe me !—over its being denied me, of all men, to have a peaceful refuge of my own ! The first step toward my relief, in this sense, will be your telling me that you intend to settle down. You shall be entirely mistress of your choice and the establishment ; yet, after the maturest reflection, I recommend you *Carlsruhe*. Let us see if your acquaintance there will keep her word and easily find you a pleasant abode. Then try and soon come to a stand, that all may be nicely set up and I can visit you the 24th November [wedding-day], from that day forth to know—in spite of all adversity—where I'm at home again !—

I am taking everything in sober earnest, you see, and cannot join in the jesting strain with which you air all kinds of crotchets. I'm sore at heart, and with great affliction do I see how, with the approach of old age, so little has been granted me by Fate for all my labours, that I can scarce offer my poor wife a good shelter. And yet ! that shall be cared for ; just you commence, and we'll see if peace won't visit us at last !—

You will understand that in such a frame of mind it tempts me little to narrate you much about the Weimar dissipations : there was no sense in it all, and I did next to nothing but crack bad jokes. When I'm in better humour, tho', you shall also hear of Brendel and the rest. But Esser has this moment come into my room, to take me to the Dustmanns' in the country ; therefore I must conclude by merely giving you the following rough sketch of my last adventures. Of a sudden the *Olliviers* changed their plan, of going to Dresden, and decided to visit C[osima] at Reichenhall, which lay on my road to Vienna. Consequently we travelled together to Nuremberg and Munich, where we inspected the really extremely tasteful edifices and art-collections of the old King Ludwig. At Reichenhall, very beautifully situated in the Tyrolese alps—where we found the B[ülow] looking very well again—I parted from them, to complete my journey to Vienna.

This the outward history of my life since my last letter.—Now I must see how to accommodate myself to my new position and the delay in studying my new opera ; you shall soon have reports on all that from me. Write me soon—and give heed to what I've said respecting Carlsruhe ; then if you concur with my wish, we'll discuss it all in detail.

So farewell for to-day ; be cheerful, and—don't envy your husband ! ! Greet your human and animal house-mates : I will give greetings for you to *Fipsel*,* who often —often meets me now, both dreaming and awake : the dear, dear creature ! Farewell, and be very heartily embraced by

Thy
RICHARD.

Address as above.

212.
VIENNA, 26. August 1861.
(Seilerstätte 806, 3rd floor.)

Thanks, dear good Minna, for your exhaustive report. Your having suffered so much from hoarseness and coughing again, however, was very unwelcome news to me ; you are too careless with regard to chills—my old complaint against you. There's absolutely nothing for it but to entreat you to take better care of yourself ; you have no use whatever for coughs and such-like.—

I'm glad you yielded to my wish at once and had a look at Carlsruhe. As for Baden Baden, I really never dreamed of it, and the very last thing I should care to agree to, would be your idea of taking rooms there. All I had in mind, was that a happy chance might bring you up against some eligible abode in Carlsruhe itself which would take your fancy and determine you to settle there. I see quite well that such a thing can't

---

* Who met his untimely and " mysterious " death a fortnight before Minna left Paris.—Tr.

easily occur upon a hasty visit, and yet I admit, it would please me so if you could quickly form a resolution quite agreeable to yourself. Indeed it would be all the same to *me*, as for my part I've fallen into such great uncertainty this time, that I can contribute nothing more to a decision, but fain would accept everything as the ordinance of Fate. I am scarcely to be blamed, then, if my chief concern is to know that *you* are spared this roaming, and brought to speedy rest.——

For that matter, the one characteristic of *my* position is its *incredible uncertainty*. I appear to myself as new a being as if I had only just returned to this world. No sooner do I try to form a plan, than I encounter vagaries : everything may turn out *so*, but also *otherwise*, and never have I fallen into such fluctuation and fumbling. Thus it was doomed to happen to me that precisely now, when I believed I should find my hands full in Vienna, I am put off from week to week through *Ander's* hoarseness, without ever learning how far we shall get by the next week. Myself I'm forced to guard against upsetting him, and have to do nothing but soothe him, since he is excited enough as it is and his health can stand that least of all. I had already got the length of abandoning all thought of my opera for this winter, and considering what to do instead ; for everything depends on this poor tenor, who can't possibly study so exacting a part if he doesn't feel perfectly well ; to rid him of all fear of it, has been my chief endeavour. Well, on Sunday I went to the country again with K[apell] M[eister] Esser, and dined with Ander ; when I plucked up hope once more : he certainly is better, and expects to be able to sing again soon. I succeeded in reassuring him greatly by promising to alter everything he might really find too trying in his part. Indeed he's very fond of me, and quite unhappy at occasioning me such difficulties ; so he will now begin to make closer acquaintance with the part. Hitherto, you see, I had had to let him off entirely.—

Luckily it is different with the Dustmann ; yesterday she sang the first act to me so beautifully, that it gave me great delight. She will sing the rôle quite perfectly !— But I still must keep on waiting, cannot foresee a serious commencement of rehearsals from one week to another, and—for all my disappointment—can only tell myself it's very well that I came when I did and am sticking on, as otherwise the whole winter would have probably passed without Tristan, especially since there of course is no lack of " good friends " here as well [Hanslick etc.] who decry my opera as impossible.—

I cannot conceal that I am in a very melancholy humour through it all, and my kind host, Dr. Standthartner, has a pretty bad time with me. Nevertheless I am glad I can remain in his house a few weeks longer; by then the *Ander* question must have come to its full resolution, and once the thing has a definite good purpose, I shall find more heart to hire myself a room in case of need. Even as it is, my stay here costs an awful lot of money, particularly through all my singers being away in the country ; I've also had to pay upwards of 50 gulden for my luggage ! So that I still must brush aside all thought of our residing in Vienna some day, because it would be impossible to make ends meet here without a handsome salary, and permanently to let myself in for such a theatre-rumpus again would be bound to become the fresh source of unspeakable sufferings. Ah, a look behind the scenes deprives one of all heart at once,

and I can't conceive quiet and small enough the place
where I should care to make my home.—

For all that, I'm making agreeable acquaintances
here every day : e.g. a young Prince Lichtenstein, who
is a passionate devotee of mine ; a sweet old Countess
Banfy (ancient protectress of Liszt), who has taken
Winterberger into her house (at Hitzingen), where I have
already dined a few times.   Metternich also is here (by
himself), and has invited me to dinner to-day.   I have
twice dropped in to dine at Laube's, where I'm fairly at
my ease ; we talk a deal of you, and the dogs are petted
almost more there than with us.

At the Burg theatre the acting is quite excellent,
one must admit, and I have spent many a very entertaining evening there already.—At the opera-house I'm
finding out the weak spots now, particularly since those
operas cannot be given in which Ander sings.   In
Fidelio, however, I was much pleased with Beck (Pizarro)
and the Dustmann, who sang the aria wonderfully finely,
just as she is the most gifted of them all in general.
At this performance, which I attended in a parterre
box, not far from me I also discovered a nice old
gentleman, who was equally delighted to meet me.   It
was friend B., just taking his honeymoon tour.   I
devoted one evening after another to him until he
left.   His young bride is a regular bread-and-butter
goose, of the most deplorable Zurich breed : they won't
be able to bite each other, as she also has only a few
black stumps left in her little jaws.   Lord, to think
that even Nette might have had a chance, then !   Bon
voyage to them !   Otherwise I was highly delighted
with the old chap : he most heartily entrusted me with
a thousand regards to Frau Minna.—

Well now, with the great uncertainty of my future, all I can say is, Wait, and let us postpone a decision. Only it distresses me not to know you're better housed. If we had a thoroughly well-to-do family among our intimate friends who would make it a pleasure to put you up for half a year, I should say, Good!—but I can't let you go to Zwickau or Chemnitz for any length of time; that's clear as daylight. So I also tell myself: To leave *everything* to chance is not quite worthy, especially of a man of my age, who after all should be able to judge his own position and take some sort of measure himself. Listen, then, to what my reason tells me in this regard:

My *new* works will certainly establish my fame and honour in Germany even still more firmly; but I can't count on substantial takings with them, as they're too difficult and only to be executed at a few of the theatres. Accordingly I must look about for other lasting means of livelihood.—*Paris* alone, as is shewing itself past denial, may still be the source of important receipts if I can only hold out. I have fresh evidence of that: the interest in me there is prodigious, and the directors will soon be taking up my operas as lucky speculations. More about that soon.—Therefore the whole question would be that of securing oneself a modest, but solid and lasting foundation. After all I've heard of the Grand Duke of Baden's good-heartedness and perspicacity I now consider it my duty, after mature reflection, to write him candidly and confidentially again and inform him of my exact situation and needs, telling him that I shouldn't like to come to a decision without him, that I should prefer to settle in his country, but can't take that step unless he can assure me a yearly income of at least 2000 gulden [*ca* £200]; in return for which I would promise to assist his Opera and musical affairs in general with advice and deed at all times, though without dislodging any other official from his post. This will prove difficult as regards K[alliwoda], who is a very good fellow, but a musical nightcap, and already somewhat out of favour as such with the serene couple (a fact I've learnt for certain).—

I shall write and send that letter off within the next few days; so we'll at all events await an answer to it before deciding on anything further. In the meantime, however, I believe you would do wisely not to go too far away from Carlsruhe, but after Soden to pay it a visit again—instead of Weimar—perhaps stay a fortnight at Mad. Fränkel's, or if that can't be managed, take a furnished room for the same period. Then you will also have leisure to make a thorough search for an abode.—*Weimar* is hideously displeasing to me, and I consider your visit there completely futile and objectless—so far as I'm concerned. *Money*, I quite understand, you'll be very soon wanting: I have already assigned a Coburg fee to you on the quiet, and am expecting an answer from there very shortly; should it linger too long, and you be in immediate need of money, please write me at once, and I'll promptly send you some of my small store.—

Badly as things stand with Dresden, still I believe that in a few months' time (after I've been duly watched and observed in Vienna) my fate will undergo a radical change from that quarter. I also mean to discuss that thoroughly with Metternich to-day.—

Now then, poor Mutz, in spite of all misfortunes,

do have a little courage ! Perhaps all will come out
quite endurably yet, and I don't suppose it will be a
case of the almshouse for you. Farewell ; accept best
love ; and soon send comforting news to

Thy

GOOD HUSBAND.

Mille choses to Jacquot !

213.

VIENNA, 4. September 1861.

DEAREST MINNA,

This letter was to have been written yesterday,
and—as I calculated—to arrive at Weimar on your
birthday. I received your last letter from Soden early
the day before yesterday just as young Prince Lichtenstein was already waiting for me in his carriage at the
door ; I had only time to read it quickly through, and
then—as previously arranged—to accompany the prince
across country to Count Náko's, where my visit had
been announced. They wouldn't let me leave that
evening, especially as it was too late to catch a train.
After sleeping the night there, I drove straight to
Ander's at Mödling, where I had given Winterberger
rendezvous ; I had a regular torment coaching my tenor
in his new part, got back to Vienna very tired that
evening, and thus at any rate had missed the proper
day for the congratulatory letter. So I mean to make
shift with a telegram tomorrow morning, and at least
prepare you for this letter's following it.—Front rank for
that, to explain the confusion.—

Your letter itself, which I have now read through
again, has tranquillised me in rather a singular fashion.
I perceive that *I* am really the impatient one, and have
been more eager for that settlement which was to assist

you to rest, than appears to you to be of need. Well, *I* too am more against excessive hurry than before, and if you don't find this nomading uncomfortable, but on the contrary it yields you distraction and suits your taste for the moment—as seems in fact to be the case with your journey to Weimar—then I may be truly satisfied at present, since it greatly facilitates a sound decision for the future, as I should really like to leave it tranquilly to Fate for once to deal me out good chances ; and who knows if something fortunate in this respect may not turn up unhoped for ? Nevertheless, to arrive at certainty for good and all on what I intimated to you, I have already written to the Grand Duke of Baden. Myself I am very pleased with my letter ; without importuning, it is very distinct, and in particular explains to the Grand Duke why I cannot settle in his country—for the present at least—if he is unable to ensure me a pension as basis of my subsistence. Thereon he will soon determine whether he *can* make that charge on his revenue ; for I believe I have no need to doubt his *will* to. Consequently—we'll wait in patience for his answer. And so I'm almost glad you turned your footsteps somewhere else at present. True, I don't quite understand what you expect in Weimar, of all places ; but you're right, that's your affair, not mine. At any rate I'm happy to think the Wartburg must have pleased you ; the whole neighbourhood of Eisenach much attracted myself again the other day.—I presume you'll have looked Frau Röckel up at once ; so I shall send my Weimar telegram to her address tomorrow. Give my kindest regards to the poor care-worn woman ; she knows it was impossible for me to pay her another call at the finish, I have spoken to Laube here [artistic dir. Burg theatre] about her daughter Lulu : he says he recently had information from someone who had seen her in a rôle, and that information turned out sufficiently unflattering to make him dispense with Lulu, especially as another young girl had been engaged already. I told a little fib in rejoinder, and though I haven't seen the girl act, I pretended she had declaimed me a poem—which she really rendered at an earlier festival of Liszt's—and thereby given me a favourable opinion of her talent : I thought I might allow myself this fib, as Liszt had assured me she recited that poem quite exceptionally finely and feelingly. That seemed to shake Laube a little. I hope to be able to return to the charge another day, and heartily wish to be of some use to the girl and family.—

Please don't forget to pay a call on Regierungsrath Franz Müller (who visited us at Zurich, you know, with his wife). He's fabulously attached to me, and both of them will certainly do all they can to make your Weimar stay agreeable. Give my very kind regards to these little people too, and thank him again in my name for the delicate, if distressing consideration he shewed me in holding rigorously aloof at last, no doubt because he saw I needed rest. Greet Musikdirektor Lassen also for me ; he is a very excellent, refined, and cultivated man.—

Your expecting to make your money last till mid-October much affects me : all the same, please count on a remittance from me even sooner.—

As for me, you may also set your mind at rest about the hair-combing * ; really I attend to that myself at

* Obviously employed by Minna in the metaphorical sense of " a dressing."—Tr,

present, since the barbers here aren't friseurs also, as
in Paris, where one can't get shaved without having
one's head dressed for the same money.   I am delighted
to see you are in humour enough to adorn your letters
to me with such admonitions.   For the rest, I am really
much troubled by my stay in Vienna turning out far
more expensive at present than I had presumed ; and what
is chiefly to blame for this, is the highly inconvenient
circumstance that my singers are scattered all over the
country, causing me a wicked outlay on conveyances etc.
Neither have I any regular meals [provided me], and for
the moment at least I'm saving nothing but the cost
of lodgings : if I could accept invitations to the country,
it would be another matter.   Still, I hope for some relief
with the approach of autumn, especially when everybody
is in town again.—My host, Dr. Standthartner, has gone
to join his family at Salzburg ; I'm quite alone in his
abode now.   *Tausig* and *Cornelius* haven't come back
to Vienna yet, so I'm happily protected for the present
from the injurious influence of too youthful company on
my views of life and general morals ; tho' I hope to
expose my weak mind as little as possible to such con-
tamination even later.—

Ander is gradually improving ; he expects to make
his reappearance the middle of this month ; meanwhile I
have begun coaching him, and thereby gained a little
peace of mind myself.   He is very devoted to me, and
I haven't the smallest ground to doubt his zeal ; added
to which, he's a really fine fellow.   Certainly, he was so
improvident as to transfer the half of his salary for a
number of years to save a brother in military service from
being cashiered on account of an embezzlement of 20,000
gulden ; he has also been having a sister educated as a

singer at great expense, and given shelter to his father,—
which has saddled him with a fairly heavy establishment ;
and the worst of it is, that during 5 whole quarters,
having lost his voice through a sham cure, he had to
forfeit one half of his salary because he couldn't sing,
whilst the other half was ceded to his brother's creditors.
All this, as I perceive from your communications, has
given him the appearance of a reprobate in people's eyes !
I am glad to take such a crying example, to disclose
to you once more the sorriness of popular judgments
on men, and hope it will make you more chary in future
of echoing the like vulgarities.— —

The Dustmann goes on diligently studying her part,
and already is almost quite at home in it ; so that she
is most brilliantly refuting per fact the kind verdict that
my new opera can't be learnt. I'm spending almost
the whole of my time now between Mödling (Ander) and
Hitzingen (Dustmann). The other preparations have
also been made as far as possible, and the middle of this
month I hope to be able to begin the regular and serious
practice. Therefore I deem the production quite possible
the commencement of November.—

At the magnificent, extremely tasteful and wonderfully
situated country-seat of the Counts Náko (to whom I
had been commended before by the Metternich) I entertained myself agreeably ; these people were among the
first in the higher aristocracy to declare themselves
enthusiastically for Lohengrin. I have taken a great
fancy to a young, highly-cultured Prince Lichtenstein.
At Metternich's also I have met a very respectable
company in my favour. They all believe and hope in
me, and I think I may tell myself I'm preparing my
new work under very good auspices.—Now let us see if

my good Baden Grand Duke can make his mind up also, and don't let our courage sink !

May the above console you in some measure, and also give you hope ! And so heartily accept my congratulations upon your birthday. I am enclosing a pair of photographs into which I've been betrayed here, that you may plainly remember your good Husband who, after many storms, still holds his head erect, you see !

Farewell, and be most fervently embraced

by   Thy

R.

214.

VIENNA, 17. *September* 1861.

MY GOOD MINNA,

You won't be surprised at my not having written you for so long, when I tell you that absolutely nothing has occurred to effect any change whatever in my situation.   Everything has remained so completely as it was, that it really needs great patience to wait on like this from day to day, from week to week, without seeing anything brought the least step forward or the awaited arrive ! That tells you all the history of my sadness, and what is weighing me seriously down.—Please realise that even to-day I'm only taking up my pen against my will, and merely writing you to prevent your being plunged into any other fears about me ; else I would gladly remain silent till I could tell you something a trifle satisfactory.—

Here I am leading such a useless life of waiting, that it often seems to me without an object ; and last week I already was next-door to despair over Ander's condition, which remained so uncertain that simply nothing could be settled. Really, I had to ask myself: What's to be done, if I must forgo a production of my new opera in Vienna this winter?—If a favourable decision of the Grand Duke had arrived of a sudden from Carlsruhe, I believe I should have started for there that instant, at least to set something in order. But everyone keeps silent there as well; which doesn't astonish me, for that matter, when I remember that much must doubtless first be pondered and arranged upon my patron's side, before he can let me have a definitive answer such as I desire. Moreover, he is certain not to be exactly at Carlsruhe just now, and that would temporarily complicate the legal path whereon alone he can decide my case as man of conscience.—

Half in despair I had already heard a new tenor whom the Director wanted to let make a début; he really had a very fine voice, but proved so terribly talentless, lazy and pitiful, notwithstanding his having sung at other theatres some years, that after one rehearsal I myself concurred with their not allowing him even to appear. Meanwhile the Court Intendant had insisted on Ander's condition being submitted to an official medical inquiry, to ascertain whether he would be in a position to study a new fatiguing part this winter and at the same time fulfil his obligations in the repertory.—Luckily Laube, who sets great store by Ander, had already re-inspired me with courage: he knew Ander, he said, and he had been much worse than that before, yet against all expectation he had always rapidly and completely recovered in the end. And now the medical report has revived Ander's own courage and dispelled his hypochondria: the first physicians here have examined him carefully, and given him—or rather the Intendance—

the certificate that he is suffering from quite an ordinary hoarseness, which is merely not completely got rid of yet, but may easily have vanished entirely within a week. So Ander also—whose nervousness had made him really imagine he was in for quite losing his voice— is suddenly on his mettle again ; he will remove to town at last next Saturday, and with the first of October, they now say, the rehearsals of Tristan are to begin in earnest. God give his blessing ! My heart is still heavy enough, and declines to brace itself as yet to any good belief ; only, the affair has returned to a point where I dare not break off anything, but must patiently just—wait ! !—

Naturally we don't entirely trust the fresh hope set on Ander yet, and the Director is indefatigable in his look-out for a new tenor. Thus I was invited by him at short notice to accompany him to Frankfort the day before yesterday, there to hear as Masaniello on Sunday [15th or 22nd ?] a Herr Richard who had been recommended to him as good. I telegraphed to Schmidt, but he hadn't heard the man himself yet. Besides him there is further in prospect a superlative tenor, a German, who lately made a furore at the Italian Opera in Madrid under the name of Morini, and is said to be one of the very best in every respect. So Salvi [Director] is off, to go on from Frankfort to Paris, where he thinks of coming to terms with Morini (Schrumpf). He much wanted to have me with him ; but honestly, the proposal was too much exertion for me, and in particular it wasn't quite clear to me whether I was to travel at my own or the theatre's expense ; wherefore I stayed behind, unfortunately having also lost all faith in something decent.

Remarkably enough, however, I could almost have repented my decision to stay behind. For, on the very same day I was asked by telegram from Paris whether I would give my consent to Roger's singing Tannhäuser's scene from the 3rd act at the Opéra comique next Tuesday. I telegraphed back that I left the decision to Truinet and Flaxland [Paris publisher]; but I also wrote to Roger himself, and committed everything to his judgment and responsibility. Certainly I might have been able to see to this performance turning out at least correct; but Lord knows, on the other hand, it struck me as so idiotic to treat the thing as of importance enough to be tumbling head over heels into Paris myself for it. One has become so circumspect and cold, that one thinks nothing worth great exertions and sacrifices any longer.—Otherwise I have no tidings from Paris at all; merely I've learnt that the Flying Dutchman has been deposited at the *Théâtre lyrique* (?). I am expecting an answer from Truinet.—I have made the acquaintance here, however, of a Herr Marchesi, an Italian, who is quite bent on translating Rienzi into Italian and being the first to produce it in Paris, at the Italian Opera. As Paris is his actual home, and he is very well known there, I am giving him free scope for the present, and shall wait and see what may come of it.—

There you have a précis of my last events: the upshot, as you see, is:—Uncertainty, Waiting,—Trial of Patience!!—Add to it, Nothing ever coming off: answer from Coburg, "Regret inability to give Lohengrin this winter"; and so it goes on. To enliven the proceedings, fresh effronteries and bothers from the side of the lamented Meser's worthy Dresden successor regarding the Paris edition, occasioning me constant agreeable correspondence etc. again. So you may ima- gine how blissful and bubbling I am, and how I've heart for nothing, not even for excursions into the country, to which I'm frequently invited !

Whilst *I'm* in such deadly uncertainty, my only pleasure is your feeling tolerably well for the moment. Your accounts of the Wartburg gave me great delight ; I'm always glad to hear that sort of thing from you ! So take your walks at ease in the beautiful park, and look on Weimar as a soothing after-cure, since the cure itself so ill agreed with you, which I heartily regret.   I thoroughly approve of your intention to consult our good Pusinelli again about your malady directly after ; nay, I thank you with all my heart for having hit upon this good idea, so reassuring to myself as well.   In that way, too, your Dresden visit will have a very apt ground in the eyes of the world, and I may hope the place itself will best assist you to endure the uncertain time of expectation we both are now going through.   (I wrote to Pusinelli immediately upon receipt of news of the bereavement.)   But I can't say much more to-day even about *yourself*, as I unfortunately am so powerless to interpose with any safety in your situation,—which, believe me, is no small grief to me.   Yet do not doubt, my good Mutz, that every atom of your news appeals to me most keenly, and I always feel somewhat comforted and cheered when I can gather that you at least are feeling fairly for the moment.   How glad and happy it would make me, if I soon could tell you something really good and satisfactory.   Indeed I *hope to ! !*—

So please be content with the little I bring you to-day, and console yourself in all adversity with the thought of your husband, who in truth has still more troubles to put up with ! Farewell; write again soon, and accept a thousand heartfelt greetings.

Thy R.

(You are right about Lulu, as always and in everything ! So: entirely of your opinion !—)

(I am eternally plagued with colds and catarrhs here ! !)

215.

VIENNA, 26. *September* 1861.
Kaiserin Elisabeth. Weihburg Gasse.

MY GOOD MINNA,

I have moved out, had to pack and unpack everything once more, and got terribly cross with it this time ! My host's family will return to their abode in a day or two ; I hunted for a furnished lodging—lost hours and days over it—found nothing in needful proximity to the theatre, and finally struck up friendship with the landlord of the hotel named above, who is an art-enthusiast, constantly harbours famous musicians, and has let me have a big parlour with bedroom on the 3rd floor, looking over the court, for the same terms as a private furnished lodging (all of which are dear enough !). So I'll here await the consummation of my Vienna fortunes.

Those—God be praised !—are gradually assuming a rather propitious aspect. *Ander* has come back to town, and will reappear in a week. He boasts that his voice has grown better and clearer than ever ; whilst he is as full of zeal for Tristan as before. Moreover, the Director has also returned from his travels : he really has engaged the tenor Morini. I saw the latter yesterday ; he's a very handsome man, and is said to have a great success.

In Paris the *Théâtre lyrique* was just wishing to engage him, for—Tannhäuser; only he doesn't want to sing French, but to revert to his mother-tongue. *He*, too, will soon appear here, and then we shall have two first tenors of the purest water, with whom there'll be a chance of doing something.—So—my heart is considerably lightened on that score at any rate, and the only thing I have to bewail is the long delay and the loss of a hospitable house that eased my so protracted sojourn in Vienna. I seem doomed to have everything fall out incredibly hard now; God knows when Luck will smile on me a little once again!

From Paris I've received the oddest tidings. The only person who has written me, is our good Truinet. It turns out to have been a Benefit for Roger, at which he is said to have sung and acted the Tannhäuser scene from the last act quite transportingly: the act began with the Star of Evening (sung by Troy), all in costume and full scenery; before it came the overture. Truinet merely says that everything was very warmly applauded, and not a trace of opposition displayed. In Lorbac's Journal it is further stated that Roger was interrupted four times over by fanatical applause, and the only difficulty is how to give it oftener, as certain statutes strictly forbid the Director [to present] translations. Two days afterwards, so I read in the papers, there was a repetition. Roger is said to be behaving quite charmingly, and I confess I feel inclined to leave the thing entirely in his hands. At any rate he has deserved extremely well of me, and the results of this revival, however curious in itself, may be of great importance. This adventure with the work is most remarkable. I'm waiting eagerly for further accounts, and have written Gasperini to-day.—I

couldn't help laughing at a letter of the Princess Metternich, who wrote me a few days since, from her Castle
Königswart in Bohemia, exulting over the éclatant success
of Tannhäuser at the Opéra comique which its director
had just announced to her by telegram. So the rascal
had briefly made her believe the whole of Tannhäuser had
been performed. I had to undeceive her.—The Metternichs will be returning to Vienna for a time in the second
half of October, when I shall see if I cannot arrive at
something decent through them. A post that would suit
me famously has been vacant here for years : that of an
Imper. Court-composer with 4000 gulden pay, and nothing
to do for it but personally conduct one's compositions.
That keeps running in my head now, particularly that
such a berth is nothing new here, and would therefore
only need to be filled up again. By God, a thing like
that might just as well come my way.—

No answer yet from Carlsruhe ; which is not a bad
sign to me. Moreover, I've seen in the papers that both
the Highnesses have been continually away travelling,
and only quite recently returned to Carlsruhe. What a
deal of time everybody takes, to be sure, especially if one
wants anything !—

In a few days, good Mutz, you will receive at least
100 thaler direct from Berlin, to go on with. It came
very pat that a couple more performances of my operas
have taken place this month there. As I didn't want
to let you wait till mid-October, I have asked Bülow to
obtain payment for them at once. By the end of next
month there'll be more at your disposal, as I really must
get myself at least paid an advance on my fee here.
(People are much astonished at my not having asked for
the whole of it long ago !)

So we poor folk will take a little breath again ! Ah
God, I need it ; I can't tell you how depressed I've been
of late. Now just you give me the delight of hearing
something good about your health ; look Pusinelli up, and
leave everything else to take care of itself. I really fancy
things will come to a good and relieving issue in course
of this winter.

Liszt is going to the Olliviers, and perhaps to Athens.
His marriage seems to have fallen through. He hasn't
written me, only I've heard it from others.—With the
Pohls you may very well consort : we're charmant friends ;
greet both of them. It's quite desperate, your having
even heard of the child's-games at Tieffurth : Liszt
thought fit to romp about ; so I believed I mustn't
appear stiff, and at least behaved as if I were joining in.
Pardon ! But then you know how often I have had to
entertain my tiresome guests before with sky-larking and
standing on my head : it seems to be my lot !—Now
fare splendidly well ; hope, trust, and—hold dear

Thy

GOOD HUSBAND.

Please don't forget the story about Jacquot !—

216.

VIENNA, 16. *October* 1861.

DEAR MINNA,

I really must write you at last, just to let you
hear something of me again before your departure from
Weimar, but—without being able to give you the smallest
good news ! That sounds sad—and is so, too ! I am
not to be blamed if I see things very black now, and ask
myself how it's all to turn out, and whether I really must

die outright before people arrive at an inkling of what
they ought to do for one, to conserve themselves a force
like mine !—Enough : from nowhere, nowhere have I
as much as a vestige of news ; not a cock crows after me.
Merely the Frommann has answered me, that she wrote
to the Grand Duchess immediately on learning my wish.
(I am really afraid of that Devrient now : to me it's as
if he were doing his utmost to keep me away from there !)
I wrote to Seebach several days ago : it certainly is of
moment that the Dresden question should be completely
disposed of as quickly as possible.—

The worst of it, unfortunately, is that I have had
to make up my mind to forgo a commencement of the
rehearsals for Tristan for the present. You may imagine
the mood I'm in ! It won't and won't come right with
Ander yet : first he was to have appeared at the beginning
of this month ; now he hopes to have got that length,
perhaps, by the beginning of November ! The truth is,
as soon as he has sung a high note a few times in
succession he grows hoarse at once. In any case his
vocal chords are much relaxed, and everybody fears that,
even if he does recover for a time now, it won't last long
with him ; he will never have much staying power again.
The management has really shewn me the greatest consideration hitherto, and not allowed anything else to be
taken in hand ; but at last I've had to put an end myself
to this objectionably uncertain, nay, impossible situation,
and so I've brought about the following arrangement :
The rehearsals of Tristan will begin the *first of January*.
If Ander by then hasn't sung all his parts with full vigour
again for the whole month of December, neither can he
take that of Tristan this winter, consequently the new
tenor *Morini* will have to sing it. *The latter* will make

his first appearance the 25th inst., and sing three different rôles in quick succession ;—my and all our hopes of him run very high. He is a Strassburger, and has spoken German from his childhood ; but as he has only sung French hitherto, or rather Italian, he has to learn up every part again in German. So far, he has had a success here through his good looks and educated, elegant manners ; he is thoroughly musical, and yesterday went all through the Tristan with me, which lies well within the compass of his voice, so that I shall have to alter nothing in it for him, as for Ander. I shall wait for his 3 débuts, however, to be quite sure of my affair. I confess that if it comes to that, and this robust young man (aged 28) with his broad chest, strong voice, perfect vocalisation, impassioned delivery and acting (just because he has no need to spare himself), sings my new opera's difficult part in lieu of the half-invalid Ander,—in the end I shall have to regard it as a piece of good fortune. It would never have come to this—this costly engagement of a tenor previously unknown to all of us—if *Ander* hadn't fallen ill ; and again, the latter wouldn't have strictly contented me, whereas the former has far more of the right stuff for it. Consequently I almost might call it a stroke of good luck, if only my whole situation were such that I lightly could bear such a postponement. If my Tristan had come out the beginning of October—as intended—what different chances I should have had for this winter in Germany ! All that is now set back another year : how hard it makes everything for me again ! !—

In any case I don't care to spend those two months, November and December, here. I wrote to Paris at once, to ask if anything were in the wind there, and whether my presence might help my affairs ; I'm awaiting an

answer. Anyhow the Opéra comique has its mind fixed
on Tannhäuser still ; Roger is engaged for it : only,
I also know that great difficulties confront it. I may
soon have an answer, too, touching Rienzi (Italiens) and
flieg. Holländer (lyrique).—Finally, I also believe it will
be needful to present myself in Berlin before long : the
Frommann has put me up to a good idea about the
tantième, whilst I believe I shall do well to remove
sundry prejudices from Hülsen's mind through my
personal acquaintance. Consequently I shall try to turn
the time to good advantage.—

You will receive the 100 rth. in full from Berlin in a
day or two ; all the same, Bülow was wrongly informed
when they told him at first there were 130 odd thaler
lying ready for me. With the great and touching
economy you are shewing me, I hope this money will
be sufficient to take you to Dresden. Thereafter I shall
see to more ; rely on me !—

You may well conceive that you delighted me uncommonly by the news of your improvement ; I give
your Weimar doctor, even tho' he is a homœopath, my
greatest thanks !—Your being so pleased with Weimar
in general, has given me no less food for thought. Have
a look at Dresden, and see how *that* pleases you again
now : in any case it oughtn't to be too long before
you set up house again with the furniture. For my
own part, I remain firmly resolved not to embark on
a definitive setting up and settling down until I've
arrived at a sufficient fixed income. Should that delay
too long, it really would be more advisable that we should
let the furniture all come to you ; you would select from
it whatever could be got into a smallish *logis* (with only 1
room for me) and meanwhile stow the rest away. Exactly

as you feel disposed ; and if it pleases you, I'll vote for Weimar too.——

Greet the Regierungsrath Müllers, Pohls, and so forth. I know *nothing at all* of Liszt.—So soon as anything good occurs to me, I'll despatch you a courier at once. Now look after yourself as well as you can, hold good Jacquot in honour, remain on the high road to health, and love

Thy

Husband

in spite of all.

Adieu !   Most heartfelt greetings !

(Kaiserin Elizabeth.)

217.
VIENNA, 19. *October*, 1861.

MY DEAR MINNA,

You are tormenting yourself to no purpose, I assure you ! Your letter, indeed, is meant too seriously for me to dispose of it with so brief a rejoinder ; yet— believe me—with the best endeavour to enlighten you, I shall be unable to do much more than amplify that You are tormenting yourself to no purpose ! Among all the incidents and declarations of that troublous time you continually abide by *some* alone, forget their con- nection and whatever else was milder and more reassuring, and go on weaving from the most defective recollections a veil through which, to your self-torture, you look un- clearly and erroneously upon events which thus are bound for ever to appear to you in a desperate light. I re- cognised long, long ago that it must ever stay impossible to provide you the true light on those relations ; I also admit that such passionate excesses then took place on every side, that all self-possession tottered ; neither

will I defend myself against having lost my own head
at times. It was just because of this, that an end had
to be made then, to obviate renewal of the conflicts. To
be sure, my good Minna, *you* find an excuse for all your
past faults, alike for breaking open that letter which
was to make you so unhappy, as also for your having paid
that fatal call, against my reasoned and solemn entreaties,
which was to deprive me of my Asyl and make both of
us homeless for long—who knows for how long?—Still,
I know the uncontrollable nature of a woman's heart :
discretion in such things is beyond it. —

Now, the serious effect on our future has been that it
never became possible for me really to enlighten you, even
by letter thereafter, on the character of that relation ; just
as I perceive from your letter afresh that it will be impossible to-day once more. Consequently I felt that if we
were to come together and live together again, one chief
and fundamental bargain must be struck between us :
never and in no way to refer to that relation or those events.
In strict observance of that bargain lay the only possibility
of our dwelling together in peace : simply to *make that
possible*, by no means to have laid down which of us
was in the right or wrong, I was compelled to insist
on that bargain. So, after we had come together again,
as soon as you shewed even a sign of infringing that
bargain, I was beside myself, for I knew that an understanding was impossible and all depended on our greatest
mutual discretion. You are unlikely to remember how
often your feelings got the better of you, and betrayed
you into openly breaking our bargain. I soon had
to recognise that I had demanded too much of so acutely
suffering a woman's-heart, and could only deplore your
embittering thereby your own life in particular. On the

other hand I still hoped to be able to carry out my
fixed resolve, namely, as often as you should shew an
inclination to infringe our bargain, to meet you with
the most unruffled calm and silence. That I was unable
to carry out this resolution at all times, and in the long
run less and less, is undoubtedly regrettable. When I
credited myself with the strength for it, I certainly
counted on a quiet, less troubled and agitating life on
my side ; but it is with positive dread I look back on
that Parisian reign of terror we lived through a second
time, when trouble, care, annoyance, exertions and sufferings of every kind ultimately brought me into such a
wretched state of over-excitement, that I only wonder how
I survived it at all without losing my self-command
entirely. And could anything worse have been added to
the numberless worries I had to experience every day,
than these untimely reminiscences of earlier events eternally misunderstood by you ? No matter how erroneous
I deemed your whole idea of that relation, no matter
how conscious I was that everything had really been quite
different, infinitely more tranquil and seemly than your
imagination depicted : the faintest taunt, the slightest
allusion on your side—in the tortured condition I already
was in then—was bound to lash me into a fury at last.
Your refusing to understand this, your constantly insisting
on seeing in those violent outbursts of mine only the
explosion of a suppressed hatred of yourself, or ardent
passion for another,—please reflect—could only make me
still more furious ; so that death at such moments must
really seem preferable—there being no cure in sight
for the calamity, confusion heaped upon confusion. It
was for *that very reason* I had made up my mind always
to meet you in such cases with silence and calm ; and the

mere fact of my fate in Paris having been so woful
and perverse again that, everlastingly upon the rack,
I could not keep my self-control, and again it came to
such dreadful useless scenes,—it is just *this* that teaches
me prudence for the future.——

How full of the most mistaken views of that relation
you still *remain*, I see quite plainly from your letter
once more. It has become a fixed idea with you, that
I am longing to possess another woman, and hate and
often have treated you unkindly because you stand in the
way of my reaching my goal. That, after those atrocious
rumours which compromised the honour of a whole family,
and suggested God knows what criminal scenes ; that
after all this I won the full, devoted friendship of a
husband who had been dishonoured by those rumours
in the eyes of all the world ; not only won, but lastingly
ensured it to myself for ever—and *how*, by what behaviour
I effected this, the grappling to me of that man's completest friendly confidence,—you take no count of that
at all, do not think it advisable to ask yourself *what* must
have occurred here, *what* well-founded opinion this husband
must have formed of myself and my relations to his wife,
to be able to receive me tranquilly into his house and let
me hospitably rest beneath his roof ! Can you consider
me capable of taking advantage of a hospitality open
to me at all times under such conditions and convictions,
of profiting by the fullest domestic confidence to woo this
husband's wife ? Tell me, Minna, is it not a perfect
maniac's dream that stands before you ? From my
relation cemented with her husband *after* those events
[*cf.* letters 169 and 192] can you draw no conclusions as to the
character of my relations with that lady herself ? If
passion ever mingled in an originally delicate and pure

relation—which, to my tristful regret, I cannot deny—can you not conclude from the fact of this relation's having at last so shaped itself, after such calumnious assaults, that he who had been so wounded by them found his reassuring place in it as third—cannot you conclude from this into what paths that relation was reconducted,—nay, can you find fault with its profoundly grieving me to see you bent on excluding yourself therefrom—as fourth—for ever? I can't conquer your obstinate determination to remain entirely shut out (through your persistently regarding that relation in a false light), and have given up all attempt to do so. Only, your blindness will never induce me, merely to humour your hallucination, to break off my intimate communion with that family, who—husband as well as wife—are attached to me by unshakable friendship : it would simply amount to an admission that your false ideas were true. Consequently I have also made up my mind once for all, that —if you do not alter your opinion—at least you shall place no obstacles in the way of my intercourse with them ; under which I necessarily include your refraining from all comment on, nay, any allusion to those relations ; for your continued mistrust is an offensive insult, which I cannot permit without making myself a partner in that insult.—Wherefore, complete silence on your side, total ignoring ! Not because it concerns anything doubtful, or anything suspicious, but because you either won't or cannot recognise it *as it is*.

Will you be able to do and keep to that in future—for your own peace of mind ? ?—In spite of the certainty of your disputing your not having already done so hitherto, I know from the experiences of these latter years that neither will it be completely possible to you in the future.

Be sure, I only deplore and am angry with you for it because you give *yourself* such needless pain ! As I am well aware of what I owe you on the other side, and that upon me rests the profound obligation to provide for your tranquillity, your utmost possible comfort ; and as even the opinion of truly well-wishing mutual friends cannot persuade me to seek in a permanent separation the best appeasement for you : so nothing afflicts me so much as the nonplus in which I find myself regarding your future. Indeed, Minna, I'm fond of you; I am immensely sorry for you, chiefly because you surrender yourself to such false notions about me. I myself would fain contribute to your calming, and not even yet will I abandon the hope of preparing for you by my side that care-free bright old age you've earned so well : you ought to be convinced that all I ask is rest and peace, not any sort or kind of fresh possession. Only : how is that to be made possible to me ? The experiences of our last Paris sojourn have shewn me how little I can depend on myself, on my best and calmest resolutions, so soon as to the hidden inner discord are added the intense excitements of a tempestuous outer situation often filled with cares to the despairing point. Fully conscious of my own best will ever to treat you tranquilly and kindly, no doubt I *can* imagine well enough how we two might rub along quite capitally in course of time, and comparatively enjoy our life quite comfortably ; but only on condition that my livelihood were thoroughly ensured to me, that a definitive settlement in some pleasant spot, where I might find suitable occupation and be guaranteed a completely sufficient income, were placed at my disposal once for all.—Should I attain this—and I'm working for it with all my might (for my own thriving needs it also)—I should be the most heartless of men if, after so many storms and troubles, I didn't offer you, poor much-tried Wife, to share that longed-for haven ; why, I should call to you with heartfelt joy : Come, dear old girl, let's make ourselves a little snug at last !—And surely, I've no doubt of it, contentment, peace and happiness—after so many sore experiences—would not then keep away. What satisfaction, what genuine pleasure to me, to be able at last to offer you that ! My old good-humour, my love of home-comforts, would return to me : if you had a fit of the blues again, and the old fudge began its humming in your head,—I should simply let you quietly come round, until you thoroughly got rid of it at last !—

So—let that be a bargain ; perhaps I soon shall be able to offer it you !

But for the present, my good Wife !—do help me bear this present *misery !* Take a good look at my position, and see how, with all the terrible cares and worries that are almost crushing me, you do very wrong to conjure up such bootless torments for yourself and me as—with however good intention—you now have done again. Consider how things stand with me ! Not one of my endeavours for a fixed appointment has met the smallest notice yet : an ordinary Kapellmeister's post would be the death of me. My older operas have gone the round : with my new works I stumble on all but insuperable difficulties. With my new works I've sped far —far ahead of my age and what our theatres can execute. Carlsruhe has already been of harm to Tristan : my enemies spread gloatingly abroad, "My best score, in sooth, but unperformable." I come to Vienna : Ander ill : at last it turns out that the whole of this winter he can hardly be reckoned on. This fresh misfortune is seized, in turn, to bring the opera's unperformableness once more upon the carpet. The new tenor Morini, to whose débuts I'm looking forward, has first to learn up every opera afresh with the German text : if he's to be of any use to the repertory, it will be difficult to hand him over to a new opera for 2 months in the middle of winter; I have to accustom myself to the idea of not expecting the production before the autumn of next year. Under such circumstances, irresolution prevails even in the management : it comes hard to me to claim a big fee, though I also do not want to prejudice myself in any way. To get up Tannhäuser and Lohengrin anew, and thereby direct attention to my exploits as conductor (which might easily have led to an appointment as General Music-Director), has also proved impossible. So that I can do nothing—nothing for myself in Vienna, for the moment. And how does it stand elsewhere?

Not a creature asks for me ; I absolutely have to begin from the beginning again. Nowhere is a need felt for my art, and the times in general are very unpropitious to artistic interests. I mean to go to Berlin and see what sort of a personal impression I can make there. But what to hope? Very little. Nothing encouraging from Paris. The director of the *théâtre lyrique* an undecided, faint-hearted man, eternally pursued by money troubles. At the *Opéra comique* all the statutes against Tannhäuser : Roger was only allowed to bring off his performance *once*. There is talk of Perrin again, and a new theatre under him : *Rienzi*— distant future. Everything problematic for the moment ; through my departure from Paris everything dried up that I might have expected in the way of succour.

That—poor Mutzi—is my outer situation, truly

helpless and desperate.—And how do you imagine it
stands with my inner? For years again torn from my
works [*Ring*], which alone could have kept me on end:
everything I might work at, had I still the least heart
for it, bound to strike me as chimerical. How produce
it, in this miserable condition of our opera-houses? I
feel it deep within me—if things continue thus, I'm
done for; I've hope or trust in nothing more. That
makes me bitter; nor is chagrin upon chagrin spared
me. Often I say to myself: Ah, couldst thou only
vanish altogether from the world!—Myself I seriously
see that if there still is any chance for my artistic future,
the only way to give it a bottom would be for me to
be able to concern myself permanently again with the
charge of a theatre. For that, however, I need the very
post for which I'm striving, but of which I still have
not the faintest prospect; not for a year can I look for
anything from Vienna. How preserve patience, then?
How keep up pluck and heart for so eternally hampered
a life?—

Ah! I could continue that tale by the hour, and
yet not exhaust all the grounds of my, I might almost
say, desperate mood. True, I still keep my head above
water; I'm neglecting nothing that might be of use to
me in any way. Not long ago I wrote to Seebach: the
amnesty, the *amnesty* is of far too great weight. Yesterday I also wrote to Pourtalès again. I mean folk at
least to know how forsaken I am, that if I should really
go under, they mayn't say they knew nothing about
it!—

Now what, poor Wife, can I offer you in such a
doleful situation, with such a doleful conscience?—For
God's sake do not make my heart still heavier!—Rest

assured I don't lose sight of care for you : I hope to
effect something in Berlin that may tend to your relief
as well. That's where I intend going next. Whether
to Paris again after that, must depend on my news.
If Tristan should come off this winter in Vienna after
all (with Morini), I should regard it as a great stroke
of luck, which certainly might have weighty consequences. But—everything is so at sixes and sevens,
and all one can do is just to try and eat one's way
through from day to day.—*Mighty fine auspices for a
silver wedding !*—Ah, my child, it's there that lies my
heart-ache ! I almost think we should do right to ignore
that day this year completely ; Fate is cruelly adverse,
you see. However, there's still a little time twixt this
and then : possibly something good may turn up ! If
that's the case, we'll try to celebrate it quietly after
all. Presumably I shan't be far from you about that
date :—we'll see. But—for Heaven's sake don't multiply
real trouble with imaginary ! Of a truth we've enough :
I truly can say nothing else !—

So fare as well as you can for to-day ; and—let Fate
determine as it may—I implore you, keep silent, completely silent on all that ! You seem doomed to continue
in darkness about it for ever !

Once more, farewell—and be good to Thy

HUSBAND R.

[*Between this and no.* 218 *there clearly came at least one missing
letter. Wagner did not go to Berlin, as intended, but on the* 26th *of
October a semi-private rehearsal of parts of* Tristan (*without a tenor*)
*was held in the Vienna opera-house. About a fortnight later he paid
a flying visit to the Wesendoncks in Venice—see those sad "resigned"
letters* 124 *and* 125 *to* Mathilde—*returning to Vienna the* 13th *November.*
—Tr.]

218.

VIENNA, 13. *November* 1861.

DEAR MINNA,

Last Wednesday [6th] my friend Dr. Standthartner (as deputy physician in ordinary) was summoned in haste by the Empress to a consultation in Venice ; as doctor and friend he insisted on my accompanying him, since I needed a change, some distraction, if I meant to hold out here. I returned this morning, and shall hope it has benefited me : at least I had no talking to do for a few days running, but only sights to see, which really did me good. For, after all it's a mere question of whether I can really hold out !——

I didn't reply to a certain portion of your last letter because I believed it agreeable to yourself as well to let the matter drop. For my part, I wish this emphatically, and *nothing in the world* shall induce me to return to it any more. That I don't reject your arguments with contempt, you might have judged by my having entered at such length into your first letter about it. I deeply regret not having pacified you, but am unequal to dilating thereon a second time. If you chose to read that as contempt, you would be doing very wrong.——

I forgot to answer your suggestion about *Prague* because I had something else to say, and it is useless to speak about things that can't be executed. For I have made very careful inquiry into the conditions there, and that through inhabitants who would much like me to come, and have found it generally confirmed that the Prague theatre is now beneath all criticism, and its director the most miserable creature ; even the orchestra is said to be vile. To furnish everything

brand-new there, is consequently bound to strike me
as more difficult than merely to procure a tenor here,
where I otherwise have everything and of the best.
You would have done better to infer from my silence
on this point that I recognised the plan as unfit, than
to think I disdained your advice. On the contrary,
I shall be thankful if you can give me good hints from
time to time.

Touching the stockings—pardon ! I've often thought
of them, but they always slipped my memory precisely
when I was writing to *you*. Be so good, then, as to
address them here at once ; for presumably I shall
remain here long enough, in any case, to be able to
expect them. From my heart I thank you for this
present.

Make my provisional excuses to Cecilie : when she
wrote me, I didn't exactly know if I should be coming
or not, so put it off. Since I firmly made up my mind
not to go to Berlin before they summon me, I've had
so much letter-writing etc. to do every day, that people
must excuse me if I do not come down on the nail
with a thing of less moment. Whoever reflects that I
daily not only have to experience disagreeables—i.e.
non-successes—but also to discuss them with each
person I meet, and therefore to repeat the selfsame disagreeable some 10 times every day, will understand
that it isn't much amusement to keep referring to it
by letter also. But there, who ever gives a thought to
how things look inside one ? !—Everyone believes that
he has first rights !—

To give you at least a clear idea, however, I'll tot
you up the following about my situation.

All our hopes of *Morini* hung on one sole thread,

as I've explained to you already. But in his second rôle too he has proved himself not the man they require here, and his engagement, projected on a most expensive scale, has fallen through. Taking a rapid survey of the situation, I offered the Director to bring off a starring of Tichatscheck ; as the latter didn't particularly please the Viennese once before, also is aging, he [the Dir.] wished me to write to Schnorr instead, and ask if he could get away for December, January and February. To-day Schnorr has answered me, that he *can't*. At the same time *Tichatscheck* writes to me : I gather from his letter that he's at liberty for 7 months (beginning with December) ; so I have just telegraphed to him at once, asking if he can and will come here the first 5 of them. If Tichatscheck makes this possible, I hope to induce the Director to engage him for that period ; it would be the *only* chance now open of still bringing out Tristan this winter, for I can't think of *Ander* any longer. Tichatscheck therefore has it in his hands alone, how my fortunes are to turn. You in Dresden will perhaps learn earlier than myself, then, how my undertaking stands. If Tichatscheck *fails* us, I must strike off a whole year again as lost.—I have also been pondering how to bear the dénouement last named. The only thing that can preserve me then, will be to take a new work—of lighter build—in hand at once. Metternich has offered me for that event a quiet undistracted retreat in his house.—

So we shall see !—

The Grand Duke of Baden has now written me : he sets forth very circumstantially and sensibly why he cannot comply with my wish.—

I have to proceed very warily with the management

here. I had already learnt that they're shabby in money-matters. I've succeeded, however, in retreating with full honours.

It is the Frommann's opinion that *only* Pourtalès can assist me to anything at Berlin in time.—

Under such circumstances, I've cast my eye on something which may provide me with the needful funds without requiring to ask favours of anyone. It is connected with the draft of a new and easier work, about which I do not wish to speak yet.—

I am able to send you 100 thaler again to-day, tho' ; I'll see to something more by the end of the year, that you may have a full 250 thr. quarterly [*ca* £150 p. a.]. Only give me the solitary pleasure of your soon coming to a rest : I still think the old Dresden plan the best, with the chamber for me, as I scarcely dare *hope* for a big appointment yet. But you—with your poor Jacquot—you must come to rest : it grieves me in my deepest soul to think. that I drag so much misery behind me for others ! As soon as you tell me you want to have the furniture at Dresden, I will find means to send it you and provide you with the where-withal for setting up : rely on that.—What you can contribute toward enabling me also to make a temporary stay again in Dresden, please do ! You'll find much pioneering done already ; I rely in this matter on Seebach's good heart.—

So, dear Minna, let the above suffice you for to-day. I'm rather done up, as I travelled all night ; also I found a deal of agitating business waiting for me, which had to be disposed of at once. But rest, composure—is so terribly wanted by myself as well ; *I*, too, already often suffer from protracted thumping of the heart, and the doctor tells me—as yourself—that all my various maladies arise from that one point alone, continual excitement and worry !—

So—best greetings to Jacquot, the last of the faithful, and keep him too at rest and out of commotion—: otherwise, I see it plainly, all three of us will come to grief soon.

Adieu !   With kindest love,

Thy

poor HUSBAND.

If I've forgotten anything again, please just remind me !

219.

VIENNA, 22. *November* 1861.

MY GOOD MINNA,

It gladdened me much to get your last letter yesterday !   Ah, God, how afraid I was again, and looking toward your news, as ever, in wavering suspense !   But you write me tranquilly and kindly : even Jacquot is merry again ; yourself, you have done with your roving at present, and are in the position to await further developments in a supportable state without fresh wanderings in front of you.   We may trust the permit will be granted to reside ; you are lodging in the house of an old friend, who will look after you in case of need ; you have old acquaintances in plenty, your seat in the theatre, and—above all—that good Pusinelli, whose orders you now can follow for some time without intermission !   God, my heart quite expands a bit, under it all ; for, to know that you're somewhat calm again, or at least in a state of equilibrium, is so essential to myself in turn, if *I'm* to carry through my next decision ; which

certainly will keep me at a distance from you for a while
again, but during whose execution I likewise hope to
find complete repose, and in its result the means of
becoming master of my own position.—So, what I have
already hinted to you shall now be carried out !—

What I have suffered here in Vienna, is not to be
described. Almost every week a fresh project to make
Tristan still feasible this winter : every week a fresh
disillusion. *Ander* discovered to be utterly shameful : a
thorough . . . wight, who has done me incredible harm
by unscrupulous chatter. Enough, as the Director and
everybody else at the theatre remained true to me, those
plans were conceived to import Schnorr or Tichatscheck
at once—whichever could get away the quickest : to
arrive at finality, the whole thing was conducted at last
per telegraph. Tichatscheck seems to think it quite
impossible to get out of his starring engagement [else-
where], even by paying damages ; so I finally had to
resign myself. It's now decided to engage Tichatscheck
for my operas next winter ; Salvi will come to Dresden
himself on Monday—for Rienzi—and conclude with T.—

The die accordingly is cast, and I have a full year
before me to—wait. The Grand Duke of Baden has
declined my request ; with Berlin, through fishing
enquiries of the Frommann and Pourtalès, I can arrive
at nothing ; Pourtalès got Hatzfeld to write me the other
day that Berlin wasn't ripe yet, I had better wait. The
only friendly token to occur to me has been Metternich's
cordial invitation to occupy a quiet little room with my
piano in his Paris Embassy hôtel. By itself even that
wouldn't have determined me ; but—I no longer can endure
this life, in which I'm quite dependent every day on outer
influences, and have relish for no occupation, not even

for reading ; I feel I shall come to utter grief if I don't
turn my hand to something that will snatch me altogether
for a year—this fresh year of waiting—from a world so
hostile to me. So the truly desperate nature of my
situation has inspired me with a capital plan. I'm
determined to give ear to nothing more, to abandon
Tristan and the rest of it for the nonce, shut myself
up in my room at the Austrian Embassy in Paris, and
write a new opera so constituted that it shall go the round
of all the German theatres next winter at one blow.
It will be something quite different from what I've ever
done before, neither requires a first-rate tenor nor a great
prima donna, but can be cast with ease by any operatic
company. The subject is highly original and thoroughly
merry, which *alone* makes it possible for me to engage in
it now, when a serious, sorrowful poem would do for me.
Content yourself also with these hints, dear Mutz, for
as soon as I conceived the first thought of this project
of rescue I solemnly swore to myself to tell *no one* a
word of it, but leave the whole world in completest
uncertainty about my plan ; which I fancy will be to
my advantage. There is only one person I have had
to tell ; the one without whose aid I cannot carry out
my plan : my new *publisher Schott*. He has just paid
me the needful advances to enable me to get away from
here, which—luckily !—has also made it possible for
me to refuse a single gulden from the local management.
(What a good thing that was, you may judge from the
hounds having nevertheless written in the papers—on
Ander's gossip—that I had received a *solatium* from the
management by way of forfeit ; which I've fortunately been
able to contradict as a mendacity.) But Schott himself is
pledged to preserve the fullest secrecy. Not before *July*

is the textbook to be sent out to all the theatres, and the
appearance of the full score announced for the beginning
of October. I am now on the point of binding myself
by a strict contract with Schott to deliver the finished
poem on the 1st of January, and a finished act of the
score every 3 months thereafter. Heaven grant that
nothing may interrupt me ! This time I hope for complete undisturbedness, to which you can contribute so
very much by constant good news of yourself. For the
rest, Schott must keep paying me the needful advances,
so that alike for the present, during work, and probably for another year after, I shall want money from
nobody. Consequently I have also written to the Frommann and the Grand Duchess, earnestly dissuading them
from any step to obtain me pecuniary relief in Berlin ;
everything of that sort would only turn out trivial,
and compromising to me now. On the other hand they
are both to do their best to extract for me the following
in course of time : a summons to conduct *Lohengrin*, a
reading to the Court, *commission* for the *Nibelungen*.
People must make acquaintance with my personal
abilities ; when all the rest will follow.—Accordingly
I leave them *time for that*—that's the chief thing, time
to reflect—whilst I shall be drawing all men's eyes to
me again by a new and uncommonly popular work.
What do you say to it ?

See, Mutz, so I'm taking the reins into my own
hand at last ; it was impossible to hold out any longer,
and everyone was regularly plotting for my downfall.
But I am going a step farther : if a few good tenors
don't turn up at last, I have another new subject in
store, a *more serious* one, for which I also need no heroic
tenor, but the principal rôle is high bass, which is to

be had everywhere, for instance quite excellently here
itself (Beck).   Then I shall write this work as well
[*Die Sieger?*], and then find out at last what I've effected.
Enough : without taking up works that at once afford
me pleasure and the possibility of their rapid circulation,
I should have succumbed now.—

Now then : help me yourself, Mutz !   Take a *thorough*
rest for this year, until next autumn—while I keep
myself shut up for work.   You shall lack nothing, be
entirely free from care, and have everything you wish.
As soon as agreeable to you, I'll get whatever furniture
you specify despatched from Paris ; so make yourself
comfortable, and set up provisional house for a year.
When I've finished my opera, I shall have a roving life
of it again, be obliged to go hither and thither, and
probably not get much rest myself awhile : we shall see
each other often ; you'll come when I produce my comic
opera—perhaps *at Munich* first, and wherever else it may
be.   But we won't take a fixed *habitation* for the *pair of
us* before I obtain a solid appointment with good salary ;
which won't and *cannot* fail to come—according to my
plan—for prudent and dignified waiting.—*Then*, my good
Minna,—on the day of entering our last *logis*, we then
will celebrate our *silver* and our *golden* wedding both
together, won't we ?   So—patience, patience to-day !
We shall be repaid for it.   No tears, then, no grumbling !
For to-day let us simply glide over it, to fix our eyes the
firmer on a certain goal !—Courage, courage !   You see
how it has returned to myself.   Peace to your heart !
Tend yourself, get strong and gentle !   All will come
right !   Many greetings and kisses from   Thy

good HUSBAND.

220.

DEAR. MINNA,

God, what an excited letter you poorest soul have written me again! Who would have ever expected it! That sleepless night explains much, it is true, and on the whole I must say I had fears for you on *that* day [the 24th, Silver wedding]; only, the letter previously received from you seemed just meant to reassure me about it. It was *that* which pleased me in it, after your earlier letter from Chemnitz, in which you complained so much of the unrest of travelling, had made me anxious. I was thinking of nothing else whatever when I lately wrote you that I always grew anxious if a letter took longer than usual; do banish all else from your head!—

On one point you are right: your having to receive the announcement of so late a Wiedersehen precisely now, was bound to depress you; I had no need to touch on that at present. Only, God knows, Mutz, just think of me, too, and the position I'm in! As if I could always keep my tongue tied, or always have calmness enough to smother up the seriousness and hardship of that situation. Indeed it's bad enough for me to have to regard an invitation such as Prince Metternich's as a kind of harbour of refuge to enable me simply to tide over a hard year of patience in front of me! It was no sugarplum, suddenly to have to decide on forgoing all my other plans for a whole year, and—as nothing save a new work could help me to survive that period—have to be glad that somebody had offered me the needful sanctuary where I could pass that evil season undisturbed, without direct *outlay* for lodging, board and firing.—To have thought of deciding on and carrying out a home for both of us *at once*, would have really been sheer folly, nay, impossible.   Hotel life, on the other hand, I could no longer have continued under any circumstances : I require much more than you, to tell the truth, and can only be rescued from very dear living through such an invitation.   Then, I was so glad to know that you would be able to pass this equally hard time for yourself—(ah ! I grant you that !)—at least in such similarly tolerable circumstances as you had described to me from Dresden.   I knew you'd have the best surroundings there—for such an evil time !— at least would be fairly at home—and that (under these sorry conditions !) was something of a consolation to me. On the other side, I was honest enough not to conceal from you that this acceptance of the Metternichs' hospitality was calculated for as long as my work's completion should demand.   The thought of my not even seeing you throughout that time indeed was gloomy to myself as well ; but it seemed to me a necessary consequence of my truly unparalleled fate !   And then—indeed, Mutz—I'm also bound to consider it good that you should likewise live exclusively for your repose, for your medical treatment, awhile now ; nay—before I come to a permanently better position, or at least am personally attuned to a better, calmer, less irritable mood—I should have accounted it a crime to urge you once more to a premature step of reunion that might simply renew the old mischiefs between us.

Consequently, my meaning was simply this :—My situation is perfectly hopeless till next winter ; I shall try to bear it through complete retirement and concentration of all my powers on a new work that is to provide me a great improvement in it : to *you* I cry— " Employ that time on your recovery and resting ; I can't assist you to that better, than by making an undisturbed life possible to you for that period."—With next autumn I then shall reappear, and in course of next winter I expect to settle my fate for good, in one way or other, and as result thereof to gain a definitive domicile. Then, by when you'll also have recovered— moving in, Silver and golden wedding at once! What person of common-sense, after a careful survey of my situation, will not rather admire, than blame my courage, my endurance, my firm adherence to the hope of a final good turning! Only regard it thus, and whatever is hard in it—for yourself as well—don't lay at *my* door; but rather reflect that I shall suffer under it as much as, perhaps more than you!—Great Heavens, do tell yourself that, and remember me too, and my tribulations!—

For that matter, this certainly does not exclude our seeing each other even earlier. As a rule I hate the life at spas, but if a spa is specially ordered you next Spring to which I can go also [i.e. not in Saxony], and where one can succeed in finding me a quiet lodging, no doubt it will be possible to arrange for me to complete my work there at your elbow. All that remains to be seen; I merely sketched you out the general plan to begin with.—

You made a correct guess, you shrewd Wife, with the Meistersinger. *But keep it to yourself now, do you hear? Not a word to any one* about it!—

Immediately on receipt of your letter to-day I *telegraphed* to Tichatscheck, telling him I would remain at Vienna for the rest of this week if he would come here at once. Did I do right?—True, I am longing to get away from here and to my work, but it has turned out that I may still devote a few days with advantage to the study of some books I can obtain from the Library here;

consequently, that would be no absolute waste of time.—
In any case, too, I can't start before Thursday [28th] ;
I'm so preoccupied to-day, that I cannot get to packing.—

So, if *Tichatscheck* still comes to me, you can write
me to Vienna at any rate once more ; which would give
me great joy, particularly if you let me off this time
the bruises I already feel on leg and arm. (God, what a
woman you are !)—If Tich. doesn't come, I shall write
you again before I leave, and you shall hear all particulars.—

I mean to write to Lüttichau as well, thanking him,
and begging him to give you that seat at the theatre
for the whole of your sojourn in Dresden.—

Now farewell ; it's to be hoped you will have passed
a better night since, and write another time by day !—
Child—Night is man's enemy : one should write to
nobody one's fond of then, but bear in silence what is
paining us, and pray the Redeemer for assuagement and
rest ! I've my nights, too, believe me !—

Two nights before the Wedding-day, however, I had
very pleasant dreams. Listen : 1. You received me in a
most comfortably furnished abode ; I recognised our own
old things, and said : See now, how good it was, that I
wouldn't have anything sold ; it's quite a pleasure now !
—2. I was a very young lad again, and heard my father
in the next room tell my mother : " Only think, our
Richard has won 7000 gulden ! " I reckoned it out
quickly in francs, went in, embraced my father, and was
congratulated by both my parents on the prize.—

Those dreams, I confess, have put me in somewhat
good humour. May it be the same with you ! You see,
my thoughts are really running on what we need.

So, farewell ! Add no new crotchets to the old !

Help me to bear, and console yourself with me ! The
very best and fairest wishes,

Thy

poor HUSBAND

R.

221.

VIENNA, 30. *November* 1861.

DEAREST MINNA,

If you had any idea how it goes with me ! Only
this instant can I tell you what is to become of me !
What has kept tossing me undecided to and fro, you
shall learn from my more circumstantial next letter.
I've only just made out for certain that I start to-day—
or tomorrow, should I be too late [for the train]—for
Mainz, and thence for Paris. Consequently it abides by
the plan last declared to you. Write me, if you'll be so
good, to Paris : 101 *Rue de Grenelle*

St. Germ. Paris

((that is : Austrian Embassy.))

Give me the pleasure of good news ; I need it, for my
pluck's below *zero*. Adieu, my poor good Wife !

Thy

poor, care-laden HUSBAND,

who is strictly all homeless and wretched.

222.

MAINZ, 3. *December* 1861.

DEAR MINNA,

I have been here since the day before yesterday,
and go on to Paris this evening.—I've brought off my
business with Schott fairly swimmingly, and tell you this
for your relief. Therefore I shall take my work in
hand directly, and thus expect to tide over the hard time

in front of me from my own resources and in full self-action. Give me your blessing on it!

For the rest, I've arranged to turn my footsteps hither *to the Rhine* at the beginning of summer and for the remainder of my work-time, if only to have the proof-correcting etc. more at hand. They will see to some *nice* summer abode for me, and if you don't need any special distant baths, we'll pass that time together. So—until then!—I can't help it! Adieu, good Mutz! Just these few lines in haste, to let you know something about me.

Madame Schott sends you kindest regards. Soon more from

Thy

good HUSBAND.

223.

PARIS, 8. *December* 1861.
19 *Quai Voltaire.*

Ach!!! Minna!!!!—If you only knew what lies behind that exclamation!—A quiet home-life!!—nothing beyond on this earth!—why should it not be granted me, of all men, who need it so much? Why must I wave off in despair each enticement to regain the needed prematurely, not to fall into still worse straits afresh?—But, everything must have an end: I shan't run short of patience!—So—to the point!—

My last few days in Vienna I did not know from morn to eve again what really to proceed with, or whither turn. However, I don't want to depict to you my psychic reactions, but simply the events.—I had announced to Metternich my advent, as he bade me when in Vienna, and everything was fixed for my departure. Then I get a telegram asking me to defer my journey to Paris awhile, a letter would follow. I read that as preliminary to a refusal, and supposed it had occurred on Pourtalès' instigation, as the latter is not in favour of my undertaking anything in Paris this winter (but not in Berlin either ! !) I confess, this assumption that the Metternichs had suddenly withdrawn their invitation made me extremely sad, because I struck myself forthwith as a person with whom absolutely no one would have anything to do. I couldn't remain in Vienna ; what to do at Berlin without jeopardising my whole future there ? Neither did I want anything else at present, than to be put up somewhere quietly and at my ease, to be able to turn out my new work.—So I wrote the Olliviers, asking if they could find me a quiet room in their house or its vicinity, with private board. In the first instance this was merely a try-on, in the hope of still teaching the Metternichs better manners.—But on the top of it came another letter from Schott, which suddenly set all my expectations of a prompt conclusion of the projected business tottering. In truth, I felt thoroughly wretched !—Then at last came Metternich's *letter*, and I discovered (I admit : to my great joy !) that I was mistaken in my supposition of a change in the Prince's mind. In the most friendly fashion he repeated to me that I should be extremely welcome, and could calmly work away in his house for as long as I pleased : only, in consequence of the sudden death of his mother-in-law, a near relative had just arrived who would remain for the month of December and occupy the apartment reserved for me ; but this would stand at my disposal from the 1st of January onward.—

So I decided after all—not to give up my *Hans Sachs*, but instantly proceed to Schott's at Mainz and set all in order personally. In that I succeeded, as I briefly notified you from Mainz. Schott consents to engrave the partitur straight off while I'm at work, and to make me the needful advances : he had already sent enough to Vienna to enable me to settle honourably all round, so that I didn't have to give myself the least away to any-body.—Wherefore I also decided to make direct for the place of my proposed longer stay. As I haven't to compose at first, but only to make the verses, I needed nothing but a small quiet room without piano, and wished to find it at once for those few weeks. Olliviers had nothing decent to recommend me ; so I have hired a small room for that brief time in a hôtel garni on the quay here (Hôtel Voltaire. Quai Voltaire 19.), and think of commencing my versifying tomorrow, God willing, so that I may meet my piano again at Metternich's the 1st of January and start the composition.—

Much other matter, e.g. my incredible deprivations, inconveniences etc., I reserve for laments by mouth : it will be abundant enough. For the present, just one point :—I mean to remain quite unnoticed in Paris, not to give myself the look of seeking something here this winter after arriving at nothing in Germany ; indeed, without Metternich's invitation and my resolve to do nothing but work in the greatest retirement, any idea of Paris would never have occurred to myself. I shall see no one but Nuitter and Gasperini (apart from my Ambassadors)—with whom I have bargained to deny my being here and say I'm in Italy or somewhere. I *shan't* go to that side of the Boulevards etc. *at all*, but remain upon this side of the Seine, take my promenades here—Luxemburg etc.—keep indoors all day, and work. That is my plan ; and my main prospect in all Paris is the good housing, convenient attendance and feeding, at the

Metternich hôtel. *Nevertheless* I have arranged for *Truinet* to spy out what's becoming of that theatre of Perrin's and so forth. As soon as any decisive step is taken, which often happens [of a sudden] here, he is to inform me at once, and I shall be on the spot to seize the opportunity.—

That's my plan. You perceive that visits to the Szemeres and such-like will not work in. Even the Olliviers won't see much of me.

But I'm thinking of the future also, and in that regard I must say the Rhine-land much attracted me this time. As it will also be of great assistance to the publishing of my new opera for me to be close at hand there, I have promised the Schotts, who very amiably put me up, to pass at least the 3 summer months, *July*, *August*, *September*, in that district. Themselves they will see where to find us a suitable summer abode in the Rheingau. I've also been thinking a little of Baden Baden, which pleased you so greatly the last time. When the time comes round, and if you care to, you might look about there for a dwelling for us, after all, where one could also get the furniture sent in at once. The latter plan would be peculiarly practical if a Berlin pension were secured me meanwhile, such a thing being already on the cards through mediation of the Grand Duchess of Baden. —So—there you have ideas for the future !—

In the meantime I've still to recover from the exquisite present. I confess I am a riddle to myself, what I endure, and yet keep regaining my courage and relish for things. I arrived here ill and with a shocking cold, in awful weather, so that I remained in bed the first day, the second in my room. I got your letter from the Embassy at once, however, and thank you for the Good luck you wish me.—Probably I shall write to Tichatscheck

also to-day.   You might give *Schnorr* a message from me ;
for he wrote me that his means were unequal to the third
act of Tristan, since he felt that not a note in it could
be altered.   Tell him really to have no scruples on this
last point, as I recognise myself that shortenings must be
made in that act ; I had already resolved on it, and would
let him know them presently.   Consequently, if Salvi
speaks to him, beg him not to talk about the part being
inexecutable on *his* side also : on the contrary, he may
rely on my putting it altogether right for him.—

Now write me soon again, best Mutz.   Make life easy
for yourself (and thereby for me as well !), and hope for a
silver and golden future !

Greet Jacquot, and love Thy poor

HUSBAND.

I shall write to Schott's about the stockings : kindest
thanks ! !—

224.

PARIS, 15. *December* 1861.
19. *Quai Voltaire.*

Best thanks, dear Minna, for your letter.   Even
without my assurances you no doubt will believe that
it did me much good to learn how well you're looking :
it lets me infer an improvement of your whole state of
health with certainty ; and that in turn revives my
never-flagging hope of a cosy, calm old age for both of
us.   In truth it is conceivable that, if only Health will
re-establish itself to some extent, the storms and trials
of life at last must render us so wise and pliant, that—
we finally should understand to prize the peace of an
agreeable home as if with doubled power of enjoyment.
At least—I have got so far myself as to prefer a fixed,

well-ordered home to any other conceivable stroke of
good fortune. Let us take good thought for it, and
sharpen our wits in advance to obviate all friction then,
and ensure ourselves peaceable intercourse. In the end
it's sure to come to pass !

Meanwhile I'm paying a terrible penalty in my own
life. I am no longer in a state to rough it : after so
often having housed oneself entirely to one's mind,
inconveniences and deprivations become extremely trying;
and how much time one wastes, before one can even
shake down ! When I read your letter yesterday
morning, the passage struck me where you say the S.
had told you on behalf of St. that he was expecting
me in his house. So listen !—In October, when I
already detected that things would go wrong with Vienna,
I wrote a friendly letter to St., foreshadowing the
possibility that I might take advantage awhile this
winter of the hospitality he lately had offered me again.
He promptly answered me that he was very sorry, but
he was expecting relatives, etc. I wrote you nothing
of it, as of so many other disagreeable experiences.—
Well, having to fend for myself here till the first of
January, not before when can I move to the Metternichs,
it occurred to me while reading your letter that I perhaps
might pass this fortnight more conveniently—and above
all, cheaper—if I really went to St. for it. So I made
off to him at once, expecting he would broach the subject
on my call (as he was supposed to have said so to the
S.). But, God preserve him, he listened very sympatheti-
cally to the story of my invitation to the Metternichs,
also of my lodging in a garni till the 1st of January,
but never rose ! So I took my leave, not knowing what
to make of the S. and her chatter, till I reflected that

this good lady is very fond of chattering, and at times may not be accurately informed.—

Certainly my presence in Paris hasn't remained such a secret, but I am sticking to it that I'm merely passing through. As I had a severe chill, I wanted wet-cloth rubbings given me, which I can only get done properly and comfortably at the hydro in the Rue de la Victoire (oh, that's another thing I once had so much handier !—). To cross the boulevard is tantamount to my being recognised by all Paris ; so I ran into that wretched E. as well : the creature wouldn't leave go of me, and insisted on my coming to dine one of these days. When I got home, however, I wrote her a little note to excuse me : I was ill from too much speaking, always did myself harm by my talking, and had made up my mind to go nowhere, for a long time yet, where I should have to talk. Thus I shook off that lady,—but I mean to pay a call on the S.'s some day.—

I have written to Schott's about your parcel, and may expect it now. Best of thanks in advance.—You make me most inquisitive about the big work you speak of so mysteriously : I hope it will come to daylight in our future establishment ! What you take this occasion for telling me about my under-rating of your [needle-] work in general—I swallow as an injustice done me.— At Christmas you'll receive a tiny present from myself, which is certain to amuse you. Guess what ? Jacquot will be equally delighted with it. The poor chap, by the way, must be terribly missing his cage !

—To repair an omission, I assure you that the tale about the laurel-wreath in Vienna was a pure invention : I didn't mention lies of that sort, or I should never know when to stop. Thus the Emperor of Austria is said to have sent a grand piano expressly to Venice, to boot, for me to play at a court-concert there on the Empress's birthday !—

It has seemed droll to be mixing with my Nürnberg Meistersingers here in Paris, opposite the Tuileries and Louvre ; I often have to laugh out loud, when I look up.

Here you have a small sample of my new verses : Hans Sachs is musing on the formless, free, and yet so stirring song with which the young cavalier had failed at the singing-trial, but won Sachs' heart : he says one cannot pick it up at all, just like the song of birds which everybody understands but can't note down, because it's something so entirely different from what humans sing : however that be—

> " Dem Vogel, der so süsse sang,
>   dem war der Schnabel hold gewachsen ;
>   ward auch den Meistern dabei bang,
>   der Sang gefiel doch wohl Hans Sachsen." *

Then [act iii] :

First the Marker has been plaguing him about his shoes,—then comes the young maiden also, and, annoyed with Sachs, in turn complains that her new shoes are pinching here and there, and so on.—Finally Sachs shews her that he knows where the shoe is pinching her, and admits her lover ;—then he complains : " hat man mit der Schuhmacherei nicht seine Noth !—

> " Wär' ich nicht noch Poet dazu
>   ich machte länger keine Schuh ! "

---

* I consider it quite needless to translate these lines, as they differ so very immaterially from the final form appearing in the textbooks.—Tr.

Enough of the sample,—you see the world I'm living in !   I thank God that I hit on this subject : it helps me through in every way now, whereas I should otherwise have downright not known what to do !—Now just you stay friends with me, too !   Continue with your looking well, and help me to bear ; just as I myself, or far or near, shall ever stand true by your side !—

Adieu, dear old girl !   All will come right in the end, indeed it will !   Patience !

Thy

loveliest HUSBAND.

Many greetings to acquaintances : above all to *Pusinelli !*

225.

PARIS, 21, *December* 1861.
19. *Quai Voltaire.*

DEAR MINNA,

True, I had been expecting a letter from yourself to-day, but must e'en write you without it, that you may be instructed in good time how to start getting something pretty played you on the Paris hurdy-gurdy upon Christmas Eve.   Accordingly I've written you out the necessary directions on the accompanying sheet ; you will soon find your way.—Agreeably to orders, the other small presents will likewise have been delivered to you in good time, I hope.   Pay nothing ; it is settled that I defray all that here.   May my good intention to give you a little surprise for Xmas be received by you kindly !   Gasperini trotted round a deal with me to buy the bonnet : so you'll receive a voucher of our united taste.

Luckily I haven't spoken to a soul the last 4 days.

I had to go to Flaxland's last Tuesday (Madame Flaxland has put up *bonbons* for you) : Lord knows how
weak I am now ! in short, at the end of dinner they
served us ice-pudding ; on the top of it I had to discuss
that loathsome Dresden publishing affair (! !) for three
hours at a stretch. With that I ruined my digestion
and everything, had a ghastly night, and have sworn
to look up no one more till I feel perfectly well again.
God, it's a wretched life !—My only hope is in my
work.—

But I had also forgotten to answer you re Beust.
I retrieve it by allowing you a free hand to do what
you think fit : that is to say, you must behave exactly
as if you were doing it on your own account. For my
part at least, I truly am not in the humour just now
to do a mighty deal of cringing there ! They're really
too, *too* contemptible, and if they amnesty me, you may
be sure they won't do it for my sake—or yours—but
merely for shame's sake, and because at last it's got
to be.—

Since I've been here (where I—purposely—haven't
yet seen my Ambassadors) no news has reached me from
anywhere except yourself. God knows if Alwine is
hatching something : I wrote her quite calmly and
clearly from here again.—If Pusinelli were to order you
Wiesbaden for this summer, that would suit me nicely
[close to Mainz] : I hear one can live quite agreeably there,
and—relatively—cheaply. Ah God, how I'm longing
for a last den of one's own ! Only take care of Jacquot :
one must have a couple of good dogs then, and if possible
also a horse. In the streets here I do most of my talking
with horses, for instance on the cab-stand. When the
good beasts flinch, prick up their ears, shake their heads,

and begin stamping their feet, I'm as pleased as a child.
I've quite taken the dear omnibus-horses to my heart.—

Frau Schott writes me to-day that the things for
me are on the road : I have asked them also to send me
an old Chorale book and a collection of old folk-songs,
which I should like to have handy.—I have not yet
looked after our things here : I dread it, ah ! and above
all *talking*.   Silence does me such good !

And now I'm hoping for a speedy letter from yourself ; I've little matter for writing—remember that.
Nothing whatever has happened to me ; I read and work,
take my walk, now and then go to a minor theatre in
the evening to win a good night's sleep.   The other
day I was at the Ambigu with Czermack, whom I had
met on the Quai.

So farewell ! Have a tolerable Christmas, and if
things are bad with you, reflect that they are not going
grandly with your husband either !—

The very kindest Christmas greetings

from

me !

226.

PARIS, 28. December 1861.
19. Quai Voltaire.

This morning, dear Mutz, I received your Christmas
letter. You may imagine how it gratified me ; for,
candidly speaking, it really is a good sign when one
sees that a pleasure is still to be given to somebody one's
fond of. To be sure, you take it very ill of me if I refer
to your state of health ; and then you say nasty, nasty
things to me which certainly had better stay unsaid, nay,
even unthought : but I myself am in none too sound a
skin, not to place Health in the forefront of communica-

tions to persons who lie close to my heart. I often have evil days, when I leave my bed after a bad night with a profound inward shudder, and in mute despair review my wretched toilsome life that hangs on nothing save my utmost courage now : don't you believe I would gladly see a kind and willing partner of my life approach me then to cheer, distract, encourage me ? Again, when I have slept well for once, feel peace and comfort budding in my tortured nerves, the sun laughs in at the window, then maybe I think : Were it with thy wife as now with thee, were peace and comfort to re-enter her shaken frame, why shouldn't it be feasible for you both to pass a blithe old age together yet ? Health helps toward everything ; without it no good fortune would avail !

So I rejoice when I hear you're picking up, that you're looking well, that even your tormenting heart-ill may abate at last. And I brew my tea, help myself, trip myself up, sigh over the discomfort of my situation ; finally I form plans how and where to make oneself cosy again some day : soon everything looks feasible, because the strength to hope and will has found a base once more. Then I write you, tell you of my joy, my wishes ;—your answer comes: the harmless castle in the air is blown to shreds ; the Wagner Family is shot upon me, and——

Don't be cross with me, but—when I wrote you last about your health with hope and joy, quite innocently I was only thinking that the best good luck in life might come too late if Health had vanished. Allow me this time, surely ! to excuse your reprimand on the sole plea that you still are really ailing ; for which I profoundly pity you—and more than you'll believe !—

But let us drop that !—I couldn't quite pass it over,

though I certainly am bound to think I act unwisely to
reply at all to such odious observations, which wound me
to the quick, nay, drive me to desperation. Does remorse
never seize you, then, for such a thing?—

Ah ! !—enough !—*I'm* suffering too, you see : a little
mercy ! nothing more !—

I dined at Flaxland's again to-day : I delivered your
greetings, but spared them the kisses. They were greatly
delighted with your delight. Another hint about the
hurdy-gurdy : if you wind up the barrel as far as you
can, it goes too fast ; with only one winding, it plays very
slowly : so just a few turns, and the tunes will be played
slow enough.—

I wrote to Leopoldine yesterday, inviting myself to
dinner for Sunday ; to-day she answers me that her
children have measles and scarlet fever, which her husband himself is afraid of catching, so I mustn't think
of risking it. I've dined with Gasperini several times
at the restaurant. I learnt the death of Count Pourtalès
from the Journal ; I went to the embassy at once, but
was unable to catch Hatzfeld until some days after. This
bereavement has certainly been a great shock to me, and
moved me to genuine sorrow ; I shall call on the Countess
in a day or two.—Imagine it, that poor Roche [joint translator of *Tannh.*] also died a short time back !

On your advice of to-day, I've left a card on the
Eberty.—I shan't present myself at Metternich's till the
last of this month ; I purposely wouldn't embarrass them,
as they really cannot take me in before the beginning of
January. Should this fall through again—which I refuse
to fear !—undoubtedly I shouldn't know why I need
remain in Paris. God would know whither then ! Perhaps to Wiesbaden.—But there,—I won't think of it !—

How I'm racking my brains every day over a speedy re-settlement! If you only knew (unfortunately you don't!) how things stand in my innermost depths, what resignation on all sides is confirming itself more and more in me! I want rest, nothing save rest: equilibrium, full undisturbed home safety! My last glimpse into the ways of German Opera has contributed so much to that: ah, to have as little as possible to do with it! I shall let them present my new comic opera wherever they like, and not take a peep at it! Simply and solely—rest, and—work: for it is only at work I am quite in my element, safe, cheerful, and myself; I cannot be responsible for the performances!—With the Meistersinger I expect to do good paying business soon: then the Tristan will surely also bring something in at last; whilst I still have other easier-given subjects in my head. I daresay one might even manage to pull through unhelped, at some cheap place where one could carefully install oneself in peace and quiet. It would be well, of course, if the Berliners would pay me at least a small fixed pension in lieu of the uncertain tantième; but—I can't wait much longer, I absolutely need domestic order and convenience. Otherwise I'm accustoming myself to live simpler and simpler: I no longer sport silk and velvet in the house; I dress complete the first thing in the morning, and wear a short cloth jacket: I catch in things less like that, and also feel less weight. But that by the way. Where I'm to live, at what spot, among what people,—all that's becoming more and more indifferent to me: I find that every place has its good and bad sides, and the main consideration is a quiet life free of care in one's own house—for *work ! !*

For some time past I haven't been quite well again;

God knows if it is chagrin, care, disgust? My stomach won't get right, and sometimes I'm afraid of last year's fever; only, people tell me that doesn't return so soon, after one has had it. Mad. Flaxland gave me salts to-day; I hope they'll do me good.—For the rest, I'm in my working fit now; you know no day dare pass then, without I've been at it. At 10 I breakfast; then from 11 or ½ past until 3 or 4 I sit at my rhyming, which constantly enlivens me. Then a little walk, an errand, food; after which back home, as a rule, to my 10 ft long by 9 ft broad cubicle, where I write letters—as this instant—or read a book. I have also been a few times to the minor theatres, to procure myself good sleep. Above all I avoid much talking, and therefore very seldom pay a call.

Now for finances. I can imagine you are running dry; yet it's difficult to send you anything from here at once. My last Schottian advance won't go much farther, especially as the little tailor, whom I owed 500 *fr.* still, has dunned me hard; I was obliged to shew my face to him, or he'd probably have made awkward enquiries at the Prussian embassy. As I shan't need to spend much more myself when—and if I go to Metternich's, I shouldn't care to ask Schott for a fresh advance before February, when he is coming to Paris,— in fact, that is what we arranged. There accordingly remains my Berlin tantième for you to go on with: they've given something of mine, I know, so there will be something ready for you there in any case. I hardly suppose you can wait until the 15th January; therefore allow me to give orders to Bülow tomorrow to make enquiries and send you something anyhow.—

The *stove-screen* gives me great delight: you know

how often I've reproached you for giving away the first
specimen. So I may hope to have it always in my study
in our future home ; you will accustom yourself, let us
trust, to the idea of its being admired by me yet in your
lifetime. Accept my best thanks in advance for the
attention !—The splendid socks, too, have arrived at
last, and with them the Silver-bridegroom's cup, which
affected me very peculiarly. The whole Silver notion
doesn't quite appeal to me : my God, one celebrates such
festivals in the bosom of one's family when everything
is standing well and prospering. But what family have
we ? We have drifted far out of touch with our relatives, you know, and there's no true bond whatever
there. No : if we really taste the happiness of rest and
fixity *at last*, then—then we'll celebrate another wedding,
and that might rather be the Golden right off ; which
folk might surely grant us harassed pair to take a little
early. This time it wouldn't let itself be forced, and
every allusion to it has had something too mournful in
my eyes for me to dwell upon it willingly. Put a good
construction on that, please !—

Now my greetings to N. : she might at least have
been keeping her Pewter wedding by now !—Reciprocate
the others' greetings also, but don't let yourself be
pestered with the photographs ; it's sheer effrontery, and
mendicancy into the bargain : infamous new fashion !
These things aren't got for nothing ; and why the Devil
should one pay for such rubbish for every goose who
keeps a silly album ? Don't promise it ; I haven't any,
and should have to get them sent expressly from Vienna
for hard cash !

There, I've been and got quite cross again, after
writing myself back into a good temper ! Ah God,

indeed, indeed I am good !   I'm always glad when I can
smooth my brow again and shew a smiling face.   If you
could only cease your worriting at last, Heaven help us ;
you can't think how nonsensical the crooked stuff appears
to me !   Yet it seems to do you thorough good, continually to paint yourself black pictures of me !   God
bless me, tho', I shall be catching it again, however well
'twas meant.   You *must* be in the right—there's nothing
else for it ; and however much your in-the-right may
hurt you, no matter, you are not to be talked out of it !—
Do be sensible, old girl, and realise what needless agonies
you give yourself !   Furnish me a nice home this New
Year, a fine big working-room for me (now become my
chief passion !), quiet, good living, two dogs, ach ! and
then a horse besides !—Get fat cheeks (but don't take
that amiss !), be good and let bygones be bygones (I
promise you to do the same), and—you shall see what a
good husband you have !—

I wish myself the above with all my heart for the
New Year : if you want to share it, share my wish !
For my part I wish for nothing more on God's broad
earth !   Amen !

Good luck !   Thy
                    most affectionate
                         Spouse and Husband !

227.

PARIS, 4. [1 ?] *January* 1862.

DEAR CHILD,

Merely two lines to tell you that the (insane)
father of the Metternich can't leave Paris, on account
of illness, and I therefore can't go to the Metternichs.
That has been my New Year's gift !   Not to get into
too hot water for this affair, however—even with yourself

—I send you herewith the last letter Metternich wrote me to Vienna, upon which I determined to go to Paris after all !—

But I have written to *Schott* at once, and am inclined to have a good long look at *Wiesbaden*, to see if that might altogether please me : there is much to be said for it. If you have anything to tell me quick, please do so to the old address still. Once I have settled my day of departure, I'll write you properly. Farewell for to-day. I should like to get the verses of my first act done here, all the same.—

Beautiful fate ! ! Don't you think I need patience ?—

Now adieu ! Soon more from   Thy
                                        buffeted
                                           HUSBAND.

228.

PARIS, 7. *January* 1862.
19. *Quai Voltaire.*

Only to-day, dear Minna, can I tell you something definite again. I shall remain here in my roomlet till the end of this month, to complete my poem without a break. Several things combine. A few days ago I had finished the first act,—a letter from Schott hadn't come ; I had some happy thoughts for the opening of the second act, began it, and now shouldn't care to let a whole dreadful winter-journey with its packing and unpacking, finding lodgings, installing myself etc. in a strange place, fall between it and termination of the entire text. On the other hand, Schott begs me by letter to-day to have a little patience regarding a fresh cheque, which would incommode him for the moment. But you can easily imagine what an unforeseen plight the falling through of the Metternich invitation has brought

me into ; having to swallow this bitter, bitter disappointment again, makes me quite sick and weary. I am
plunging right up to the ears in my work, simply to
forget the wretched world I'm placed in !—

Under such circumstances, and with my fresh all-
dominating bent to work, I'm longing more than ever for
a domicile again. So I shall have a thorough good look
at Wiesbaden, with that intent, from next month onward.
As one will perhaps be compelled to live by the labour of
one's hands alone for life's remainder, and certain home-
comforts, good attendance etc., are the main consideration,
much less the company—which has its good and bad
sides everywhere—the exact spot is becoming more
and more indifferent to me, provided one has a pleasant
abode, and—cheap living. So I confess—please laugh—
this instant I'm even thinking of a look at that fabulous
Bamberg.—There you have the sort of ideas that form
a running accompaniment to my work : meanwhile,
suppose *you* win something handsome in the lottery !—

There's another thing, however, I don't intend to
leave untried.—At the end of this month I think of
getting on the march ; I shall travel viâ *Carlsruhe*,
and announce myself to the Grand Ducals, with whom
I'm on quite a good footing still, for two things :
1°, a recital of my new poem (completed by then) ;
2°, a performance of Lohengrin under my direction.— —
Remains to be seen !—The Grand Duke in any case
took too grave a view of the affair, and friend Devrient
will certainly have done his honest best toward that ;
so I shall let him know, I'll settle in his capital if he
only gives me 1200 gulden a year [*ca* £120]. After all,
that's something, and it will be a last attempt on my
side. Shall see !—

So just write me once more ; I know you have only been waiting for news of my whereabouts.——

Before I leave here I hope to see Seebach also, who is in Dresden just now.   Perhaps you might call on him ; in any case he'd be of most use to you.   If this Saxon fix would only cease, it would be a good job in every way !——

Now excuse my writing more ; as I've to send news of my decision in various directions, I still have a deal to attend to to-day.

May these lines find you in good spirits and humour ! Lord knows that's needed, and if it weren't for my Apprentices, who have to open the second act, I shouldn't know where I'm to get the humour from.   The saucy lads afforded me much fun in the first act before, with David as ringleader !——

So farewell, remain——or *become*——good to me !

Thy

RICHARD.

229.

PARIS, *Sunday*, 12. *January* 1862.

MY GOOD MUTZ,

You gave me great, great joy with your last letter ; and indeed, believe me, you've succeeded in imbuing me with courage !   Thus things will go ; thus I see all coming right.   Thanks, then, and true heart's reward !

I fancy I shall get another letter from you in a day or two, however, as my last informed you that I intended staying on here till the termination of my new poem. At that I'm now working with an eagerness beyond belief : it pleases me so, and yields me such exhilaration, that I'm only sorry each time I've to cease for the day, since I see nothing else at all before me that can give me joy. Unfortunately this keenness is somewhat deranging my diet ; it makes me over-pass my luncheon hour, and consequently my hunger ; in result whereof my digestion itself is fairly out of order, and I'm suffering somewhat severely from abdominal pains. Still, I shall probably hold out to the end, and hope to have finished for certain by the end of this month.—

Your letter has also turned the scale as to what I shall do then. I keep to *Wiesbaden* for this summer at any rate, there's so much in its favour ; but your description has really put me rather out of conceit with it for the present, and in particular the idea of tumbling into the midst of utterly strange folk and surroundings in winter isn't very inviting to me. Many things combine with your suggestion, on the contrary, to influence me to pass the remainder of the winter in Berlin. At first I wanted to avoid it, as I was afraid of somewhat compromising myself by a premature appearance there. However, who's going to force me to appear in public ? I've a couple of friendly families there, who will make life pleasant to me ; and I look for nothing beyond. Bülow has offered me full hospitality, full tranquillity for work, full unconcern, and everything besides. Now the Avenariuses offer me the same ; [but] they won't take it ill of me, if I prefer the Bülows. Hans invited me to them so long ago as last summer ; they're furnished for it, from Liszt's visits to them ; with him I am intimate, have the pianist, the practical musician, and uncommonly attached comrade at hand, and shall be glad to work in such surroundings. The family Avenarius, on the other hand—in spite of sister—is quite a stranger to me now ; neither does Cecilie deserve it : she never came to Switzerland. That would be a sort of constraint, as said, of unhomeliness, which couldn't have attracted me to Berlin ; [whereas] making music with Hans, especially at a time when I'm composing there, will be most agreeable and stimulating to me ; moreover, in any case he was the first to speak. I shall see the Avenariuses often, and with that they'll be content.

But sundry other influences are at work, which perhaps may conduct to an issue of some kind in Berlin. Eh, it seems, it seems to me as if my remarkably erratic fate were about to undergo a change there. Lord, if it were nothing beyond a small pension, how greatly it would serve our settling down anywhere else ! I have had myself announced at Carlsruhe, to conduct Lohengrin there, and to read my new text to the Grand Ducals. Already—I happen to know—the Grand Duchess (*between ourselves ! !*) has taken steps in Berlin. So we'll see what I can thaw out on this winter-journey, and in consequence thereof.

One thing stands firm, however, Mutz : from this summer forward we'll try to bring our domiciling definitely about. I'm thinking of having the furniture and piano despatched to Schott's at Mainz ; but in any case we soon shall meet again, even if only on a flying visit to Berlin. I leave it entirely to yourself how you regard that, and whether you'd care to leave Dresden this winter ; but in the Spring at any rate, somewhere about the end of May—if your heart isn't absolutely set on something else—we'll take up our quarters on the Rhine, have a good look round, and if Fate's at all propitious and we're well pleased with some place—if we find a thoroughly suitable nice abode where living isn't dear— why, the furniture will be close at hand, and by the autumn all will be ready for entry. Without a settling down I cannot do : I can't go on like this ; and even if I had to get collections made for me throughout all Germany, it *must* be. And if *you* won't settle down with me, why, I'll take unto me somebody else : settled down it must be, even if I had to marry the A. [Alwine?]. There, you've got it now, and know what to expect ; let's hope you'll catch fire !

When my Prentices are chaffing poor David over his old Magdalene, they sing :

> "Johannistag ! Johannistag !
> Da freit ein Jeder wie er mag !
> Der Meister freit,
> der Bursche freit,
> da giebt es Geschlamb und Geschlumbfer !
> Der Alte freit
> die junge Maid,
> der Bursche die alte Jumbfer !
> Juchhei ! Juchhei !
> Johannistag !——"

I hope you will find the rhyme quite pretty ! I wonder if it will please the A. ?—

Na, it's going with me, you see !—

Apropos : call on Seebach and remind him. The Countess Pourtalès is also going to Berlin, and has begged me to call upon her at her father the Minister's. Might also be of service to us !—So a best God-be-with-you ! More hearty thanks ! Yes, courage, courage : I've something in me still, I feel it ! Adieu, good Mutz !

Thy
R.

230.

MY GOOD MUTZ,

I'm writing you so soon again because I really am bound to keep you *au courant*, and that you always may learn from myself whatever is up. —

So then : immediately after writing you last, I had letters which have taken much of the gilt off the idea of a longer sojourn in Berlin ; in particular, from the Frommann. The thought of frightening anyone by my arrival is repugnant to me ; and if I mean to plant myself there for 3 months, nobody will believe that I don't contemplate staying for good. That's one point.—

But I also now learn from the Bülows that they would have to put me up outside their house ; something quite different, then, from what I gathered from their first invitation. Consequently, not even an entirely unreserved welcome. Neither can I imagine its altogether pleasing me at Cecilie's for long ; whereas I now need great repose and equability for my work. I see, all that's nix, nix !— I must and will refound my house as soon as possible. Oh, if you only could have made up your mind last summer ;   I foresaw the event of its becoming imperative to me to hunt up a sheltering home ! That *must* be speedily remedied, and to lose no time over it, I shall make a beginning. And that was the second point.—

Wiesbaden has lately been again described to me as just the thing, by the Frommann among others. You must have had a very unfavourable glimpse of it. Remember it is a capital, has its Court-theatre summer and winter, where they continually give all my operas and bear me on their hands as nowhere. So, diversion even in the winter, especially for yourself. Then, only

$\frac{1}{2}$ an hour to Darmstadt ; not much farther to *Mannheim*, *Frankfort*, even *Carlsruhe*. That offers distraction and change, whilst one can be wholly independent and sequestered at the place itself. So I mean to have a good look at it soon, at any rate, and—which will be very easy at a watering-place in winter—take a small furnished lodging to start with, for us both if you will. That shall be in the first days of February. Then—listen !—I'll pay a brief visit, of about 4 to 5 days, to Berlin, and alight for that at Avenarius', who pressingly invited me the other day. The main affair to me, with that, is to see yourself ; so, *if it isn't too much trouble to you*, I heartily beg of you also to come to Berlin for a few days, for the time of my visit. I have just written to Avenarius that, if they cannot put up both of us, they're to send me to some inn close by. So place yourself en rapport with Cecilie ; we'll agree on the exact time later. Perhaps I shall make a couple of days' halt at Carlsruhe first, if it comes to my conducting Lohengrin there ; but, we will defer all particulars. At Berlin we'll have a thorough good talk, when I will bring you precise and self-gained information as to Wiesbaden.

I quite see I shall have to make myself full master of my destiny again ; I am determined rather to work myself to death, than wait for those wretched f——— any longer. Now I see that a publisher can be got to pay me enough for a new opera to enable me to live during work with cheap and quiet housekeeping, good : when I've finished the Meistersinger, and if things go on like this, I shall take up something else at once ; I've enough in petto !—Tomorrow I shall probably have completed the 2nd act of the poem, which is turning out capital and is sure to have enormous success !—

From Berlin—in addition to the 50 thaler already—
you will be receiving upwards of 80 thaler in a day or
two. The tantième was tolerable this time, Lohengrin
packed.—So—this for to-day, that you may know how
you stand with your poor husband ! Adieu, good Mutz.
From his heart

Thy
R.

231.

PARIS, 31. January 1862.

BEST MINNA,

Work has made me forget *much* this time : it
has been and is my consolation, without which I
shouldn't have known what to do to make head against
my fate. Unfortunately, though, I have forgotten all
writing as well.

On the 25th I finished the poem, and was hoping
to be able to make the necessary fair-copy in about
another 3 days. In spite of an industriousness that has
damaged my health in the end, I couldn't bring it off
before to-day, as I always make a thing like that most
accurate.

For the last fortnight I have seen or spoken to only 2
people : Truinet and his father, whom I've met each
day at dinner in the *Taverne anglaise*.

Now I have got the length of departing tomorrow
evening. First for Carlsruhe, where the Highnesses
expect me Monday for my reading of the new poem.
From there I shall write to you properly.

The Berlin visit, which strictly is a pure luxury—
alike as regards money and fuss—shall be finally decided
on my part within a few days. In the meantime I want
to look around in Wiesbaden, Mainz or Biebrich, for an

abode for my immediate needs. If I come to Berlin after all (which might just as well be another time) it will be about the 7th or 8th of February.

All particulars as to that, however, from Carlsruhe.

Meanwhile be of good cheer ; my poem has succeeded beyond all hope !—

I have just received the stuff from the Szemère, and paid 12 *fr.* for it.

Farewell, then ; greet Jacquot, and wish me bon voyage for tomorrow.

Adieu, good Mutz.   Thy
                                        RICHARD.

If you have anything to communicate to me, or if you want to delight me with a message of any kind, address to

J. B. Schott's Söhne

in

Mainz.

232.

PARIS, 1. *February* 1862.

DEAR MINNA,

Cecilie has written me also, telling me that you have declined staying with them.

You will have your own reasons for it,—but so far as I'm concerned now, this circumstance turns the scale with me *not* to go to Berlin for the present. It would be a distasteful thought to me, you see, not to be under the same roof as yourself on this occasion. It spoils me the cordiality of the proposed few days, and as I've *nothing* to seek at Berlin in and for itself, whilst all I seek in general is peace and harmony, I have made up my mind to keep clear of every single thing that bears in it the smallest seed of discord.

Without naming the true reason, I'm informing Cecilie forthwith of my highly presumable not-coming. I shall shortly be able to write you more at length ; to-day I'm in the act of packing for departure. Therefore merely these few words.

Kind love from

Thy

RICHARD.

233.

MAINZ, 6. *February* 1862.

GOOD MINNA,

Here is Cornelius, who will take the place of a longer letter—which I couldn't possibly bring off to-day —and tell you how it goes with me, and what I purpose. Imagine it ! I wrote from Paris 7 days since to this Cornelius, at Vienna, that he must be at Schott's in Mainz the evening of the 5th, when I meant to read the Meistersinger aloud for the first time. Sure enough, last evening at 7 enters Cornelius at Schott's, in spite of inundations and unheard-of travelling adventures ! That will give you some notion of *what* I possess in Cornelius. The man's a perfect angel.

I shall answer your letter, which much rejoiced me, in a day or two. Now I require rest and firm foothold. That need alter nothing in your plan of cure at Reichenhall ; but—about that shortly.

So, goodbye for to-day ! I'm besieged, and only just wanted to give Peter, who is starting back for Vienna to-day, these lines to take with him. He's making a break at Dresden *solely* to bring you my greetings by mouth ; you see what we possess in him !

Adieu, dear Mutz. Soon more and better from Thy

RICHARD.

234.

BIEBRICH (*on the Rhine*) 9. *February* 1862.
Europäischer Hof.

DEAR MUTZ,

Here I am in an hotel again ! A nice life this ! And with it all, to have no other wish than to be able to work in peace and quiet ! I must admit that if nobody will credit *me* with patience and endurance, I should like to know to *whom* those qualities should be imputed !—

Your having seen Cornelius in the interval, affords me great delight ; I feel as if I had been with you myself. So far as I remember, you took a great fancy to Cornelius when you were at the Altenburg [1854] ; myself, I only drew towards him in Vienna very gradually, but ended by discovering that he's truly a most rare, uncommon creature in *all* respects, alike as regards character and mental ability. He really is the only one among the younger generation (although he's well on in the thirties) to whom I can attribute actual genius ; whilst his temperance, modesty, contented mind and great moral worth, place him on a pedestal apart. I could only wish this winning soul would come to us for ever ; but he is following his own independent plan of life, which I respect.—

Well, he will have told you much about me and my plans. With everyone else, he considers a settling down at *Biebrich* by far the fittest for me. The advantage of it lies in this : if I never mean to enter fixed relations with a theatre again, it is highly important that I should be able to reach them all by way of easy *trip*, while retaining my actual place of residence in quiet and agreeable retirement. Now, in this respect the situation

of Biebrich is quite unique : in 10 minutes by steamboat
I'm at Mainz, where the Schott family spreads its hands
beneath me, and quite a passable theatre, outwardly in
fact most imposing, offers a certain interest ; Schmidt
(from Frankfort) is kapellmeistering there now, and I
fancy will be for some time, which suits my book. In
10 minutes also I'm at Wiesbaden, which has a good
theatre both summer and winter (to-night I'm to see
Gounod's Faust there). In an hour and a quarter,
Frankfort ; in $\frac{3}{4}$ hour, Darmstadt ; in $1\frac{1}{2}$ hour, Mannheim
(all considerable theatres). In 3 hours, Carlsruhe : i.e.
about the distance of Leipzig and Dresden from each
other. For Vienna, Berlin and Paris, almost exactly
in the middle. Then, the place itself is charming : on
foot, the pleasantest of walks to Mainz or Wiesbaden ;
to the right, down stream, the heavenly Rhine-lands
for expeditions at any moment. Moreover, at the Schloss
a wonderful big park with glorious trees. Adjoining this
park I've noticed very pretty dwellings ; if I were to find
one of them completely suited for [our] domicile, it
might prove very difficult to me, so tossed about and
craving for domestic order, to resist the temptation to
rent it. For my own part, *I* should be quite satisfied
that such a settlement would fully meet my needs ; for—
I have come to know myself now, and can lay down the
measure for the rest of my life. *Work*, new creation,
that's my element : producing it, well and good if I'm
begged to, and if people meet me at all points ; then
shorter or longer excursions, but always with the prospect
of returning to my quiet work-hearth directly after the
exertion. *That's* the main consideration : *that* I must
keep alone in eye, for that depends upon *myself*. All
outer things are out of my control, may come or not

come ; for my tranquillity I daren't depend on them.
Such is the lesson this last year has painfully taught me
again !—

At Carlsruhe I had a whole hour's talk with the
Grand Duke (his wife was taken ill) ; he will invite me
to come again in a few days' time, and if possible—
conduct Lohengrin also.　I can't help saying that I gave
the dear fellow a hearty squeeze of the hand on taking
leave.　It was palpable that his relation with me had
been preying on his mind since the last letter (which I
hadn't answered him); he really was pained, and supposed
I **was** vexed with him.　I found him in a strange confusion of ideas regarding my circumstances, and almost
think our good excited A. must have caused a little
muddle here.　Thus it transpired that he actually hadn't
grasped the simple nature of my proposition, and assumed
other things (such as heavy debts etc.) behind it.　Nevertheless it delighted me that he repeatedly confessed he felt
it his duty to stand security for my mental repose and
freedom from care.　Thereon I told him very quietly, I
had defined that in my letter plainly, and therefore simply
reiterated to him : As I was without any inherited
property, there were only two ways open to me of maintaining myself : $1°$, to turn out works such as should
quickly provide me with a capital on the interest of which
I could live—which, with the wretched scale of fees in
Germany, was impossible ; or $2°$, to accept a post as
Kapellmeister, which it was to be hoped that *he* would be
the last to ask of me, since one could use other people for
Kapellmeister service to better purpose than productive
poets and composers of my stripe.　The Grand Duke didn't
raise the least demur to that, but declared I must be so
disposed of that not the smallest obligation should be

laid upon me ; it must be left entirely to my own free will, whether I would bother about a performance or not ; the *only* thing, was for me to live in peace and free from care. Very well, said I, that is perfectly simple : let those who recognise it club together to pay me an annual pension ; but no one seemed inclined to understand that. Liszt had told me he had conveyed that to the G. D. of Weimar, but found no hearing ; I had already told him [G. D. of W.] something similar myself, and again he hadn't found it feasible. What remained for me, then, but to scrape through a wretched life from hand to mouth, and be glad if I found a publisher who would advance me about enough on my work to enable me to keep alive while engaged on it ?— No, exclaimed he, that must not continue ; I will place myself at the head forthwith, and hope by my example to influence a few other princes friendly toward you to unite with me in seeing that a fixed pension is ensured you. Tell me quite candidly : how much do you believe you'll need as annual fixed stipend ?—God, said I, if I got it regularly and for certain, quite a little would suffice ; and if you can guarantee me 1500 to 2000 gulden under those conditions, I shall know where I am, cut my coat accordingly, and make both ends meet with my other chance receipts. He was very glad to hear that, and undertook to see to my desire being fulfilled as speedily as possible. Not to fall out of rapport again, he then begged me to visit him once more at Carlsruhe shortly, attend a rehearsal of Lohen- grin, and if it satisfied me in all respects, give them the great pleasure of my conducting this work myself. Which I promised, of course.—Beyond that, my plan of settling down at Biebrich met his full approval ; he wished me entire independence, but would account it all the higher to me if I would favour him from time to time.—

In spite of this really very beautiful, and (I do not doubt) eventful resumption of relations with the Grand Duke, I have completely abandoned the notion of a settlement at Carlsruhe ; and chiefly on account of *Devrient*, whom I didn't even call on this time.   I could never get on peaceably for long with that stiff old pedant, who makes it a set principle to bolster up the mediocre, and moreover has continually harmed me with his infamous talk about the unperformableness of Tristan : my patience would give out some day, and—Lord bless me ! peace and quiet is my motto now !   It might happen to me, you know, to get into a thundering passion with a dodderer like that.   If I go there now and then, on the Grand Duke's invitation, it will be another story.—

That, good Mutz, is about the present complexion of my outer affairs.   I have told you exactly my require-ment, my desire, ay—under circumstances—my inten-tion.   One sole thing fills me with anxiety : how *you* would feel about it.   Would you care to settle down at Biebrich ?   Would you like it ?   Would you not prefer another place ?—You will understand that if I've made *my* needs my first consideration here, it's bound to worry me whether my choice will also correspond with yours ; consequently I have a dread of carrying anything out which might possibly be repented again before long ! The place is excessively quiet, and offers few resources in itself—for winter ; to which *I'm* naturally most indifferent, as I have remarked in Paris and everywhere that I strictly like nothing but being at home.   True, even in the

winter here we can at the same time be living at Mainz
and Wiesbaden, for the journey is no longer than if one
took a fiacre from one end of a moderately big city to
the other, only much cheaper and handier. It would
therefore be a question of trying it. As for *myself,* I'm
glad to be commencing here in winter, precisely to see
how it answers. I can have company at any moment ; I
only need to invite [myself] in Mainz or Wiesbaden.
The very trip is a refreshment.—So I think I shall just
let it depend for the present on the success of my studious
endeavours to find a quite fitting abode. That would
have to be the case ; for one would never care to be
merely roughing it under such circumstances. Whether
I shall find that abode, is still a very open question, [but]
things are said to be most *cheap* here, provisions and all :
one can get a whole tip-top flat, they say, for 250 to
300 fl.—So—I mean to set about it leisurely and hurry
nothing, as I have had a thorough sickener of remorse.—
Let us see, then. If I find it, my need of home convenience is so great now, that it will really turn the
scale : *you* would then have to try if it pleased you
also.—

A little dog will soon be procured !—

Probably I shall quite give up the Berlin visit now, in
any case. My God, I hadn't a soul in Paris to whom I
could have shewn as much as a verse of my new poem ;
so I just thought of an evening with you, the Fromm-
jumbfer * and the Bülows : which certainly would have
been very nice. We should have convinced each other
we were still alive, and had a talk : all of which would
have been famous ! But now this ado to begin with even

---

* Alwine Frommann, old maid ; see the verses in no. 229.—Tr.

as to where one is to sleep and dwell 2 days, one of us at one place, the other at another; then the Albert's— concerning whom I really hadn't given it a thought that they were still in existence there; the Fromm-jumbfer with her terror of the King; the Jews no doubt, too, and reporters; and God knows what besides! Ah, I could do without all that! No: that was not exactly what I wanted! I hope Cecilie will allay her sisterly affection, and arrange for it another time. I am thoroughly sick of this travelling, packing and unpacking; ah, and the money it costs! I'm not speaking of the regular expenses, but merely the tips. No: God preserve me!—last even- ing, when I reached here and had another good hunt in my trunk for this and that, salt tears ran down my cheeks, poor devil. And that with such a splendid work in my head, for which one cannot even find a quiet nest: it's shameful!—

I'm expecting the Erard in a day or two, when the Devil shall be loosed!—Congratulate me on it, and hold me a wee bit dear, you old Dresd'ner.

Farewellkie for to-day.

Thine most sincerely,
R.

(You shall have some more money in course of this month, self-understood, Mutz!)

[*March* 4 *he writes* Cornelius: "*I am most unhappy, and want to breathe my woes to somebody. . . . You know how I was longing for a regulated home again, and how I believed I could only attain it through reunion with my wife. Well, while I was sadly trying to install myself in winter quarters here at Biebrich, my wife, appealed to by my straits, suddenly decides on following your example, in a sense; instead of answer- ing me by letter, she appears in my chambers here herself* [ca *Feb.* 20], *just as I had completed my shake-down. My heart leapt within me, and my great emotion and delight should easily have shewn her how things stand with me. . . . Next morning came a strange intervention of Fate* [vide *p. 747 inf.] . . . That letter arrives here on the second, the little box on the third day of my wife's stay with me, and both fall into the unhappy woman's hands at once. Incapable of viewing my relations with that lady in any save an odious light, she refuses to understand a single explanation, but indulges in that vulgar tone again which makes me lose all self-command : she reads my anger as an effect of that lady's agitating hold upon me, and—the whole mad house of cards stands stark once more ! It was enough to make me lose my senses : this woman on the very selfsame spot as four years since ; the same invectives, word for word, the selfsame common tone !—These ragings over, I composed myself again, tried to regard them as a last mad thunder-storm,—still hope, and abjure no possibility. But then appeared the sad old sequel : mistrust, suspicion, misconstruction of my every word ! And that in total solitude like this. . . . They were ten days of hell. And yet those ten atrocious days at least had one good side : a final warning. . . . My own eyes have taught me that, in any circumstances, my wife has better health away from me ; nay, I plainly recognise that the feeling of true love for me does not exist in her at all ; she knows no injury save what is done to* her, *and her heart is quite incapable of e'er forgiving it. Yet—as the only world we know is that within* us—*I figure to myself it* may *be otherwise, true sorrow, deep affection may make her suffer—and* my *heart bleeds. Since the day before yesterday, when I said goodbye at Frankfort to the unhappy, but still resentfully self-pitying woman, it has kept gnawing at me ; and nothing save the certainty that by weakness I should only prolong the agony on* both *sides, can bring me—resignation in the end. Ah God ! and then the tears well up in me, and I cry for a kind woman's soul to take me softly to itself ! ! But I have shut that off from me ; and so, I fancy, all the sufferings of my wife are venged !"*—Tr.]

235.

BIEBRICH, 11. *March* 1862.

Don't be surprised, dear Minna, at my not answering you until to-day : but I should have written to-day in any case. I was at Carlsruhe, to tell the truth, and didn't find your letter till I got back last evening. Unfortunately I can well imagine your having had it so cold, for I thought of you with apprehension even on my small return-journey from Frankfort to Biebrich, when I fairly froze, myself. Since last Friday, however, Spring has put in a sudden appearance ; in fact it's so warm now, that I have quite given up fires. Let us hope it

will soon travel to your part, and may the milder weather
then contribute to restoring you, after the great and
varied hardships of your winter trip.   I deeply have had
to deplore the strange coincidences that became matter
for troubling our mood during our brief meeting, but
perhaps the most regrettable part of it to me has been
the discovery how extremely irritable and unsteady my
temper is.   That gives me the most food for thought,
because I see that it needs a great deal of good luck,
success, and cheering transformation of my circumstances,
if I am at last to arrive at that calm equanimity I so
desire.   For the present, however, and after the unparalleled reverses of the last few years, with my acute
susceptibility I can only wonder at my holding out at all,
or giving breathing-space to hope in any mortal thing.
I trust you also will consider that, and take into account
my sorrows, the everlasting obstacles that confront my
every step, the never-ceasing worries that beset my mind
and turn it from its natural occupation.   You know, and
surely have perceived that, alike inwardly and outwardly,
I should be unable to subsist at present without a work
in which I can engross myself entirely, and from which
nothing shall deflect me.   Unspeakably hard as it has
proved to me even to win the hearth for it again, let us
be glad if I can only get to this work now, and stick to
it without disturbance till its termination.

As regards yourself I have the comfort with it, that,
so long as I haven't inwardly and outwardly attained an
easier position, your life with me midst cares and cramps
would be less refreshing to you than an equally undisturbed leaving-alone ; nay, your health positively demands
that you should stay spared the agitations my now so
irritable and impatient temper continually exposes you

to—against my best will. I *know* it, and you feel it in yourself. I am so clear about myself, that I make it my most deliberate aim in general to keep as little company as possible. Nothing save the completest solitude suits me, in such circumstances : then I do not have to speak (which always increasingly heats me), compose myself, collect my wits, and thus regain a mood in which, as you behold to-day, I become gentle and just, and willingly assume the blame for much that I inflict on others when in company.—Let us hope that thus in course of time, during which I am wholly restored to myself by a new and prospering work, I also may recover in other respects through rest and quietness : for sure, a new good turning will appear then in my outward lot, at present so deeply at ebb, and—then we certainly shall also strike the channel to conduct us both to that reposeful life we wish. For our mutual future let us cleave to one experience from these latter days : the motive which impelled you to that arduous journey in the depth of winter, and the heart-felt joy with which I welcomed you—cannot but shew you and myself how it stands with both of us !—If each will now care for himself, *his* rest, his prospering, at like time he'll *thereby* care best for the other.—

For the rest, I refer you once more to what I deem the most expedient, and most acceptable to myself as practical upshot of our agreement : namely, that you should settle down with all our household goods in Dresden—on a moderate and modest scale, which in fact we *mustn't think* of exceeding there, of all places. All else to me seems whimsical and without sufficient ground, new surroundings exciting, old ones on the other hand soothing, especially for yourself. I think of sending you the whole this autumn, placing at your disposal the needful sum for an equipment altogether to your taste, and leaving you to act entirely on your own initiative. After our having always had such bad results when *I* set up house and you came *to me*, I really am looking forward to coming *to you* for a change, and *hope* it will then have good results for ever, as I am confident I shall not feel too ill at ease with it. Seek out then a dwelling large enough to serve us to the end of our life : if *I* in future need a spell of total peace and quiet for a major work, no doubt I shall find such a haven in some castle of the Grand Duke of Baden's ; or should our circumstances very much improve, one might fit up a little country-box besides, whither I could withdraw for the summer, or even for winter. By which I mean that before fixing on a *definitive* abode in Dresden, this future outlet must be allowed for, so that we mayn't exceed our means to start with : therefore, something like a raised parterre suite of 3 to 4 living rooms, at a moderate rent : try for one in the Räcknitz neighbourhood. How I shall manage coming to you precisely by the time when you've moved in, I know already.—

Perhaps it's premature of me to be indulging so far in these plans and proposals to-day, but you will see what I'm preoccupied with, and that my thoughts are friendly to you ; whilst I hope my rough proposals will answer to your fondest wish.—

For the present, alas, I haven't yet got rightly back to rest. You know that even my financial position is giving me trouble again for the moment and a while ahead : I have had to find a means of not approaching Schott again *before* a certain time, and fancy I've succeeded ; so that I may also hope to let you have at least a little more quite shortly. Have no fear about the summer; I can count on Schott for certain *then*, and you shall lack nothing for your comfort and cure.

Before finally setting to work I much wanted to have another interview with the Grand Ducals, and therefore wrote to him anent the reading of the Meistersinger: for your amusement I enclose the telegram the Grand Duke himself despatched to me forthwith. After spending Friday at Schott's again, I travelled on Saturday to Carlsruhe, was at the Grand Duke's on Sunday, and returned here Monday night. The Grand Duchess had hit upon the idea of surprising me with a performance of Tannhäuser on Sunday evening. I had to miss the first act, as I was at the palace from 3 to 6 o'clock, and then had to get some food before I could go to the theatre: my recitation lasted that length because we had a deal of conversation before and after every act. On this occasion I was also greatly pleased with the young Highnesses again: as they dine at 5, I proposed to break off after the second act, but they wouldn't hear of such a thing, provided I weren't overtiring myself; so they kept their dinner waiting a whole hour, and nevertheless were at the theatre long before myself. Their attentiveness and approval were great: alike the serious and the mirthful made a fine effect, and in the last act their irrepressible laughter made me laugh so much myself, that I was obliged to interrupt my reading. In brief, my success was complete, and I am glad their belief in me has been strengthened in this way afresh, and that they know I'm not yet done for.—For the rest, the Grand Duke didn't seem to have got the length of being able to disclose any results of his promised steps in my behalf: I had to give them my word to come again soon; still, I gained so much trust, that I continue firmly reckoning on the amiable, steady young prince.—

I have weighed it in my mind, how easily I could extricate him from the difficulty if I were to declare myself prepared to accept the Kapellmeister post there : only—I am bound to deem a thing like that impossible for ever. True, I have made it up with Devrient, since he proved to me that *Ander* had simply fabricated that conversation with him which so annoyed me. But—but : theatre fish remains theatre fish, and whether it's Devrient or Hülsen, the same story holds good ; with this artistic management the cause doesn't stand a hair's breadth otherwise than anywhere else. I sat out the performance of Tannhäuser like a lamb on the altar, and let the whole representation pass over me to the secret accompaniment of this one vow :—never to place myself in such a position again !—My God, no : I really should have looked for a shade more common-sense under knowing Devrient's command ! Of course he had valid excuses for everything : precisely ! that's just the trouble, that such things can be excused at all. No, dear Minna : As far away as possible ! remains my ever stronger resolve : I *can't* abide it ! Work, write, and that practically—shall still be my amusement and unique delight ; but let them leave me out of their performances. The dearth of thought and talent is too, too great, and were I to keep on interfering, I should simply make enemies all round and anger myself to death. No : tranquillity—solitude ! else I cannot hold out !—

However, I mean to have another try with Lohengrin, if *Schnorr* does come : only, *not* with Mad. H[ewitz] as *Elsa ! !*—I've told them that. Devrient maintains that she's capital ; but he let himself be over-reached by

this person at a time of fix, and conveyed her a per-
petual engagement at 5000 gulden. And *I'm* to pay
the penalty ? No thank you !—

Now fare you well, and treat your poor distended heart
to rest. I think I've supplied you enough news for a
while : tomorrow, God willing, I shall set to my work at
last !—When I returned last night, the little white dog
went quite crazy : it was funny to have to view him
as a hired chattel of attachment ! The charwoman is
shaping very well ; she is sharp, and does everything
tidily. She also made me an egg-bag at once ; so,
with the aid of the sand-glass, I cook my eggs quite
admirably now. In fine warm weather the apartment is
truly charming already ; they tell me there are so many
nightingales here, that it positively deafens one ! Good :
I'll let myself be deafened !—

Enough of chatter now : nothing else has happened ;
I have heard nothing from anywhere. Till I've brought
them an easy, attractive new work again, I shall regard
myself as dead. It's high time : so now to work ! I
hope you will give me your blessing on it ; yourself you
need my bringing something off again for once.

So, God be with you ! Greet Jacquot, to whom
I'm very partial still, notwithstanding he loves me
no longer. Think of a Fipsel soon : somewhere about
autumn ; then we'll christen it together !—Hearty thanks
and faithful greetings from

Thy
Meistersinger.

236.

BIEBRICH, 22. *March* 1862.

DEAR MINNA,

The letter to the King will follow tomorrow. I
am unwell and in bad humour. All these things prevent

my coming to rest ; furnish a little help or money—
they won't, you'll see.   Also, I should have thought I
had written the King and his ministers enough already.
Various people, as I read, have already been authorised a
free return ; I learn from Köchly that he could have
returned to Saxony without any fuss even last year.
Consequently it is with great bitterness and resentment
that I approach such a letter, which will only be made
an instrument for my public humbling.   You might
aptly have informed the Minister, he need merely remind
the King of my letter, for instance, transmitted through
Seebach last summer.

I really don't know whence to draw a further string
of needless words ; it puts me in a shocking humour.
I've torn up several rough drafts already.   Why is it
so pressing of a sudden ?   Should not the permission
to tread Saxon soil again be regarded simply as the
final long-awaited answer tendered *me*, after countless
requests ?

Well, perhaps I may have a more placable moment
tomorrow ; if I hit on a brief sufficient form of wording,
you shall have it.   But do understand that I have other
things in my head besides, which unfortunately I can
never get to ; whilst my whole load of cares is still left
on my neck upon all hands.   I'm heartily sick of it !

Now adieu for to-day, and thanks for your good
will.   No doubt it will soon be done, too ; only I'm
a bit refractory just now.

Best greetings and wishes from

Thy
RICHARD.

237.

DEAR MINNA,

Once again you don't judge me correctly. I should have to put up with that in the end, if you didn't invariably convert it into an injury to yourself. Do please believe in earnest that I can have a mind for nothing now, for nothing in this world, save for bringing about a new opera I may get given next winter if possible. Can you shut your eyes to the certainty that nothing can be of such importance to me as this, and everything which distracts and turns me from the needful mood, after such long and trying obstacles, is bound to culminate in my utter despair ? An evil star reigns over everything connected with me, letting nothing appear at the right season, and what would otherwise be most desirable too late, if not in fact untimely. After those four months on the rack in Vienna, and when I had to form the quite monstrous decision to give up Tristan altogether for the present and undertake a new and easier-given work instead, how gratefully, nay, with what veneration—I needs must repeat that to you—should I have welcomed the message : '' You are amnestied ; I'll get the furniture sent, set up house, and you can come and work in peace here ! '' *Now* that I've passed another winter full of hardships, succeeded with unspeakable toil in at least getting straight here for my work's requirements, at last am taking up my pen to jot down the first notes of my music, of a sudden comes the news, His Majesty is in a melting mood, the thing will be arranged now.—

Do you refer it wholly to *yourself,* then, if I have been quite indifferent to this arrangement now, and positively nothing but *disturbed* by it ? Do you wholly dis-

regard, moreover, what I tell you of my money troubles?
While I am racking my brains, not with musical invention, but with the discovery of ways of procuring
the monetary means so soon needed again without giving
myself away, what so joyful impression can it produce on
me to learn that I may just return to Saxony? What
have *I* to seek there; what sources of help will be
opened me there; who will give me a thaler there? Do
not all my hopes repose on prospects that can be realised
only altogether outside Saxony, nay, only on the assumption that Saxony is nothing to me? What value to me,
under circumstances such as those, is this so atrociously
long-delayed amnesty?—

Very good : I will not deny that last winter, when
the Bürde[-Ney] was still in vigour, it might have been
of the utmost use to me to have the Dresden theatre
at disposal with Tichatscheck for Tristan. I will hope
that the Opera may regain its full rating there, and consequently I admit that artistically it is of value to me to
see Dresden open to me again ; but let us also hope the
Intendant will summon me one day, as I shall obtrude
myself nowhere any more. Further, it is good that
through the amnesty the blot is now expunged which
hitherto, and as late as last winter—in the Frommann's
opinion—may have withheld certain very high personages
from dealings with me : if the amnesty had arrived *last*
year, I should have gone to Berlin this past winter,
and tried my luck at Court there.—

But now this has all grown late, I feel done up,
embittered, and fancy I am doing right to set no more
store by it. Consequently I had *one* sole true and urgent
reason for writing to the King *once more*, and that was
my concern for *you ;* since I know that none but a

Dresden residence will appear to you a last and im-
mutable. For *my* part, I have much to overcome in
the notion of settling in Dresden again, and any other
place where I can live quietly to myself is preferable
to me at bottom. But for your sake I wished for this
settlement—long ago ; that turned the scale, and I have
done all that was needful towards it. What would you
more, then ? Am *I* not left all, all other cares of man
and artist ? Has aught whatever been transformed
thereby in my truly all but desperate situation, save that
I now know we can settle down where *you* would liefest
come to rest ?—

I pray you : think yourself into *my* situation and mood,
too, and do become a little juster—for *your own* sake !—

For the present let me devote myself to my so greatly
needed work ; grant me the right humour for it, and let
me spin it off the reel in good time. *Then* much will
stand otherwise, and I can breathe again. I will see
to the money for you to rent quarters in Dresden at
Michaelmas : until then please give rout to your blues,
and—be a little juster to me. I need the most jealously-
guarded repose now : how do you think I can compose
after this letter to-day ?—

I will attend to my missive of thanks when the
customary official intimation shall have reached me—in
answer to my [previous] letter ; I always got the refusing
letters safely, so I suppose they'll let the consenting also
reach me this time.—

Now be tranquil ; this last award has been of great
importance to yourself. Think of a dwelling such as we
discussed : in no case must we do the grand in Dresden,
for many reasons.—

After your first-rate looks at the end of the past

winter, dear Minna, I entertain no fears about your health ; take care of yourself anew, and let us pay heed that it be not so easily shaken again by disagreeables in the future !

Adieu, farewell, and be of good cheer ! But also grant rest and good humour to him who needs them both so urgently !

Kind love from

Thy

RICHARD.

238.

[German ed. " 239." *]

BIEBRICH, 9. *April* 1862.

O Minna !

Peace !   Peace !

Here is the letter to the Minister, in which I express my thanks, and at the same time beg him to lay me at the feet of the King !—

These scanty lines came very hard to me again, else I should have given you a sign of life still earlier.—

Julius's death, which had already been briefly notified me by Luise (no one else has written me from Dresden), we will pass in—silence. Your interest in him, and the tone of your more detailed report to me, do your heart and self great honour ; I thank you for it ! Beyond that, Fritz Brockhaus's conduct in particular has touched me much ; I beg you to give him my most cordial greetings : he has something very affecting to me !—

My trust in your health—which, strange to say, you interpret as envy—has not been shaken by your protesta-

---

* In the current German edition this and the following letter are printed in the inverse order, evidently owing to an editorial miscalculation of the " Easter " date.—Tr.

tions. It isn't nice of you, to threaten me so often with black thoughts, which hardly ever come to you, I'm sure, except when you converse with *me*. For myself, I'm not afraid of death, especially of such a calm and peaceful death as Julius found it.—

If my communications about my money-troubles only produce on you the sad effect of covert reproaches for yourself, it will certainly be better if I am somewhat more chary with them in future. Only, it is scarcely a fault in me, to be so eagerly desiring some results on that side, in particular as it so distresses me not to be always able to provide you with all those comforts to which the troubles you have gone through give you such just claims, and claims so deeply felt by me. This is my only sentiment toward you in that regard.—

I am hoping you'll soon be also taken with the wish to look around for an abode. The provision of everything connected with that settlement in ease and order by next autumn, largely depends on my having got so far with my new opera by then as to be able to anticipate results from it. Till now I've been unprecedentedly delayed, and am much behindhand with my work; which no doubt is contributing to Schott's close-fistedness with me. Only the other day, and mainly through the influence of fine weather—which is greatly enhanced by the delightful [situation of my] rooms—did I succeed in seriously sinking myself into my music in spite of many things ; but I believe I shall soon have got the length of sounding that productive mood whence not even the most untoward occurrence can tear me any more. You, dear Minna, know how much you can assist toward that. Don't think of *my* weal, but solely of the very needful thriving of my work !—And make this comprehensible to all the rest.—For which matter, you may tell the Messrs Dresdeners that, if they're so anxious to have me back in Dresden, they should furnish me also with something to live upon.—

I saw *Jacob and his Sons* at Frankfort, and met the regisseur, Hysel (known to you also from Magdeburg days). Thereon the local Kapellmeister [Ignaz] Lachner wrote and bade me to a conference on Tannhäuser, which is to be got up there afresh ; which took me there a second time. I saw a Spanish tragedy (very good !) and was introduced to Herr v. Guaita, who interests me much. Being a very rich Frankfort patrician, he has been placed at the head of the Theatre-committee, is a man of the most cultivated taste, and prepared to cover out of his purse any deficit thereby arising. I was quite astonished at such an encounter !—

Hr. Bürde—as you say—is an agreeable, lively, educated man : as actor, I've seldom met anyone of less talent ; such affectation and unnaturalness had absolutely never come my way.

I thank you kindly for your news about the Holländer. A pity if it never succeeded at Dresden ; in Vienna they have given it innumerable times, and yet the Viennese are rated far less serious and profound. It seems it always needs a great deal else, to hit the Dresdeners' taste.

Now forgive me if I've forgotten anything. I am very mean with letter-writing now : when I'm working, I always find little free time to keep a free head for my letters !

Farewell, and the very best greetings !

Thy
RICHARD.

I did put something in the Frankfort lottery, but drew a blank.

239.

[Germ. ed. " 238."]

BIEBRICH, *2nd Easter holiday* [*April* 21] 1862.

Kindest thanks for your letter, good Minna.—Ah God, one's getting old, you see, and the " certain years " assert their rights ; how hard it is to say what's happening in one then !   Lucky the man who at that age need cherish no wish for himself, but solely for his progeny. Under the ill conditions of my life, I'm striving all I can to secure at least tranquillity for work,—yet nothing will rightly speed with me.   To be dead, would please me well enough ; but to be alive and never in sound health, is not agreeable.   Scarcely had I got a little under way at last, than I was overtaken by all sorts of threatening symptoms, so that I have the doctor in the house again.   Good God, this constant agitation !   The bowels are in a miserable state with it all ; but it had also invaded the chest with quite novel oppressions, and the thumping of the heart became so painful and sleep-disturbing that at last I really had to seek advice.   The doctor finds nothing amiss with the heart,—they never do : but your humble servant has the torture (you can sing a song of that yourself !).   Now I drink bitter-water of a morning, and walk it off.   My humour has been much upset by it, and an overpowering melancholy seems to have been trying to master me.   Coarse as you think me, I'm an extremely delicate plant as a fact ; at least it's astonishing the uncommon influence the slightest change of weather, for instance, exerts on me.—However, I must grin and bear it !—

I am entirely without news from Carlsruhe once more ; will the Lohengrin performance take place before the holidays, or not ? I know not, and don't much care to ask : it would look as if I set such store by it. That was to have occurred in the second half of May, during Schnorr's starring. If it were still to come off, it would disappoint me as regards my birthday, which I meant to keep in Dresden this time. If I'm prevented by Carlsruhe from coming to Dresden about that time, it shall certainly be done before ; so prepare your mind for it, and try to lodge me somewhere near you.

Your getting on with the Brockhaus's, and your seeing so much of each other, is pleasanter news to me than perhaps you think. There are reasons for that : I don't make much account of anything in the world now, but— peace I wish to have around me, and strained relations simply drive me off. I'm fond of solitude, but merely as a second-best : if no great claims are made on me, I'm very partial to fairly sociable company. In the end, too, one much misses a family : a little young folk belonging to one, and by whom one gets a trifle petted, is not a thing to be at all despised ; if one looks too strictly into character, one ends by finding ground for reservation everywhere.—I have been unable to write to the girls ; tell them I'm soon coming to Dresden myself for a day or two. And give my love to Fritz and Luise.

We'll have a talk about the dwelling on the spot. However my outward circumstances may shape, really we can only set up very modest house in *Dresden :* if I obtain a pension from outside, it will at any rate involve a few outer obligations, so that I am unlikely to be able to be in Dresden *continuously ;* but the most annoying, as you'll understand, is the grudging surveillance by people there

to whom I still owe money from before.   Nevertheless
we can run to 250 thlr for certain ; therefore if we soon
take a *great* fancy to one of those dwellings you now
have in mind, I don't see why we shouldn't rent it even
from July.   If the amnesty had only come just 6 to
8 weeks earlier, I undoubtedly should not have set up
here first : isn't this eternal contrariness sufficient to
put one out of humour ?   But enough of that !—

From Vienna I have heard sheer *nothing ;* but if they
are expecting me there in September for Tristan, it is
no more than in strict accordance with the arrangement
under which I left Vienna last.   Consequently it would
delight me if the management itself had adhered to the
bargain without my further importuning ; for—I have
sworn it to myself—*I'll never* ask a management again,
nor yet a singer, for anything whatever !   Amen ! !—

I forgot to tell you of G. S[chmidt]'s opera.   I went
to it ; he gave it for his Benefit.   It is the wretchedest
and commonest shoddy I've come across as yet ; he seems
an adept, however, at getting himself puffed in the
papers.   Child, in the cold light of day there isn't much
to be said for the good man : the Frankforters knew pretty
well why they got rid of him ; he isn't fit for any decent
theatre, and doesn't know how to shew respect on any
side.   His taking up my operas in his Frankfort period
was only since Schindelmeisser (an odd, but not ungifted
fellow) had anticipated him with great success at
Wiesbaden.—But enough of that too !—

In the Theaterchronik I've been shewn a poem on
myself which was recited at a party in the Hôtel de Saxe
(I fancy).   It was very pretty, and pleased me much.—
Good goodness ! an unknown " Biebricher " also sent
me a magnificent Easter-egg yesterday with Tannh. and

Lohengrin [upon it]. I'll bring it with me.—Otherwise I don't see a soul except Weissheimer, who comes out to me as often as he can. Cornelius wanted to come too. Bülows, who intend staying on the Rhine 2 months this summer (he often gives concerts at Wiesbaden), have enquired whether it would disturb me if they sought quarters at Biebrich for that length of time ; to which I naturally had no objection.—

Speaking strictly, I've done nothing of my new opera yet, except—the *overture ;* but that has turned out very well, and probably will cut out all my other overtures. God only grant good health and some diminution of worries !—So, till further orders—perhaps by mouth !—

Best love.

Thy
RICH.

I am still very pleased with the domestic : she keeps everything neat, and I don't hear her.—

240.

BIEBRICH, 26. *April* 1862.

DEAR MINNA,

As you wanted an answer by return about the rooms, I'm replying with these lines at once, and shall let a letter follow with 100 thaler, which I mean to send you in a day or two ; for money-letters, to the best of my knowledge, take somewhat longer, and you need to hear by Monday.

Please decide about the rooms completely of your own accord ; you know my views and purpose. If you believe—as you wrote me lately—you will be unable to find so good a suite next autumn—that is, when you return from Reichenhall (which I had by no means

forgotten)—then I abide by it that it will be prudent
to make up your mind already, as it certainly is a matter
of an abode that shall meet all due requirements for a
permanence as well.   I hope you won't take it amiss
of me, that with this I chiefly bear in mind yourself and
your requirement of stability ; myself I should also like
having a home somewhere, but must leave it still an
open question whether Dresden, of all places, will contribute to my special ease, and I imagine time will prove.
In my eyes the choice of Dresden is *only* of value because
I like the thought of your being there best, and you
are bound to prefer it yourself to any other dwelling-
place.   You won't take it ill of me, that this is very
weighty and decisive in my judgment ?   Of what profit
that habitation will be to *me*, must be left in the lap
of the future ; I wish and hope for the best and most
agreeable to yourself !

Beyond Pusinelli and the Krietes (the latter for the
interest on capital advanced to me and since repaid) I owe
no one any money in Dresden.

Regarding the abode, once more, decide entirely as
you think fit : if you believe you won't find so reasonable
an apartment later as the one in the Walburgigasse, and
if that pleases you, why, take it.   Roughly calculate
also the cost of your living till autumn, including
Reichenhall, and tell me what you think you'll need
till then ; you will be receiving 100 thaler (as said) in
two or three days.   For the removal of the furniture and
its doing up (when you'll have to renovate much) I hope
to scrape the needful sum together in good time ; which
very much depends on whether I have made sufficient
progress with my work by then.   The latter thus remains
the chief consideration. —

The Carlsruhe business must decide itself very shortly now.   I believe it *won't* come to a Lohengrin perform-ance there ; in which case I look forward to spending my birthday in Dresden.   Then I shall wish for all that is good, and hope and expect it !—

Adieu for to-day.

In fine weather please take a droschke (at my extra expense) and drive to the Grosser Garten (about 6 o'clock), there to do a little promenading.   I do it every morning in the park here, where the nightingales have recently arrived, and I always feel refreshed by it and put in a lovely humour.   Please do !

Kind love from

Thy

RICH.

241.

BIEBRICH, 26. *April* 1862.

I now supplement my letter to you of to-day, dear Minna, with the remittance of money announced in it. Here follow, accordingly, the promised 100 thl.

Don't ask me how I've managed it ; if the wife can contribute nothing, she strictly oughtn't to know much about the husband's burdens.   *Berlin* has somewhat helped me this time, as it brought in something over 200 th.   Oddly enough, Paris also has furnished a little, namely 238 *francs* tantièmes from concerts, *Cafés chantants* etc.   *Truinet* saw to its payment to me, and I couldn't help laughing at this droll receipt.   It always comes to very little, as it has to be divided among a mass of interested parties ; nevertheless, even this small revenue, of which one has no idea at all in Germany, has some-thing startling.

It is wonderful here now :—only the two dogs give

much trouble, as the Herr Architect [his landlord] is frequently away, and nobody bothers about the poor beasts [. .]. The architect wanted Leo kept tied up, but I couldn't stand that [. .]. Now a little coolness seems to have arisen.

Poor Weissheimer is lying at death's door in Darmstadt, where something of his was to have been performed at a concert on Easter Sunday. This very day I received a message not to come and enquire, as his illness, an inflammation of the lungs, was at its acutest critical stage.

I've hardly gone to Mainz at all since. Almost every day I make my expedition to Wiesbaden, just merely there and back, mostly on foot all the way. I pass the Bank many a time, but have never yet prevailed upon myself to stake.

Since Weissheimer hasn't been coming, I see or speak to absolutely no one ; often a longing tries to seize me, but in the end I find total solitude quite bearable, and in any case more beneficial than intercourse with unsympathetic people.

I am surprised at your never having anything to tell me of Schnorr ; is he not still going to Vienna ? They're expecting him at Carlsruhe also, I believe.—

There—I've fairly chatted myself out now, and must think of dinner. Be good and remember my admonition to drive to the Grosser Garten each fine morning : economise the droschke fare by a little chariness with present-giving, your ancient passion.

And now farewell ! Let me hear again soon. I shall soon discover if I can come to Dresden for the 22nd May !

Kind love from   Thy

RICH.

242.

DEAR MINNA,

I have been expecting a message from Carlsruhe day after day, and meant to wait for that ; but it seems they can resolve on nothing there.   I haven't the least desire left to conduct Lohengrin ; I answered Devrient's last absurd report most briefly, and really have a mind, if the Grand Duke wishes it, to tell him the naked truth about D.'s management.   On the other hand, I've proposed to the G. D. to arrange a grand concert-performance on some occasion—as formerly at Zurich—at which I would present them with fragments from my new works. Presumably that also will shipwreck on D., whom I simply think of henceforth treating as my enemy.   It certainly is woful to make such experiences with regard to wretched presentation of my operas precisely at a theatre controlled by Devr., and it robs me of the last relish for direct dealings with the stage.   How greatly you are mistaken if you believe I've been expecting to receive offers from Dresden for the theatre : I merely see by that how much you hold yourself obliged to be the only one to tell me the truth !   My God, what do all you people know of me, and how things look within me ? !

It is curious how it suddenly occurs to you—and as it seems, quite by the way—to stir up fresh confusion about the residence.   My child, decidedly you have too few real cares, too little occupation, since you always find so much leisure to think of yourself and wrongs done or possibly still to be done you !   I should really have thought I had expressed myself repeatedly and plainly enough on this Dresden question ; but as so many hair-splittings still occur to you, accept the comforting

assurance that there is no place in the world to which
I should give preference over Dresden for a residence,
and as every place is equally indifferent to *me*, I prefer
Dresden to all others because I know you thrive there
best, it being after all your home. It is and was arranged
that you should settle there, and set apart a room for me.
Thus our estimates come cheaper, the dwelling has no
need to be large ; for I also shall not be going to Dresden
to *work* there, at present, but simply to distract, divert
myself, and above all to see how one can stand it. I
have good reasons to be a little anxious on that score ;
but I shall come with the heartfelt wish to find or re-
establish peace and comfort there. In the event of new
or old troubles arising, however, and my having to prefer
for our mutual peace' sake to withdraw at times into
some sequestered work-den, it will console me to know
that the above arrangement leaves *you* at least in your
accustomed stronghold ; and for that, above all other
reasons, is Dresden well-seeming and pleasing to me.
Consequently I insist on your choosing the dwelling
according to *your* needs, before all : in an unsequestered
neighbourhood, where you can see people [passing] and
are not too distant from your female friends ; a 1st floor
or parterre, with or without sun, as you like best. You
know what difficulties there always were in finding an
abode to answer all *my* demands as well, if my principal
aim was to *work* in it ; finally we had to take whole
houses to ourselves, and then again, *you* felt remote and
lonely. So : it not being so easy to accommodate the
interests of *both* of us, let us abide by a compromise ; I
deem the one proposed by me the best, but—let us also
leave it to time and circumstances whether they can
prepare for us in Dresden what most will suit the interests

and needs of both of us combined.   It—may be—I hope and wish it, and extend my hand to everything.—

The above is my most honest opinion : if it disquiets you, doesn't satisfy you, then—don't be surprised—I should have to think you downright ungrateful.—Now act accordingly, select and begin to solidify the home !

It is painful to me beyond all notion, to keep having to reply to naggings—forgive me—of the last description ; absolutely nothing results from them, except discomposure for me.   You see how placably I keep on stretching out my hand, and trying to open up roads to the best one could wish ; so for Heaven's sake do *your* part towards it, and don't be for ever upsetting the mind of your husband, who does not belong to you alone, but to his art, to the world and posterity !

I was half inclined to write to Madame Huber this time, to tell you the above as a friend : another time I should really have to do so.   Do please be sensible, conquer this eternal mania for wranglings quite unworthy of you ; surely you can see, when all's told, that you may rely on me in every way.—

I beseech you, lay that to heart !—

I am thoroughly pleased with my work now : candidly, I shall make a break in it very unwillingly, and am afraid of evil consequences, afraid in general ; for who still should trust and hope ! I also doubt my hearing Schnorr [at Dresden] ; in the end it will be merely another vain hope : even his *not* going to Vienna makes him very indifferent to me.

Now farewell ! Greet Jacquot and Mad. Huber. From his heart

Thy
RICHARD.

243.

BIEBRICH, 13. *May* 1862.

DEAREST MINNA,

I must send you a couple of lines at once, in answer to your good-tempered letter !—Your little spies deceive you ; you're served exactly like the Saxon Police, when they also had me spied on heretofore, and got fine balderdash reported to them. My child, I am *glad* to be installed here for my work, and have but one care : namely, to keep interruption at arm's length. I was at Darmstadt for 2 hours some time ago, to call on poor Weissheimer, who unfortunately is not quite out of danger yet ; Schindelmeisser insisted on my running over the next Sunday for Tannhäuser (with Tichatscheck) ; next morning I received a letter of regret, the performance was interfered with. So I remained where I was, and have had no further notice ; neither has Tich. himself called on me, so I'm still waiting and waiting to meet him. I go to Wiesbaden almost every day by the 6 o'clock train, drink a cup of coffee in the Kur garden, take a walk, and return on foot to Biebrich, where the burning lamp awaits me regularly from $8\frac{1}{2}$ on.—Since poor Weissheimer hasn't been calling on me, I see or speak to literally not a soul ; least of all at Wiesbaden, with the exception of a Herr Städel, a connection of Schott's, whom I meet about once a week there, and perhaps of Herr B., who inflicted himself on me a little too long the other day. At Frankfort I wanted to attend a Tannhäuser rehearsal once, but changed my mind, and returned without it.

The reason why I didn't answer your punctually-received letter of the 30th of last month for some time, will have become plain to you from my last, which I despatched to you 5 or 6 days since. (Apropos : your last letter, of the 9th May viâ Darmstadt, only arrived here to-day ; nevertheless I am surprised at your not having received mine [May 8] by then.) Now I see by your epistle of to-day that I very probably attached too great a weight to the provoking questions and remarks contained in *that* letter, and find my experience confirmed that one mustn't always take things so precisely with you. No doubt it pains me to have always to be prepared for this or that slash, this or that confusion as to which you urgently demand intelligence,—especially when I am bound to wish myself such *total* peace of mind as now ; nevertheless I'll resolve not to take things in such deadly earnest for the future. This time it had quite uncommonly put me out again ; and most likely that arose from the state of my health, which makes me a great hypochondriac at times. The last time it was positively unbearable, particularly with my bowels and my chest-affection ; do or omit what I would, it made no difference (my doctor's a toper, and doesn't shew his face). I daresay it must spring from some error of diet ; mostly, tho', from my unceasing cares, the constant failure of everything I undertake, the necessity of resigning myself in every direction.

I stick to my work like a devil, and while you— who know me so well, you know !—suppose me on continual pleasure-trips, even in the worst of humour I am wresting from my muse at least one smile a day. So I really am well into it now, and a fairish portion of the first act is already finished.—Concoct what plans I may for my future bearings toward the Theatre, all, all *now* come to this alone : I must bring a fresh opera into being—since I'm still in great uncertainty about the

Tristan at Vienna.—Nothing else I might undertake has any sense or prospect of success if something new of mine, and easy to be given, does not precede it. So I keep suppressing all my thoughts, all disappointment, and tell myself : Complete the Meistersinger ; nothing else !—

I hope you will quite comprehend this, and seek no other thing behind, if I am growing more and more uncertain about my projected Dresden visit. It is no trifle, and often of the greatest danger, to interrupt one's work. Eh, if I had already finished something like the half, and needed a distraction ; but it's only 6 weeks since I thoroughly got to work : everything still is delicate, and needs careful rearing. Moreover, I have become so distrustful of anything pleasant or good assumed to be in front of me ; I believe in nothing, but simply fear commotions, disillusions, annoyances : at least, they always happen to me, once I mix with people. Oughtn't one to prefer a secure limitation, to any change ? And then the money point : would it not be better for me to save the 50 thaler the excursion at least would cost me altogether, and contribute it to you, which really will soon be of need again ?—All these are demurs which I give you to ponder, to prepare you for the event of my *not* coming just now ; but I've settled nothing as yet : we'll see !—

Everybody at Schott's is ill ; they fear that he's developing consumption. Consoling also !—From Carlsruhe—not a sign of life !—Never mind, if my work but succeeds in spite of all. I—hope so !—

Farewell, and greet all who greet me. Perhaps — — ! —

Now Adieu ! Thy
RICH.

244.

BIEBRICH, 19. *May* 1862.

Best Minna, a little ailing the last few days, to-day I feel my unwellness somewhat increased, in particular through a severe flux.   Were it not for this, I'd promptly announce to you my definite arrival at Dresden Wednesday 10 P.M.   Should it improve, and especially the dysentery (I don't think it at all dangerous), I will confirm the projected arrival by a telegram tomorrow (Tuesday) evening.   In case I am able to come, it would be nice if someone like the Brockhaus's were to expect us to dinner on Thursday with the Heines and Pusinelli. Should I have to de-telegraph, please do not consider my illness in any way serious ; it is the result of a chill and too much mineral water, which the doctor here had ordered me.   Only, there would be a difficulty with the flux on a journey.

So, look in any case for speedy news from me.   I should like to be able to travel !

Hearty greetings from   Thy
                                    RICHARD.

245.

BIEBRICH, 20. *May* 1862.

DEAR MINNA,

I am sending a few written lines on the heels of to-day's telegram, to remove any anxiety it may have aroused in you concerning my health.   A little fever has appeared with me since yesterday : I hoped it would vanish after a good night ; only the night was very restless, and I have to keep myself very passive and quiet to-day, not to increase the fever—in no case more than a catarrhal.   Under such circumstances the anyhow fatiguing journey to Dresden wasn't well to be thought of. That's all! It is a singular fate that this illness—however slight—should have seized me precisely this week. Perhaps, though, the very unrest in which my travel scheme had plunged me was to blame for it: as I always am pedantic with my work once I'm fairly into it, I had meant to let the trip depend on my having got clean through a new scene in good time. That made me rather overtax myself in the end, and now I have to pay for it by several days' stoppage of work. Rest will set me up again at once; consequently I also expect to be able to write you properly within the next two days at latest.

Kind love from   Thy
                            RICHARD.

246.   BIEBRICH, 21. *May* 1862.

DEAR MINNA,
     That's always the way! Precisely through my eagerness to make my birthday-journey still possible I have put myself hors de combat for it. I had intended if I got my scene with David finished to a T, to go to Frankfort Tuesday evening, and on to Dresden Wednesday morning. Then it happened that I so forgot myself on Sunday in the press of work, that I didn't rise from it and go to dinner until half past 6, having taken nothing whatever since my tea-breakfast. I gulped down my food, set myself in active motion by a walk to Wiesbaden despite bad weather, caught cold on my way back, and on Monday I was miserable, had weakness and dysentery, which Tuesday reinforced with slight but lowering fever. I already feel better to-day, and in any case the attack is of no further importance; but it would have been

impossible to carry out the journey to-day without the
certainty of arriving at Dresden really ill. So I will
take it as a dispensation of Fate, which has at least
this good side for the moment, that I'm able to add
another full 100 thaler to-day to your last. Be so good
as to let me know if you believe you can manage till
about the second half of July now.

I'll write to Frau v. Bülow to give you full particulars concerning Reichenhall ; I believe it's still
thoroughly cheap there, and fairly primitive.—

It would delight me, if it became possible for me to
fetch you from Reichenhall the 5th of September and
accompany you about as far as Nuremberg ; my work
will surely grant me *one* such trip—I hope !—precisely
at that season. That this work dominates me in everything now, has become comprehensible to you ; it makes
me indifferent to all else, e.g. whether I hear Tichatscheck
or Schnorr. This work alone, and my really achieving
it, is also my apology for having set up this provisory
retreat for myself here ; without such an object, I
myself should have had to regard this transitory domicile
as inexcusable. Moreover, I shall only retain it until
that object is fulfilled. I hope to have got so far by
late-autumn, and on this assumption I propose to enter
your abode at Dresden the 24th November.

I cannot help considering my decision to regard the
Dresden domicile provisionally as merely *yours* both wise
and prudent and most in keeping with my circumstances.
My position, taken strictly, is so forlorn and helpless,
that I am bound to look on any thought of permanent
and cosy quarters for *myself* as extremely unjustified.
Just now my prospects for the future are of the completest uncertainty and possible entire abandonment,

which perhaps nothing save a fresh great success can somewhat alter. Countess Pourtalès, who has just magnanimously helped me out with the most indispensable funds, at the same time implores me to expect as little as possible, or better, nothing at all from the Courts, *despite* the sure reliability of the Grand Duke of Baden. Consequently, after terminating my new opera I shall consider myself flung helpless on the world again ; and nothing save the engaging in a new work could make such transient installations as my present one of need, and therefore accountable, either now or in the future.—

Under such circumstances, in the natural order of things my wife would have to share my changeful and unsteady fortunes. However, as she has shared so many shifts and hardships of the kind with me already, my first thought is to bring at least *her* into safety and provide her an enduring hearth : and I rejoice to learn that the fittest spot has now been found for that, since you so often have declared to me of late yourself that, now you're there again, you feel best off in Dresden. So my chief thought is to preserve you the Dresden haven sure and safe, and at all times to supply you with the needful means for a decent subsistence there. For my own person, I propose to view a cubicle in your apartments as my home, leaving it entirely to *yourself* how home-like you may make it for me. In course of time, and let us hope as result of a successful new opera, once my prospects grow settled I reserve to myself a supplementing of the Dresden domicile with one that meets all *my* requirements too ; adhering to it that *you* shall still stay safe there under *any* circumstances, since that is to be accomplished with more modest means.—

And in face of these clear and distinct dispositions, I am to have the grief to be told by you that I'm thrusting you out to roam the world, and you must deem it a charity to have been invited to Russia by relatives with whom you once stood in the most hostile personal relations !—I'll say no more on that.—

After the unhappy outcome of my Tannhäuser in Paris I was advised (and that by Liszt in particular) to pay a call on *Rossini*, whom folk had been treating to all kinds of vexing reports on me ; nay, one day Rossini himself sent to tell me he'd be pleased if I would visit him. I turned it over in my mind that a false construction, humbling to myself, might very easily be placed on such a visit ; and as I understood in general that the good old man would never be able to understand *me*, and therefore nothing but confusion must arise, I did *not* go to Rossini, preferring to bear the reproach made me of thereby offending the amiable old genius.— Now I am brought a journal-article in a German music-paper of last year, where a long full account is given of a visit I'm alleged to have paid Rossini after that Tannhäuser affair to win him over to an intervention in my favour, whereupon Rossini is supposed to have dismissed me with a clever taunt. All the world of course took that for truth, and Weissheimer has entreated me to contradict this lie even now. I have serious—and very melancholy grounds for not doing so, but leaving the thing at rest. No doubt this story will appear in my biography some day ; but what besides will not appear there ? Whoever finds letters from *you* among my papers, will find it written in them that my wife describes myself and my behaviour to her as " heartless," " coarse " and " common " ; so I daresay that will get into my biography

also ! Well, I can't prevent it ! But let us drop that—
and before all else complete the *Meistersinger!* I've
hope ; and then we'll look a little farther !

Best compliments to Madame Huber, and—kind love
to yourself from

Thy
Birthday-husband.

247.

BIEBRICH, 12. *June* 1862.

DEAR MUTZ,

I see I must break my firm resolve, and once more
give you explanations I wished to be relieved from for all
time.

Between me and you stands no one, but your own
suspicion and the illusion with which you plague us both.
Lay this to heart : it is the unadulterated truth. The
arrival of letters and a parcel during your visit to Biebrich
was a most remarkable coincidence. I hadn't even informed Frau Wesendonck of my departure from Vienna,
but when I was about to leave Paris also at the end
of January I forwarded a brief account to Zurich of my
outer fortunes, together with some remarks on my new
opera-poem. Through those letters to Biebrich I learnt
that M. W. had sent me a Christmas present to Vienna,
but, after much travelling to and fro, it had returned
to Zurich. Acquainted at last with my whereabouts, she
sent the things on to me, worked by Myrrha, she said.
Afterwards her husband informed me that his wife was
very ill, which was making him particularly anxious
as she is to become a mother again in June or July.
Thereon I answered him, and there's an end of it. Now
I beg you, let Madame Wesendonck be confined in peace,
and for God's sake let no grey hairs be added to your

head on that score.—It really almost makes me laugh, to see you so madly mistaken ; but as this illusion makes you suffer so terribly, my laughter leaves me, and—as you have repeatedly experienced—genuine despair takes its place, to think that nothing can teach you the true state of affairs.—

I have had my say,—and now—please, please, not another word about it, since it drives one silly !—

What put me out so much in that letter of yours of the end of April, was your facing me with " I appear to be wanting to *impose* the Dresden residence on *you*," after everything stood so peaceably between us. For me that had a sense which quite unspeakably annoyed me, and seemed to contain the seed of some fresh discord. However, as I wrote you after receipt of a second letter, I then regretted having at any rate attached too much weight to your expression, ascribed it to my own bad humour, and to some extent apologised to you.—I can say nothing further : all the rest, that you've made out of it, is utterly erroneous. Only you remain entirely unjust to my position, and refuse to believe the clearest reasons for my arrangements as regards the Dresden household. How am I to cope with that ?

My things were already packed for the journey to Dresden, and my few acquaintances believed me on the road ; only the doctor knew I wasn't travelling, and why.—I paid for one despatch to you at Biebrich : what created the confusion of a double telegram, I do not know.—

I don't destroy your letters ; I have them all.—

I mean Dresden in earnest ; God grant you strength for it.—

For the present I can't help you, but only *you* can

help *me*, by allowing me mental repose for my work, without which things won't go at all now, and from which nothing ought to turn me. I must forgive you for my livelihood cares being indifferent to you. About a most affecting conversation with the Grand Duke regarding Devrient, and the results thereof, I will tell you another time. Nothing is so important, for the present, as my being able to give Schott soon a part of the full score ; otherwise I know not whence to draw money for late-summer.

The Vienna management has now informed me that the rehearsals for Tristan (with Ander ! !) are to begin in mid-September. On the whole I'm pleased, as I hadn't written another word to Vienna ; I don't quite know as yet, tho', what attitude I really ought to adopt towards it. I already had my eye on a production at Dresden next winter ; and I think of also going in for that sub rosâ.

So, brief and to the point : Come to yourself, shake off your illusion, and believe my words ! Thus you will profit your own health, and thereby help me too !

With his whole heart's wish for prompt recovery, and kindest love,

Thy
RICHARD.

248.

BIEBRICH, 9. *July*, 1862.

DEAR MINNA,

With all the other sorrowful accounts of your health, you could have told me nothing more unwelcome than that the letter I wrote you *poste-restante* to Reichen-hall, in pursuance of your directions from Zwickau, and which should have arrived there in the last days of June,

hasn't reached you.   Really it is the first time a letter
from *me* has got lost : I had furnished it with the selfsame address as I sent the Berlin cashier at the same
time.   I hoped that this letter, briefly giving you a
reassuring explanation of the latest incidents, might
contribute something to your better frame of mind.   I
mean to try and trace that letter ; I should much like
it to reach your hands even yet.—

Not altogether needlessly to broach that painful
subject once again, let the assurance suffice you that
my motive for writing to Pusinelli simply sprang from
your last letter from Dresden, which indicated to me
such a serious attack of illness * that I became very
concerned at having no one but yourself to discuss your
complaint with ; for my own peace of mind I was bound
to want another person's opinion at last as to how to
behave, on my side, to have as little harmful an effect as
possible upon your health, what I ought to do or leave
undone to promote it to the best of my ability,—which
I hope you won't take ill of me.   I did not appeal
to Pusinelli for an intervention : his believing himself
nevertheless bound to interfere emphatically of his own
accord may shew both you and me how seriously others
look on what to you, dear Minna, at times seem nothing
but mere conjugal disputes without ulterior moral consequences.   Your believing you must understand the
opinion he gave you from himself as if *I* too were har-
bouring the thought of a divorce from you, has greatly

---

* " On my last return from Carlsruhe I found a letter from Minna
awaiting me [see p. 749] which set me in the most appalling concern about
her.   For that letter really gave me the impression of coming from a mad-
woman.   She must be terribly excited again ; God grant that her visit to
Reichenhall may lead to her improvement ! "—to sister Clara Wolfram,
June 2.—Tr.

distressed me. Never has that entered *my* head, and never will it enter it.*—Notwithstanding, let me heartily beg you to conform in reality to the other advice he offered you as regards your conduct ; I also hold myself bound by it in my deepest conscience. It cannot and must not continue like this, that the occasion should present itself at every moment for tearing open the profoundest wounds.—Let us now restrict our correspondence to the needful messages about our outward life ;

---

* In the important collection of letters to Dr. Pusinelli (*Bayreuther Blätter* 1902) will be found a touching document of July 1, 1862, from which it is advisable to quote the following : " My creative composure is becoming harder and harder to preserve ; I am startled out of the midst of my work by this or that fresh needle-stab my heart receives from that side ! . . . How profoundly I feel obliged to you again for this last, so extremely difficult act of friendship ! Ah, I really wanted little more than to discuss the things concerning us with some third person,—to hear a voice that should cry into this chaos of mine a clear and feeling word. My dear Anton, you have done infinitely more ; with a matter that is bound to pain whoever even touches it, you felt compelled to grapple deep ; you understand it all, are just and charitable ! . . . I never seriously thought of an actual divorce from my wife. All I yearn for, comes from no vestige of desire ; no, I only ask for rest, tranquillity, if possible, oblivion. I would sacrifice even that wish, if I could believe I thereby might prepare my wife a pleasant life ; but experience has proved the opposite, and—I believe I now at least must finally desist from such attempts. So you see, we are at one ! "—A letter of ten days later to sister Clara also says : " Hitherto I had endeavoured to mix no one else up in it, and tried to pull along alone with that unhappy woman who bootlessly is torturing herself and me to death. But there's no end to be found to the madness. . . Consequently a continuance, or resumption of our living together is the most foolish and wrong-headed thing conceivable. It therefore can only be a question of the *manner* in which it is dissolved ; and that depends upon what Minna's shrewdness can persuade her to. . . The idea of a divorce [or "legal separation "—*Scheidung*] did not proceed from me, obvious tho' it may be, and excusable as it might be in me . . the right moment for that was missed long since. . . You see, dearest Cläre, how completely I agree with you ; nay more, I admire you and your clear judgment, for not having let yourself be bewildered by Minna's incredible falsifications of matters of fact between us " (*Familienbriefe*).—Tr.

and even in your answer to this letter of mine I beg
of you to make no mention of the serious point last
touched.—We have only one hope : age may make
everything worse, but it also may gradually heal and
cicatrise old sores. Let us leave the door wide and
willingly open to this latter possibility !—

Pusinelli declares you totally incapable of managing
a larger household now : God grant you may recover
strength enough at Reichenhall to take the smaller one
in hand this autumn. Last winter's stay in Dresden,
when you had to worry yourself with nothing whatever,
proved of the greatest benefit to your recovery—in P.'s
opinion also ; so, if in this respect I mean to avoid
everything that must needs be harmful to you, rest
assured upon the other hand that I shall arrange it all
in such a way that not the least humiliation can arise for
you in the eyes of the world. Unfortunately—my own
uncertain and completely prospectless position supports
and justifies me much in this.—

And now—think solely of yourself ; and while attending to your health, please stamp this deeply on your
mind : that only your returning vigour can also open *me*
the prospect of still being something to you, of helping
and invigorating you.

We shall certainly meet at Dresden in late autumn ; I
have altered nothing in my plans.—

Tristan is really to be put in rehearsal at Vienna
mid-September. The management's announcement pleased
me, and I shall let them have free play,—yet I don't
make much account of it, especially as the talk still
is merely of *Ander*. So much the better if it comes
to something after all.—

I shall most studiously see to more money ; be easy

on that head !—I thank Mathilde with all my heart, that she is coming to you.—A number of visitors are on my neck here now ; the Schnorrs among others. The plan is for them (with Mitterwurzer) to study Tristan on the quiet, so that the Dresden management may find it as easy as child's-play to give the opera some day. Only I should have to conduct it myself : will that be possible there ? ? ?—

Now farewell ! Hope ! ! On your health depends everything—believe me ! When you are feeling a little better, we'll have a longer talk about it all !

Farewell, and be heartily saluted by

Thy

RICHARD.

249.

BIEBRICH, 23. *July*, 1862.

DEAR MINNA,

Of late I have been more in request than I care for ; scarcely had the Schnorrs departed, whom I coached in Tristan, than the Dustmanns came, and so on.—In and for itself, moreover, I believe I do right not to answer your letters forthwith when they don't concern urgent affairs, but simply regrettable points in our general relations—a course you still persist in. How much I myself feel exhausted by that endless skein of incorrect and exaggerated fancies and conceptions, *never* to be unravelled *this way*, I have repeatedly sought to bring home to you ; but even if I left *my own* composure out of count, I never know how to pick and choose expressions not to yield you fresh occasion for self-torturing misunderstandings. Your last letter itself has re-confirmed this, and strengthened me in my inflexible

resolve—believe that !—not to be drawn into those points
again in any way.

What more can I say, if you really remain of opinion
that I threatened to get you " punished " by Fr. Huber !
[*Cf.* p. 738.]—Such nonsense I can only meet henceforth
by silence.—But how, in spite of my positive statement
that I adhere in all things to my views anent our domi-
ciliary relations, and shall see you again at Dresden
this late-autumn,—how you have persuaded yourself
once more to construe my assurance that I shall make
it my business to avoid anything in those relations which
might possibly shame you in the eyes of the world,
as if I didn't mean to lodge with *you* in Dresden,—is
one more evidence how hard you make everything to
me, and what I must always be prepared for ! I beg
you, read my letter through again, with the passages in
my previous letters which dealt with our future domi-
ciliary relations, and answer yourself whether I could
have had such an insult to you in my mind with that
assurance. I have so definitely expressed myself to
you about my growing need of temporary retirement
to the greatest calm, the quietest seclusion of dwelling-
place, on account of my works ; about the difficulties
of *combining* this in a big city with an abode that meets
your needs of non-seclusion, lively surroundings, nearness
to people, etc.,—I have expressed all this so definitely,
that you ought to have been in no doubt of my meaning
that I should make it my business to furnish the world
a similar reason for leading an intermittent life with you
in Dresden.—

Once more, dear Minna : Don't take things too
heavily,—but also don't take them too *lightly !* What
makes the present epoch hard for us is not merely dis-

putes from these latter years; under any circumstances we have arrived at a critical period of married life, a period that, with our so extremely different views and characters, must be passed through and surmounted with the utmost prudence. We are neither young nor old : young, we cannot make ourselves again ; so the hope of age alone remains to us. Benevolently and kindly careful for each other's weal, let us leave ourselves a breathing-time for entering that further stage wherein we may resume a peaceful care-free life in common, with all our woes forgotten. Soberly and benignantly I now offer this needful pathway of transition. We will not separate for that, but leave the door still open to the need of each. *Mine* passionately impels me to completion of various drafted works, for which I'm still in years of adequate creative power precisely *now :* for that I not only need quiet, but my whole bent, my own sore ailments, positively drive me to the greatest solitude available ; and this must now stand open to me whenever I require it. On your side, in a modest Dresden settlement you'll find the very thing that does you good, society of female friends, distraction, life all round you. There you will keep my room prepared for me ; and there, whene'er I turn my steps to town and town affairs, I shall be at home and have my home with you. Thus will it gradually be discovered what is good and needful for the pair of us, without our wearing each other out—which is really to be feared after our latest experiences—in the difficult transitional epoch we now have reached. And thus shall we at last attain that period of our age which, as I fondly hope, may still reward and soothe our undivided intercourse.—

You see, I *abide* by the plan I unfolded to you after

your return from Biebrich.   Now do not let yourself be led astray again, for your part ; compose yourself, preserve your health !

You shall have money again in a few days.   The amount required for the Dresden.installation I hope to be able to supply you in the course of August.—I'll write you upon other things next time.   Now farewell, be reassured, and understand me right and well !   Kind love from

Thy
RICHARD.

250.

BIEBRICH, 21. August 1862.

DEAR MINNA,

The day after tomorrow it will be 4 weeks that I've had to suspend my work entirely.   Even to-day I can only write these lines to you by holding the pen between the two middle fingers ; I can't so much as think of music-writing yet.   If it had been the whole left hand, it wouldn't have mattered at all, as there is hardly any pain ; but precisely the right thumb ! *   I have still to protect it from any sort of pressure, if I don't mean to check the very slow process of complete internal healing, and make it painful anew.   You may imagine my frame of mind !   I had based my every calculation upon being able to deliver to Schott the full score of the first act quite finished this month, to induce him to pay the fresh advance I need : only to-day can I even attempt to write to him connectedly about it. Upon his answer—he's at Kissingen—depends my being punctual with the money for your furnishing etc.   I hope

---

* He had been bitten by the Herr Architect's big dog.—Tr.

to !—Meanwhile I'm much à sec myself just now, and must entreat you to address yourself in my name to Mathilde for what you're short of for the journey back. As soon as you are back in Dresden, I hope to be able to send you at any rate something again.

You are quite right to be returning by Vienna. Call on the Laubes; they live in the " Stoss im Himmel " block (sounds droll enough !). The Standthartners unfortunately are not at home.

From your last letter I see that you're merry again, and feeling better on the whole. That makes amends for everything, even for the various ills that touch myself. I really must have untold patience.—

So farewell, and don't be vexed at this little ; I can't write more at present ! Kind regards to Mathilde. From his heart

Thy

RICHARD.

251.

BIEBRICH A/RH. 3 *September* 1862.

DEAR MINNA,

You will be astonished at this *empty* letter : judge how painful it must be to myself, to have to appear in this guise on your Birthday. I had been hoping to be able to send you the money for your Dresden furnishing to-day : I cannot even send you what is needed for your everyday expenses, and must address you the distasteful prayer to borrow your next few days' requirements from one of your lady friends (I specially beseech Mathilde). I trust this latest pinch will only last a few days longer. Times have been very hard with me, and I should have dreamt anything rather than that Schott would have left me so completely stranded—on account, so he says, of entire stoppage of his own receipts from America and Russia. I went to Kissingen myself, where he's taking a cure, but found him laid up with high fever, and couldn't even be admitted to him. I have taken steps, however, to beat up the requisite money on other paths, and believe I may reckon with certainty on being able to send you at least something for your keep within the next few days, and shortly also what is needed for your installation with the furniture. Console yourself with me, whose misfortunes you now have to share : rest assured in return, I shall remember you in the very first place when I'm out of the wood myself.

But yet another pleasure has been dashed for me, and I have had to defer its fulfilment. I wanted to send you a very successful oil-portrait of myself for this birthday, but the painter hasn't finished it,—I couldn't sit of late : obliged to leave now, he will only complete it quite at Munich, and despatch it thence to you before the month is out. It will look very well in the new abode.

I am alone again now, and my finger also has so far recovered that I have been able to work again without disturbance. It was highest time ; only, these momentary ·cares disturb me much still !—

The Frommann surprised me with a visit from Schlangenbad the other day ; she received a full account of my relations with Carlsruhe, and has gone on there to see the Grand Duchess. I don't believe, though, that she will be able to achieve anything for me. My whole future reposes on the completion and success of the Meistersinger ; therefore I know nothing so important as this work.—

Lohengrin was to be given at Frankfort with the

Schnorrs : he cannot come. Whether I shall bother about the performance itself *without* him, I must leave unsettled for the moment.

Now, dear Minna, don't be angry with me because of this disappointing letter ; things will soon improve. For to-day please accept my heartfelt wish that you at least may feel well and in full strength on your birthday ! I hope so fervently, and send best love !

Thy
RICHARD.

252.

BIEBRICH, 15. *September* 1862.

DEAR MINNA,

This moment I have received word that the Leipzig manager has at last seen fit to deposit the fee for the Flying Dutchman [after 16 years]. I am at once giving orders to forward the 20 Friedrichsd'or [£17] to your Dresden address, and consequently breathe again at being able in this way to let you have a little to go on with.— The rest is bound to arrange itself soon, and I hope to be able to let the chests of furniture (exactly as you wished— together with what I think I can spare from my own small establishment here) go off to you by the end of this week, so that everything may stand at your disposal in Dresden by October 1. At the very latest you will also have the needful money for your fitting up by then.

The saddest news is that I'm so behindhand with the Meistersinger. I've sworn it shall be altogether finished by my 50th birthday [next May]. I shall hold to that unflinchingly !

So, I conducted my Lohengrin for the first time in my life myself last Friday [12th]. The original cause resided in a star engagement of the Dustmann's last July :

as the Schnorrs also intended visiting me at the same
time, I proposed to Herr v. Guaita, the Frankfort artistic
director, a model performance of this opera.   But since I
likewise wished to give the opera *entire* (without the
usual villainous omissions), there wasn't time then.   At
last it got that length—but the Schnorrs couldn't come ;
I attended a rehearsal, and found the Kapellmeister
(Lachner) so miserable, that I had to make up my mind
either to withdraw completely, or to take over the
rehearsals myself.   The *integrity* of the score would have
proved detrimental to the representation if I had not
conducted it myself ; so I embarked at last—and *don't*
repent it.   You know my knack of handling such people,
so everybody was astonished at what I had made of
them ; only now—with the work in its entirety—did it
all become clear, and the success was quite extraordinary
(in spite of the strictly most limited means), so that folk
tell me they didn't recognise the Frankforters again.
Such a thing had got to happen once ; and I've promised
to conduct the next few performances also, to get them
firmly set.—Perhaps—it may profit me in other regards !

Meanwhile I have great worries ; my money matters
are not squared up yet.   Schott lies seriously ill at
Kissingen,—and life is not exactly easy to myself.—It
was pleasant to meet the Prince Metternich's on the
Johannisberg yesterday ; a meeting which will have important results, I expect.   He is going to Vienna, and will
draw the attention of highest regions to me there in
such a fashion that what I have awaited from Carlsruhe
and Berlin in vain perhaps may happen thence at last.

The Frommann is ailing at Schlangenbad, and
couldn't come to Lohengrin ; I hope to see her again,
though.

Weissheimer has gone off to Leipzig, to make preparations for a big concert there, at which I've promised him to conduct my new overture to the Meistersinger myself. That will be about the time you have got done with your furnishing ; so I shall come on to you, take a glance at Dresden, and expect to delight myself with your fortified health. Your accounts convince me that the cure has done you good, and no doubt it doesn't need my protestation, to tell you how much that relieves me and fills me with hope.

Now, dear Minna, you have a little money again for the instant, and a great weight accordingly is lifted off my heart. Mathilde can wait till the 1st of October, can't she ?—Adieu ! Farewell ! Have courage, and count on my solicitude ! Kind love !

Thy
RICHARD.

253.

BIEBRICH, 24. September 1862.

DEAR MINNA,

I thank you for your kind and entertaining letters ; your having so diverted yourself, is a happiness nobody grudges you less than I,—only don't take it ill of me if I haven't mental peace enough to enter any farther into your communications and the invitations passed me on : I have a head chock-full, and to look out for my skin ! You cannot believe the confusion Schott's behaviour has thrown me into : I can't get near him ; he really is very ill, and his considerable losses, particularly through America, by all means aren't to be denied. But what is the use of my going into all that for your benefit ? it would simply bewilder you as well. Many a time has it been easy for me to procure help in such cases : this time quite incredible ill-luck pursues me !—However—means *must* be devised in the long run !

Trusting to ultimate success, I have found time to attend to the furniture-cases : nos. 7 and 14 have been re-packed and filled up with some things I could spare : all went off yesterday, and will reach you in a week. You must and shall have the requisite money by then ; be easy on that score !—One chest will follow later, and contain a few things from my present equipment which really must be in my room at Dresden.—

For the moment, when I am driven from correspondent to correspondent, to say nothing of flying hither and thither to follow up financial operations, I really can't write you much more than just that announcement and solace !—

I am bound to tide over this too in the end, but it has taken a deal out of me this time, and I'm just earnestly seeking to obtain definite security against suchlike vicissitudes for the rest of my life. I hope Metternich will assist me to that !—

In the thick of my worries I conducted Lohengrin only once more, and then handed it over. The audience behaved very nicely again, and laurel-wreaths came down. The performance went surer than the first, but I also perceived that the singers had got the full length of their tether and weren't to be brought any farther !—

In a calmer frame of mind I will make up for all omissions ; to-day I merely wanted to reassure you and let you have the needful solace !

Patience, then, all will come right ! The furniture is on the road !—

Kind love and all best wishes from

Thy
RICHARD.

254.

BIEBRICH A. RH. 30. *September* 1862.

DEAR MINNA,

I'm on live embers to hear if any money has been paid to you ; God grant I may have a reassuring message about it tomorrow morning ! I have had to try and shift in every way, my forsakenness was past belief ; thus I am pumping my last ounce of strength to work out as much of my full score as possible, so as to get something into Schott's hands soon and make *him* amenable again. Meanwhile provision had to be found for your security, and I have made use of a kind friend in Dresden (who offered to put me up in his house before he knew anything about our settlement). I hope he'll have already supplied you with the needful ; if not, let me know at once.

The packing-cases should be reaching Dresden about tomorrow : if you haven't the money yet, all you need say is that you don't want them delivered for three or four days. But in that extreme event, perhaps Pauline might assist ?—it would only be for a few days !—

You see the commotion and worry I am in, and surely will forgive my inability to respond to so many invitations to have a jolly time of it here or there with anything except a sigh now ! Lord, if folk only knew what other things one has in one's head, than the thought of gaily trotting to and fro !—

However—that also will change for the better.—

One thing more :—for God's sake send that con-founded "*Monde musicale*" about its business ; I *won't* take it in !—So—no more

(Fragment ; end torn off.)

255.

BIEBRICH, 3. *October* 1862.

DEAR MINNA,

So I may hope you'll be receiving at least 200 thaler within the next few days, and indeed from Berlin. Pusinelli's absence from Dresden has been very disastrous to myself too ; had *he* been there, you certainly would have already had the money. However, that mournful month had been so rich in disasters of all kinds, that I had got quite used to it. In course of this month you shall receive another 100 thr. On the 31st October I shall be at Leipzig, and see you in any case ; then we'll also take more thorough steps against recurrence of such bothers.—

My local carrier's estimate unfortunately is correct ; there are more expenses with such transactions than you think. But it was contrary to my intention, that he sent the cases ' carriage forward,' whereas I was expecting to receive his bill *here*. It's done now, and you shall have it all set right by me. If it relieves your mind, I will enclose you the estimate next time.

Here it has been a case of—*preserving patience;* there was nothing else left to me. Now don't you lose yours for another few days ; I am sufficiently depressed at having put you in a fix as well !

Kind love from   Thy
                                                    RICHARD.

256.

BIEBRICH, 5. *October* 1862.

DEAR MINNA,

I may assume that at the same time as I'm writing these lines the Frommann is remitting you the value of my latest tantième from Berlin : how high it runs, I haven't been informed yet : only I know that Tannhäuser has actually been given twice, whilst Lohengrin was to have been given in September. Alwine tells me she has already placed a small sum at your disposal out of her own pocket. Now, if what you obtain in this way is *not* sufficient to cover your expenses for the current month, I beg you to make use of the enclosed two letters—according to need, and to which is the less disagreeable to you. In those lines I am asking both Luise and Pusinelli to hand you 100 thaler on my behalf at once ; I pledge myself, to the one as to the other, to refund them their money on a personal visit to Dresden in the first days of November. So make what use you think fit—according to need— either of the one or of the other letter,—or even, should it be necessary, of both.

The present catastrophe is pulling me uncommonly down ; this latest experience has determined me to think of serious means of guarding against its like in future.

—After a mere flying visit to Dresden, this time, I must be off to Vienna !—

God grant I may soon receive comforting news of the end of your dilemma !

With love,

Thy

RICHARD.

257.

BIEBRICH, 12. *October* 1862.

DEAR MINNA,

The Frommann has sent me no account yet of the dimensions of the present Berlin tantième. Doubtless the money is in your hands by now, and I'm

anxious to know if it puts you in a position to manage
till the beginning of next month.—Not before the 1st
of November can I count with certainty, on my side,
upon a sufficient haul; therefore I also see myself
obliged to beg you most pressingly to ask Frau Pauline
in my name to induce Kaskel to let the 150 thlr stand
over until the 3rd November. Only on that date can
I pledge my word of honour to refund this money to
the lender.

The fact that not a soul has helped, or could have
helped me this time, is something new to me, in a
degree, and I perceive that I must take my fate into
my hands another way. At this instant I'm no longer
busied with the Meistersinger, but with the arranging
of pieces from my other works yet unknown to the
public (particularly the Nibelungen)—so as to give
Grand Concerts with them, making a commencement in
Vienna shortly. Despite the papers, I have no serious
hope of Tristan there, as things still stand with Ander
exactly as a year ago; consequently I must try something else. This means that I'm quite overwhelmed
at present with the needful preparatory work for my
concerts. I shall be happy if by the day of the full
rehearsal for the Leipzig concert I have got the length
of being able to leave here. Social forgatherings with
good friends and relations are scarcely to be thought
of under the circumstances.

Hard as your life seems to you, please do believe
me that my own is *harder*. To all the straits and
harassments *you* suffer, for me is added the reproach
that *I* involve you in them; whereas you have a perfectly clear conscience towards myself in that regard.—
I too, dear Minna, am much upset, and the effect

upon my spirit of the quite unprecedentedly perverse experiences of these latter times is simply heightened by my having been unable to spare *you* a share in them.

However—things will alter now !—And rest assured, I'll see that you have no fresh harass to suffer.—

So—tell me whether you will require anything beyond the Berlin money before November 2.—The servant's bed is being packed : it shall go off, with several other things, within the next few days ; also the wedge-bolster.

Farewell, and console yourself with me ! Sad, but heartfelt greetings from   Thy

RICHARD.

258.

BIEBRICH A. RH. 12. *October* 1862.

DEAR MINNA,

This moment I have received notice of the Berlin tantième, which accordingly wasn't to be levied through the Frommann before : so *this* piece of pedantry was to plague me, too ! It delights me, however, to find the yield is large : it comes to 161 thlr, 25 sbgr., which amount you will accordingly get direct from Berlin by return, as I'm sending them in the receipt and assignment to-day.

Now—since Alwine, as she tells me, has also sent you something—I hope you will get on quite well till the beginning of November. Kaskel, the Frommann's and Tichatscheck's advances, and finally whatever else you still are owing, I shall repay on the 3rd of November at latest. Then I shall also arrange with you all further measures to prevent any troubles of this kind occurring again.

The above as hasty postscript. Now leave my head a little free for urgent preparations for my purposed concerts ! May calm take up its dwelling with you, and you be cross with me no longer for this last mishap.

From his heart

Thy

RICHARD.

259.

BIEBRICH A. RH. 28. *October* 1862.

DEAR MINNA,

I am going to Leipzig tomorrow on account of Weissheimer's concert, which does not take place, however, till the *2nd of November*. Should the rehearsals permit me (which I much doubt, tho'), I shall run across to you before ; but I have a good many other things to do at Leipzig, especially with publisher affairs, and am afraid of splitting up my time ; wherefore I beg you not to *expect* me till after the concert. Unfortunately I can only remain 2 days at the outside with you even then, as I *can't* go direct from Dresden to Vienna (where, on the other hand, they're urgently expecting me), but—am compelled to return to *Biebrich* first. It was impossible to beat up any money, and so I'm leaving sundry bills unsettled here ; for which reason I have had to represent my coming Leipzig journey to the parties interested as a mere flying trip, from which I should return in a few days. To have taken my luggage for the winter with me would therefore have produced a bad impression, and I'm only coming with my travelling-bag and the bare necessaries for a week in it.

God grant I may be luckier at Leipzig than I have been anywhere else ! Such a persistent quandary I really have never experienced in all my life, and I feel depressed in the extreme—nay—more than that ! It is therefore high time to make serious provision for the rest of my life, and that provision is my chief concern now. I have hopes still of a favourable issue at Vienna ; notwithstanding my being wretchedly off with the Tristan there, I am pleased to see by many tokens that the Metternichs have been of great use to me lately, and true good-will is entertained towards me in high quarters there. This—to be able to tell you something cheering as well !

I shall put up at Ottilie's (15 Poststrasse). Should you want to come to the concert on Sunday, you will be welcome !

If Kläre is with you, give her my love ; I shall soon see you again—if only en passant—and convince myself of your condition, also no doubt bring a little assistance.

So, to a good meeting !

Thy

RICHARD.

260.

LEIPZIG, 15. *Poststrasse, 2nd floor.*
30. *October* 1862.

DEAR MINNA,

The concert really is on *Saturday* [Nov. 1]. I let you know this, that you may arrange accordingly in case you care to come. Unfortunately Ottilie *can't* take you in as well ; but after all, that needn't make much difference.

I arrived late last night, and am not quite well to-day ; so I must remain indoors and keep very quiet, not to be really ill tomorrow. I expect to come to Dresden Monday ; so merely this information for to-day, and at the same time best love from

Thy

RICHARD.

[*The Dresden visit of two to three days duly took place; a few years afterwards (Dec. '68) it is thus referred to by the husband, in a letter to sister Cecilie: "It was Cläre I found at Dresden when it was a matter of making a most painful meeting with my lamented wife endurable."* —Tr.]

261.

BIEBRICH, 12. *November* 1862.

DEAR GOOD MINNA,

I thank you most kindly for your letter.—It seems as if things would come right with me at last. At Leipzig I obtained further assistance through a small loan from [A. ?] Ritters, and decided to force my departure for Vienna at all costs, without letting myself be detained by other instant hopes—whose vainness I had recognised, however; so I set forth at once for Biebrich, since I might also hope to find good news here. That happened too, insofar as it was an easy matter to find security, so that I shouldn't need much actual cash to get away from here. But then the Grand Duke, or rather the Grand Duchess of Weimar put in an oar; I received such a nice money present from there, that I am able to pay everyone off in fact now, besides keeping enough for the journey and my first start in Vienna. Finally, I'm also asked by telegraph from Weimar what fee I should demand for prompt purchase of Tristan and the Meistersinger, to which I naturally could make no definite reply; nevertheless I see that further resources are at my command there, which perhaps will amount to as much as I intended raising by that unsuccessful loan. It seems that Liszt has been of very energetic use to me there, upon C.'s intervention. Consequently I may also hope to send you the needful money very shortly; which will be an untold comfort to me. For, do believe me, it pains and shames me deeply not even to be able to give you the most essential relief.

So : the clouded sky seems clearing. I'm plucking up courage and trust in my fate again, which were really smitten to their lowest on my last return to Leipzig. Give my love to niece Clärchen, and tell her she shall also have the letter to Frau Schnorr from Vienna. The good thing about the operations just commenced is that, if brought to fulfilment, it will be no *borrowed* money, and I shan't have the worry of repayment.

Now I am just going to pack everything up and pay a few necessary calls, in particular on the famous old lady at Ingelheim ; who really might be of the very greatest service to my future, as I should then be free of any official obligation, which is always a drag. I hope to start tomorrow, though ; so expect my next letter from Vienna. If you have anything of moment to write me meanwhile, please address c/o *Dr. J. Standthartner, Stadt* 806. *Wien.*—

And so give heartiest love to good old sister Kläre ; she's to be nice and stay on with you. Also to Fritz and Luise. It seems I shan't go under yet, although a deal of care and trouble still remains !

Now many, many heartfelt greetings ! Pluck up heart yourself !

Thy

RICHARD.

262.

VIENNA, 17. *November* 1862.

DEAR MINNA,

My time's most excessively occupied, as you may well imagine ; for a few days to come I shan't belong to myself. Merely thus much : everything is shaping well, *good will* is past all doubt now. *January* Tristan —I believe, for certain !—

Only a petition :—J. J. Weber of Leipzig would like to put my portrait, copperplate, in his edition of the Nibelungen [text].   I am writing him either to get the oil-painting—undoubtedly the best likeness of me —sent to Leipzig by yourself (for a short time), or to give orders to an engraver in Dresden.   In either case I wished to let you know that the picture will be requested of you for a little while in one way or the other.—By the time you receive it back I hope to have also got so far as to be able to order a nice frame for it ; just as I only need to muster up courage again, to put a thorough stop to our hard-upness in general.—

Have hopes of a speedy remittance !   Greet everyone. Keep strong, and rejoice me with good reports on your health !   With all his heart

Thy

Once more :   RICHARD.

Weihburggasse,

Kaiserin Elisabeth.

263.

VIENNA, *Kaiserin Elisabeth.*   30. *November* 1862.

Dear Minna, things are at once going and sticking. I am annoyed at having to send you another empty letter to-day.   There's the fullest prospect of my being quite helped out of the hole by Weimar, though, and also enabled to provide for you poorest soul completely. Under the title of an immediate purchase of " Tristan " and the " Meistersinger " they have asked me, on direct behalf of the Grand Duke, for my requirements ; I have framed my answer in such a way that—unless a total change of front appears—I may hope to be quite satisfied shortly, probably within the next few days. Don't be cross with me for having wanted to await a certainty ere writing you : it gives one such pleasure to be able to present oneself with a good conscience and full hands. However, I really mustn't keep you waiting any longer for a somewhat more detailed report.—

Things here stand passably ; undeniably full earnest with the Tristan ! Yesterday we had the first complete rehearsal. Ander is shewing himself quite brisk and up to the mark : which has its reason. Hitherto things were still of a complexion in which I could put no trust at all ; so—with *very* great difficulties—I contrived the engagement of *Schnorr* for next January, whereby I'm at least certain of perhaps 6 performances from about the 10th of January on. That had its due effect on *Ander* too ; so it's possible I may shortly have two Tristans.

I had thought of giving concerts also in the second half of January, but people have advised me to begin as early as December. It is the same with me here as everywhere ; the envy of the craft is intense, and they do their best to keep me off. So it will be well, and have a good influence on the Tristan practice also, if I shew myself as soon as possible in all my glory as conductor, etc. Moreover, it will do my exchequer good ; for—I see plainly again—I shall lose my whole personal authority with the higher officials here directly I begin to dun for money. I must wait for them all to come to me, nay, behave as if it were no present concern of mine.—Under such circumstances I shan't know whether I'm on my head or my heels before long, and you will have to overlook it if you receive nothing save the briefest notes on main points.

Touching Foreign Affairs, the Weimar ones are in rather a ticklish phase for me. What the Grand Duke can give me *alone* will not suffice for my requirements ; a sphere of action with such paltry means would be quite impossible to me—who couldn't have taken up with Opera *stationarily* even at Berlin or Vienna—and none but bad results would arise, both for me and for him, if under pressure of want I accepted. On the contrary, I adhere to it that the three related Highnesses, of *Baden*, *Prussia*, and *Weimar*, should combine to allow me a pension of 3000 thl., in return for which all three could have me for *extra*ordinary occasions. We'll see what comes of that.—I have to be all the more circumspect now, as it concerns a last decision for my lifetime ; for— something *extra*ordinary may easily be compassed with Vienna also ; whilst I can't and mustn't bind myself to any place in permanence, or—it's all up with my productiveness.

My God, what I should like best of all, would be that rich old lady of Ingelheim ; but one must go to work very gingerly there, as she—naturally—is most mistrustful. It must all come as if of itself ; and that has now been capitally led up to.—All else is constraint, with great harm and vexation to follow.—

Really, dear Minna, I have nothing against the Walpurgisstrasse, but the tidings received there haven't led to much : e.g. the 100 fl. for Ollmütz preserve dead silence.—The Hamburg letter, on the contrary, brought a great stupidity : the management, having lately given Herr Gounod an ovation with be-laurelling for his Faust, invited me to let myself be similarly fêted at their theatre, for which purpose would I be so kind as to conduct my Tannhäuser in return for travelling expenses and full board ? I have replied that, since the Hamburgers had be-wreathed my friend Gounod already, I would accept that honour as simultaneously conferred on *me*, and thank them for the board and travelling expenses.—

On the other hand I have had an invitation from *Petersburg*, to conduct Philharmonic concerts there. Under circumstances, that might look more like ; but it won't fit in.—There—you know pretty nearly all about me now, and can answer people's questions.

I thank Kläre very much for having stayed on so much longer. Best greetings to the Dresdeners. If I get time, I'll send a note to Klärchen also for the Schnorrs ; but believe me, I am terribly rushed : to say nothing of proof-correcting, prefaces [*Ring* poem], and so forth. So, to full hands soon, good Minna ! Behave yourself, and be good to

Thy

RICHARD.

264.

VIENNA, 27. *December* 1862.

Ah, good Minna, you really ought to take a little thought to make things lighter for me ! You ought to soften even your just complaints to me (and those about your latest trouble *are* so !) ; but you abide by a constant illusion about me and my mode of life, from which nothing seems able to tear you. Only believe that I'm leading an utterly *wretched* life, daily, hourly —and *never*, *never* am merry !—Hold that before your eyes,—and your own griefs will appear less to you : mine are simply multiplied by yours.—

How wretched and disgusted I feel at every contact with our art-world, you neither can nor ever will comprehend.   My continual return to the attempt indeed is nothing but sheer desperation, never enjoyment !—But— enough !—

Outwardly yesterday's concert went off brilliantly. My most incredible personal exertions, however, hadn't succeeded in giving sufficiently good acoustics to the band-stand on the stage ; and to-day my work begins again, to surround the whole orchestra with a costly solid construction such as I once got made in Dresden [1846], so as to have better success with the second concert (New Year's day).   I have no accounts of the net profit yet ; the house was full, but a lot always goes out in free tickets and extras the first time, so that I shall be happy if things just balance.   The repetition, on the other hand, is bound to bring me something in ; then a third time perhaps : the same programme.

I was applauded on my entry for 5 to 8 minutes long ; I seem very popular here.   The young Empress was present from beginning to end ; I shall have to get myself presented to her now.—

It's progressing with Tristan, and I have nothing to complain of.   Still, it will probably drag on till February.   Esser is working for me like a slave, and is an excellent fellow in general.

Unfortunately I am supported in this arduous time (a concert like this is always quite a new occurrence, and one has to attend to everything oneself !) by no sleep ; I feel all to pieces, and everybody wonders how I even keep on end : increasing thumping of the heart and severe congestions on the chest, with terrible prostra- tion.   I never go out, except to see to something ; I don't know what a walk or recreation is !   That's my usual fate, and of such is my life! From New Year onward, tho', I've hopes of some repose; please do your share towards it. Among all my cares and troubles, the care for *you* has still remained the most consuming. Nothing having turned up from anywhere, at last I begged Standthartner to advance me the needful on my Tristan honorarium. He has had my wish complied with through his banker,—so now take heart, good Minna! It is certain to do you instant good, even to be rid at least of money worries and able to have things somewhat snugger. Come what may, in any case you shall receive a portion of my New Year's taking; so you may count on more money in the first days of January. Just write me—merely in round figures— how much you still need, beyond the 200 thlr, to free yourself from debt entirely.—

Let God dispose the rest! Adieu; I can no more! My hand is shaking, and I've to answer people dropping in here every instant!—

Best wishes, and—a good New Year's eve!

Thy

RICHARD.

265.

VIENNA, 8. January 1863.

DEAR MINNA,

With the greatest difficulty in finding days vacant for concerts, I had chosen New Year's (midday) for my second concert. In spite of the great disadvantages of that day and hour, I had bigger takings than anybody would have supposed; only they didn't quite suffice to cover the enormous costs (which I had been obliged to augment by the supplemental construction of a sounding-board all round the orchestra). This has very much depressed me, as I see I can arrive at nothing even on the path of concert-giving ; so I shall give a third concert (next Sunday) in the mere hope of the expected highest takings (—for the second concert's success at any rate was huge !) recouping what I had to lay out on the two first.—Very ailing through sleeplessness and indisposition of all kinds, on the 2nd of January I attended another pianoforte-rehearsal of Tristan, but again was reduced to great hopelessness, for I saw that Ander is in no sort of condition to master the part ; I cut whatever I could, but inwardly lost all belief in the thing.—From Weimar I expected to hear something good for New Year ; instead I learnt that the intended Court-concert had passed *without* the Meistersinger overture, whilst *everyone* keeps silence there.—

Under such circumstances I could find no occasion to acquaint you with anything cheering :—but that you should always put the worst construction on what I do or leave undone, as also on my motives for it, after all is your misfortune ; *I* am used to it. But how you can dream of drawing me to you thereby, would be a marvel to anyone who didn't know you.—

I am still in the greatest uncertainty what I shall do. They are imploring me *not* to withdraw Tristan. I have recently made a proposal to carry out the Meistersinger for the Vienna company which, if entertained handsomely, might tend to some alleviation of my plight. Otherwise I am hesitating as regards an invitation to Petersburg, to conduct 2 concerts of the Philharmonic society there, which at any rate would bring me in *something* certain.

You doubtless will now comprehend that I myself

am neither lapped on roses nor seated in clover. Nevertheless you may reckon with certainty on further ample
remittances from me this month ; in spite of all, I
hope to smooth *your* couch completely before long.—
I shall write to Herr Arnold, and reprove him for his
low remarks. All I beg of you, is to get a legal
transfer of the Dresden furniture, etc. drawn up as soon
as possible, and I will promptly execute it here.—

Remembrances to Heines, and wish them luck !—
Tell Clärchen that I asked *Schnorr* long ago to invite
her to music one day, but it seems *Mad.* Schnorr is
jealous ; which—in this case—I should regret !—

Farewell, and if you feel worried and downcast,
console yourself with the reflection that I also am
reaping no joy !

Best greeting from

Thy

RICHARD.

266.

VIENNA, 28. *January* 1863

DEAR MINNA,

A little light is breaking, and I regain courage
to give you an account of myself. I have had a woful
time to wade through, which at last has made excessive
inroads on my health.

My third concert, on the 11th, yielded never-ending
applause, the like of which can scarcely ever have been
heard ; I strictly might have repeated every single
number, but contented myself with three. The house
was quite full, too, so that I expected the highest possible
taking this time. But the treasury accounts made it
only 1350 fl. once more, so that I wanted to institute

legal proceedings for palpable theft. I was dissuaded, however (no doubt rightly), and had to resign myself to their having left me at least enough to pay expenses this time ; whereas I had had to shell out for both of the first ones, simply because there was no end to the costs (with all their trickeries).—Under such circumstances you may imagine how I felt ! The whole thing undertaken for no other purpose than to *earn something :* and to be plunged in debts instead ! !

One may understand my being heartily sick of existence !—

However, I haven't ceased either to hunt for aid or to lay plans for the future.

My results until now are as follows. At *Weimar* they have accorded me a fee for Tristan and Meistersinger which I am dividing in fairly equal parts with you, your share amounting to 40 louis d'or, which they're to forward you direct from Weimar (God grant they may !).— I go to Prague for a concert next week, for which I'm guaranteed 500 fl. If I find it possible, on the 9th of February I shall also go to Breslau, where they want to pay me 30 louis d'or for a few pieces at a concert. With that I shall try and pay debts and hotel bills, and see how much farther I get. At Petersburg I could earn 2000 silver roubles for 2 concerts, only I should have to be there by the 24th of February. I can't possibly contrive to get this Tristan out by then, tho' ; there's no hope of that before about the 10th of March : so another case of—sacrifice !—Steps I took to indemnify myself for Petersburg through an order for the Meistersinger for the Opera here have been rejected ; the management is afraid of my local influence, and that I might take it into my head to saddle myself on their back. Nobody bothers about me at Court except the Empress ; who was at two of my concerts from beginning to end, but *completely alone.* —

The only thing to raise my courage is the Tristan practice, which now awakes the highest hopes. *Esser's* great perseverance and pertinacity have worked wonders : he has drilled the music into intractable Ander like a starling. The *Dustmann* above all, however, is heart and soul in it ; she has moved me deeply, and will infallibly carry the whole audience away. There's no doubt about it any longer, and I count on a great, perhaps an unexampled success.—

As I've no answer from Weimar about Tristan with Schnorrs, I'm in treaty now with Prague for it. I believe it will come to my giving [all] my operas, and before all Tristan, there with Schnorrs from the middle of *May* to the *end of June.*—

Thus far have I extricated myself again, this time : it has cost me—many anxious days and nights !—

Now give me news again yourself soon. But not on yellow paper,—you appear to have forgotten that letter [see pp. 87, 89, 110].

Farewell ! Kind regards to our friends, and tell them how hard things are going with me.

Best wishes for your health from   Thy
                                        RICHARD.

(: P.S. on an enclosure : *Strauss's Benefice, Monstre-Ball (Walküren-Parodie).*) That's what goes on in Vienna while I am eating my heart out.

267.

St. Petersburg, 38 *Newski Perspective.*
5. *March* 1863.

Dear Minna,

Here I actually am, in Petersburg, which strikes myself as nothing but a dream. Last Tuesday I had the first concert, which went off extraordinarily brilliantly ; next Tuesday is the second. Should I receive no urgent message from Vienna [re *Tristan*], I would try and bring about a benefit concert for myself in addition.—Certainly, the exertions entailed on me are the *utmost* I still can expend on my livelihood : these journeys, and all connected with them, are intensely wearing. Nothing else remains to me, however, if I mean to reap the smallest particle of permanent repose.—Probably you'd have had to repent your great passion for travelling : the journey is abominable, desolate, appalling ; the city is magnificent, but one sees nothing of it. At least *I* only go out in a closed carriage to attend to the most indispensable, for the climate's atrocious ; the incessant wind, and its peculiar cuttingness, do for me the moment I step outside the house.

So, directly after my arrival and first rehearsal I was taken ill, and feared it might attack my nerves again ; but by dint of three days' thorough rest and seclusion I recovered. I have to spare myself all I can, however ; the concert took a fearful deal out of me again. Luckily they've lodged me very well, quietly and well-attended, with some Germans who keep a pension. I have exactly 10 paces to take from my house to the concert-hall ; naturally the concert-givers come to me daily, almost hourly, to make arrangements, so that I couldn't possibly have dwelt far off.

Touching the Mecks, I'm in a strange predicament ;

when I hunted for their address, I found I hadn't packed the telegram, or indeed their last letters (for good reasons) : so—how learn Meck's address now ? I thought to myself, if these people haven't entirely lost their senses, no doubt they'll enquire after me ; but nobody turned up. Finally, on my return home to-day the man-servant brought me a card from Colonel Meck [Minna's brother-in-law] together with your letter. He had called, but not left his address ; so, unless Meck comes back, I'm exactly as wise as before. To ascertain his address at the War Office would really be a very great trouble to me, who have so many other things to do ; so I must hope he'll catch me in yet.—

At present I'm still in great uneasiness about the band-parts of my new compositions, which I had forwarded direct from Prague, but haven't even yet arrived here. It's an extraordinary pickle, and I don't at all know yet what is to be done.—I should much like to thoroughly exploit the sensation I'm making here ; Lord knows if I now shall have time to.—

It certainly is curious that I should be finding here in Russia the help I strictly should have had to seek at home in Germany. But look at Saxony, my darling Saxony ; good Leipzig, ah, and that precious, noble Dresden, where I'm treated almost like a mangy cat ! My bitterness is gradually beginning to amuse me. Lawyer Schmidt no doubt has read you portions of my letter? How good it is, that I'm earning something in Russia at last to be able even to pay for those books H. B[rockhaus] took away from me ! And the shameful chicanes of the Saxon ambassadors right up to Vienna, where I still am persistently given out by Herr K. as incendor of the Royal palace ! Ah, what good this fatherlandly love and interest do one !—

Really, if I preserve patience, and renew my courage to work away and hold out, it's no small matter,— but it also is my last effort; I feel that I'm greatly exhausted, and not good for much more.

Well, preserve yourself so much the better; I'm taking care that you shan't lack! But—keep calm! Farewell, and accept the kind love of   Thy
                                              RICHARD.

268.

                              PETERSBURG, 1. *April* 1863.

Forgive me, dear Minna, for leaving you so long again without a word; my over-occupation is immense, and I have twice been ill already. On the very morning after my Benefit here I had to start for Moscow, according to arrangement, to give 3 concerts in a week, 2 for the directors and 1 for myself free of cost. Immediately after the first rehearsal I fell ill, and had to have that concert cancelled; so, to earn my Benefit after all, I had to give 3 concerts in 5 days, which strictly brought me only the profit of one. My condition is of the utmost exhaustion!

I got back here at 9 this morning, after luckily meeting a relative of the Ritters en route, who offered to attend to the enclosed bill of exchange for you; so that I'm able to write you this very day and send you money,—which wasn't possible before, for lack of time. Accordingly, I am sending you the following: 250 th. for your quarter's money, with the 50 thr you paid to Pusinelli; consequently, 300 th. for yourself. Then 362 thlr for the note of hand I gave bookseller Arnold, which will be presented to yourself, in lieu of me, for payment in our dwelling on the 15th April.

Moreover, another 150 th., which I still owe *Pusinelli*
from last time and I beg you to enclose in the accompanying note and forward to him thus. Altogether this
makes 812 thr, by my addition, which you will at
once collect from Kaskel on the bill of exchange.
Beyond that I have debts to pay at Leipzig, which
I shall liquidate there direct. Now I beg you to get
clear of your own debts; if it will not run to that,
you had better *not* pay the rent for the 1st of July
out of this, but I'll send you the fresh quarter's money
early enough for you to pay it out of *that*.

In spite of fine receipts, I'm rather sad and troubled.
I cannot repeat such undertakings without coming to
grief; that's the conviction I've won. I enclose a
photograph they took of me in Moscow; it will shew
you how pulled down I am. Consequently what I now
have earned must last for *long;* please therefore back
me up in thrift.

Now I must take a thorough rest here before tack-
ling the fearful journey to Vienna, where I shall soon
be much needed: what exertions I am going to face
there again! So I'm almost glad nothing has come of
the Berlin and the Breslau concert; I couldn't possibly
have stood it. If on the other hand I get time from
Vienna, perhaps I may give one more concert in the
Easter week here, which will bring me in more than
Berlin and Breslau combined. My local receipts really
amount to something over 6000 roubles (or thaler).
Audience and orchestra dote on me; perhaps Amalie
[Meck] has written you that? I was able to lay hold
of those queer folk at last, and allot them a box for
my concert, which they filled with their whole family;
I was highly pleased to see them again. Amalie left

me a little present for you, which I shall make over
in Germany shortly ; they have gone now.

Now, dear Minna, I must bid you Adieu again ;
I'm exhausted in the last degree, and want to write
a couple of lines to Pusinelli also. Farewell, be and
become tranquil, tranquil, and ever rely upon me !—
    Many greetings from

Thy
RICHARD.

[*He returned to Vienna the end of April, and soon installed himself at
Penzing, a semi-rural suburb, waiting for a production of* Tristan *that
was doomed not to come off, and meantime working at the music of* Die
Meistersinger. *Husband and wife appear to have never met again, but
it is obvious that further letters passed between them prior to the next
and last in our collection, also in the interval of a little over two years
preceding her sudden death ; in fact, on the* 16th *of February* 1864 *Wagner
tells his brother-in-law H. Wolfram :* " Your letter's brief description of
Minna's [mental] state quite shocked me ; I can't recover from it yet, but
weep all day. How I pity the unfortunate woman, I cannot tell you !
Of course I wrote to her at once,—soothingly and encouragingly, I hope.
If only good Cläre could visit her again, that I might have someone to
give me a clear account of her !" *For the present, however, these are all
we possess.*—Tr.]

269.

PENZING, 28. *September* 1863.

DEAR MINNA,
    Either at the time I am writing, or at any rate
within the next few days, you will receive from banker
Mendelssohn of Berlin the 250 rthr you now require.—

Don't be vexed with me for this brief note to-day ;
you shall soon hear more from me, and that good, I
hope. All I wanted to-day was to send you the message
above.

    Kind love from

Thy
RICHARD W.

[270*]

PRAGUE, 8. *November* 1863.

DEAR MINNA,

Herr v. Bronsart asked me to conduct some of my new things at a concert in Dresden the 25th November. There is something about it I don't quite like, and now I'm hesitating again as to whether I shall give my definite consent. In any case, however, would you kindly tell me if you are in a position to put me up precisely then? All I require is a bedroom, and at a pinch could even sleep on the couch in the lobby. Be so good as to let me know at Carlsruhe (Court-theatre), whither I am going from here so as to bring off at least a concert there at last. To be sure, I've great qualms about Dresden : my appearance in a small hall there, and with inferior forces—without the Kapelle—will naturally be regardable as a demonstration against the Court-theatre ; which is the last thing I should wish, as I see quite well it wouldn't have the least effect, since the hatred of Herr v. Könneritz [Lüttichau's successor] seems to pass all bounds against me. Therefore I shall still have to let it depend upon how I may feel as concerns this affair. In any event I should be passing through

---

* This letter, addressed to " MADAME MINNA WAGNER, 16, Walpurgis-strasse, DRESDEN," is not yet included in the German edition, but was published in Dr. Adolf Kohut's brochure *Der Meister von Bayreuth* (1905), and has the fullest appearance of being genuine.—N.B. The projected visit to Dresden did not take place, Wagner writing to sister Cecilie from Mainz on the 27th of the month : " Give Minna my kind love. I was in thorough earnest about a somewhat longer visit to Dresden, and probably it will come to that ere long, but—under easier circumstances than the present could have been. If I were always to explain things in detail, I should never find another moment's peace." It should be added that Minna was never allowed to go really short of money, even at her husband's worst financial crisis, and was amply provided for as soon as Ludwig II. of Bavaria came to his rescue in May '64.—Tr.

Dresden about that time, and drop in on you ; when I'll bring you money to pay off your creditresses.

Forgive my haste.   I really am dead tired [between two concerts] and have exerted myself here without the desired result ; which also makes me glum and out of sorts. So send me word, and expect me this month in any case on a longer or shorter visit.

Farewell, dear Minna.   May these lines find you in tolerable health !

Kind love from   Thy

RICHARD W.

THE END

INDEX TO BOTH VOLUMES.

In this index figures denoting the tens and hundreds are not *repeated* for one and the same reference, excepting where the numerals run into a fresh line of type; "*n*," following a numeral, signifies "footnote"; whilst curved brackets, enclosing numerals, indicate that the subject is only indirectly mentioned on that page of the text : thus

Paris 15, 8, 70, 7, 124, 9*n*, (37), would stand for
Paris 15, 18, 70, 77, 124, 129 footnote, 137 (an allusion).

As the pagination of the two volumes is *consecutive*, the reader may find it of assistance to remember that, with exception of a single half-page, p. 399, all pages *below* 400 are contained in volume I.—*Tr.*

A.

Aar glacier, 107.

Aarau, 269, 344.

Actors and singers, 5, 11, 6, 21, 2, 24, 5, 32, 4, 7-40, 3, 5, 8, 52, 54, 6, 7, 121, 67, 95, 209, 17-8, 248-9, 406, 9, 29-30, 2, 8, 551, 558, 613, 23, 36, 41, 5, 50, 4, 90, 728, 60, 2. See also Ander, Tichatschek, etc.

Adelphi Theatre, 209.

Agoult, Ctsse d', 310.

Aix-les-bains, 280, 4.

Albert, see Wagner, A.

Albisbrunn, 93-106, 272.

Albums, 458 ; photo., 695.

Allgemeine Zeitung, 485.

Alps, 82, 107, 10, 4-5, 273, 451, 62, 467, 73, 9, 92, 522, 36, 47.

Altenburg, Weimar, 441, 625, 708.

Alter, architect, 291, 5, 7.

Altkäs, tenor, 312.

Amat, Léopold, 304-5.

Ambassadors, 59, 61, 124, 305, 426, 611, 9-23, 71, 9, 82, 3, 9, 92, 694, 783 ; see also Diplomats.

America, 56, 115, 32, 236, 455-6, 463, 758, 61 ; see also New York.

Ander, Aloys, 396, 487, 540, 613, 627-72, 720, 49, 52, 66, 73-81.

Anders, E., 71, 6, 130, 67.

Anderson, George F., 168, 75, 214, 223, 6, 34, 5, 314.

Antwerp, 607, 9, 10.

Architecture etc., 40-1, 56, 121-3, 150, 91, 5, 375-7, 80, 3, 469, 73, 576, 609, 32, 66.

Arnold, Dresden bookseller, 779, 784.

Arve river, 273.

Asia Minor, 91.

Asyl, the, Enge, 301, 13, 444, 571, 589, 737 ; quitting, 325, 33-7, 340-1, 56-65, 8, 482-3, 505, 87, 657, 9.

Athens, 90-2, 652.

Atlantic passage, 236, 493.

Auber, *Masaniello*, 646, see *Stumme*.

Auerbach, B., 467, 534.

Aufdermauer, Brunnen landlord, 289, 495, 557.

Augsburg, 591.

Austria, 109, 366, 75, 85, 6, 426, 527, 32 : Archduke Ferd. Max., 453 ; Emperor, 61, 349, 371, 422, 36, 90, 537, (44), 686, 760 ; Empress, 666, 87, (769), 776, 81. See Vienna.